The Journey to the Castle

The Shamanic Journey of the Clan of Tubal Cain

by Ann Finnin

Pendraig Publishing Inc

Copyright © 2021 Ann Finnin

All rights reserved. No part of this book may be reproduced in any form or by any electronic or mechanical means, including information storage or retrieval systems, without permission in writing from the publisher, except by reviewers, who may quote brief passages in a review.

ISBN# 978-1-936922-92-5

The opinions stated in this book are those of the author and may not represent the opinions of the publisher.

Editing by Raven Womack
Front Cover design by Ted Venemann
Book design by Raven Womack

Printed and bound in USA
First Printing August, 2021

Published by Pendraig Publishing Inc
PO Box 8427
Green Valley Lake CA 92341

Visit www.pendraigpublishing.com

For Carol

Contents

Foreward	vii
Introduction	xiii
Elegy for a Dead Witch	xvi
1 The Shamanic Journey	19
2 The Sacred Circle	35
3 The Reluctant Guru	51
4 The Aftermath	81
5 The Art of Cunning	93
6 The Clan of the Cave Bear	101
7 The Moat and the Mill	117
8 The Ancestors	131
9 The Lady of the Castle	139
10 The Dark Mother, Goddess of Fate	153
11 The Keys to the Gate	163
12 The Sacred Path	181
13 The Question of Authority	197
14 The Shadow Clan	219
15 Lord of Light, Lord of Darkness	231
16 The Journey to the Future	243
Index	261
Bibliography	271

Foreward

When Ann sent me the manuscript for this book, she warned me that it might ruffle a few feathers. Knowing much of the story and some of the events of recent years, after I read it, I had no doubt that it may well do that. But if you don't ruffle feathers from time-to-time they get really dusty, stiff and complacent which can make it really hard to fly. To be sure, among Ann's many talents is definitely the ability to ruffle feathers.

Ann Finnin is a bit of an enigma. She's absolutely devoted to her path in ways too numerous to list, and has made sacrifices to her craft that are equally numerous and yet completely different from the majority of people on similar paths. I've known Ann and her equally enigmatic husband Dave for over 20 years. We have often disagreed about various interpretations of folklore and Paganism and witchcraft as well politics, social issues and so on and so forth. I've shared many "experiences" with them both in magickal as well as mundane settings as well as a fair number of Irish whiskeys and creamy stout or two. To be honest, I consider them both friends and mentors and they are without a doubt keepers of vast amounts of knowledge and lore which they share freely and without strings.

I first met the Finnins in 1997 after I opened my store in North Hollywood and by the time I actually met them I had been regaled with a plethora of stories about what awful people they were and practically heretical in their craft. It was claimed that they approved of corporal punishment in their circles, that they were completely homophobic and gun runners to boot. It didn't take me long to figure out that they were none of these things, but they were quite amused that they were rumored to be gun runners. In fairly short order, the people telling me the lies were no longer in my life or in the community that sprung up around the store, but Ann and Dave were.

This was an interesting time in the Los Angeles witchcraft community as the influence of Wicca as the main philosophy of the local witchcraft movement was giving way to what was commonly known as "British Traditional Witchcraft" or BTW. Ann and Dave were then, and always have been on the cutting edge of this type of practice in the U.S. Wicca will of course always have it's place and there will always be those that prefer it's structure, form and the safety and ease of its repetition. But BTW, is something else, something a bit more primal, more guttural and in my opinion more natural… at least to me. Some would say it's darker, but that's a debate for another time. I've always believed that was one of the reasons there were those who were less than enthusiastic about their presence in the Southern California Pagan community. Dave and Ann's coven, and their many daughter covens, were energetic and expanding while some of the other covens were imploding and dwindling to lack of interest, with some notable exceptions of course. I learned with time, that in the Pagan community the greater your success, the larger the target on your back.

Another thing that always set the Finnins apart, was their penchant for plain speak. Neither has ever been known for "pussy footing around" a subject. I have never seen Ann be uncivil, but if she disagrees with you, she will let you know it in no uncertain terms. This doesn't really set well with everyone and while it can be a bit uncomfortable and not politically correct at times it's always honest and forthright. And the thing is, if she disagrees with you, she can back it up with actual experience, training, scholarship, and/or all of the above.

While I never formally trained with Ann and Dave, we were always linked by the tenuous legacy of Robert Cochrane and his writings. When I got my "1734" initiation, my high priestess was oathbound not to let me see the then mysterious and now infamous and widely published "1734 papers" until I had been successfully initiated, such was the way then. Once I received my "papers" and began studying them, I found certain things that didn't make sense, certain things that didn't seem to belong, so I asked Dave about them. He seemed perplexed in regard to the material I was asking him about. He went home and got his copy of the papers and we compared them, only to find that there were a lot of extra papers in my set and therefore in the papers of my lineage before me. It was Ann and Dave Finnin that arranged the meeting with Mara Schaeffer to sort out the what's what. Theirs was the cleaner version which is not surprising considering that they are in fact responsible for the very preservation of many of the letters that make up the "1734" papers. This is what they do, they seek out the truth. Not because they don't believe in the continued fleshing out of source material or its expansion but because they believe it's important to know what is source material, and what is born from it.

The Finnin's have literally had a front row seat to much of the modern Pagan movement in the U.S. and quite a bit of experience on the other side of the pond. They've not only been there and done that and gotten the t-shirt, they also know where the bodies are buried… well most of them anyway.

In *Journey to the Castle*, Ann has laid bare the actual history of their journey along this crooked path and while you or I may not agree with some of her personal conclusions or opinions what I can tell you is she is honest… like I implied before, perhaps, at times, to a fault.

Journey to the Castle is a well-written tome full of lore, tradition, philosophy, comparative religion, psychology, and spirituality. It's part history, part editorial, and part magickal autobiography from someone who was often on the frontlines.

Raven Womack
Pendraig Publishing Inc
Raven's Flight

Preface

Mindful that I am presenting information with which some will take issue, I would like to present the following disclaimer.

The material in this book is mine. Everything in it consists of information that I have personally been given, both written and oral, regarding the Cochrane tradition from the time I was first given the original material in 1974 until the present day. I have consulted the writings of others, both published and unpublished, regarding this tradition only as confirmation of material which I already had in my possession.

Therefore, this book is based entirely upon the research, teachings and experimentation that I and members of the Roebuck have conducted over a nearly forty-year period. Nothing has been cribbed or copied from anyone else's work. In addition, I have refrained from quoting from the original Cochrane letters or from the personal letters I received over the years from E.J. Jones due to possible legal action from those who might desire to silence me thereby. However, I have copies of all these documents in my possession and can show them to any interested party in order to back up any assertions that I have made.

It saddens me to have to make this disclaimer. But over the last twenty-or-so years, the Cochrane writings have become 'hot property' and a number of people on both sides of the Atlantic have attempted to take possession of them in order to place it under their exclusive control and purview.

The fact that Cochrane's writings had languished for the most part unknown and ignored from his death in 1966 until 1991 when Doreen

Valiente and Evan John Jones published *Witchcraft: A Tradition Renewed* and enabled his writings and ideas to escape into the public domain. However, these same writings have been circulating in private hands since 1966 and formed a part of a number of traditions both here and in England. Indeed, that was where we first encountered it in 1974.

Attempts to copyright the letters and articles notwithstanding, the cat is out of the bag with regards to Cochrane and his version of the craft. As I hope to show in the following pages, religious and spiritual ideas cannot be copyrighted and to claim that there is only one true version of this tradition is making the same grievous error that the Catholic Church made two thousand years ago.

This present book outlines one version of Cochrane's tradition. There are other versions. We happen to think that our version works better in the grand scheme of things. Others will certainly disagree, and that is their right. We won't burn them at the stake if they refrain from doing so to us.

I consider Cochrane's work much too valuable to the history of the craft as a whole to allow it to be fought over as dogs fight over a bone. Cochrane has long since passed into the Otherworld. So, have nearly all the people who worked with him and contributed to the development of his ideas. Those of us who have inherited the tradition, whatever our background, would do well to add our contribution to its continuance, rather than hoarding it for our own gain and personal gratification.

It is in this spirit that I offer this culmination of forty years of study into the Craft of Robert Cochrane. I hope that others will do the same and allow future generations to judge the results.

Introduction

Midnight

The lights of the city glow at the bottom of the mountain, but you are far, far above them, in that realm between earth and sky. Above you is the whiteness of stars. Around you are trees, black silhouettes against the glowing sky. A stang with two tines pointing upwards stands in the north.

You stand with your clan in a circle around a small fire, tiny flames licking at the burning embers. The smoke drifts in the air, irritating your nose and throat. The magister and maid have just consecrated the cup. When it is passed to you, to take a drink and pass it along. The contents are strong and make you feel a little dizzy.

"Begin to tread the mill," the magister commands.

You turn to your right and face forward, looking over your left shoulders at the fire. You take a deep breath and start to pace around the circle widdershins, first slow and measured, trying not to run into the person in front of you. A chant begins: a succession of vowels, each sound morphing seamless into the next.

You join your voice with the others. The sounds vibrate in your throat, throbbing in your temples. They don't mean anything. They aren't supposed to. You chant in unison with the other members of your clan, your breathing synchronizing with theirs, one sound, one breathing, one note, in two octaves, the higher one from the women and the lower one from the men.

Around and around you go. The Magister quickens the pace, the circle *which was tight is now widening to accommodate the pace. The sky spins, your head spins, the glow of the fire floods your retinas with light. You can't see anything else. The trees vanish. The other people vanish. All you can do is chant, breathy now, more of a gasp for air than a chant.*

"Drop!" commands the Magister.

You crumble to the ground, panting, your heart pounding. The sky is still spinning even though you lie motionless on the ground. The sandy soil presses against your cheek, smelling like trampled grass. You don't know where you are in the circle: north, south, east or west. It doesn't matter. You are so detached from your physical body, you don't care.

"Before you is a path leading from the northeast quarter of the circle ..."

You hear the words of the Magister and you obey. You leave the circle, pass an ancient oak and go down to the bank of a river. The moon is only a faint sliver in the starry sky, and all you hear is the rushing of water in front of you. Are you in your body? You don't know. You don't care. At the edge of the river you can make out a hooded figure sitting in a boat. You discover that you have a coin in your hand. You give it to the figure, who motions you to get into the boat.

"Now, cross the river," *comes the voice of the magister.* "Cross the river to the other side."

You climb into the boat, and the hooded figure rows off into the darkness.

******

It is difficult to say, even with the passing of nearly forty-five years, just what the strange allure was in the brief life and briefer writings of the man who was known as Robert Cochrane (Roy Leonard Bowers, 1936-1966). His influence on the history of the modern Witchcraft movement rivaled that of Gardner, Valiente, and Sanders, even though they not only lived far longer, but wrote far more published works than he did.

The corpus of Cochrane's writings is scanty – a dozen or so letters to various friends and correspondents, a few articles for small magazines and journals, and a handful of students in a group he ran for barely three years. But the influence of those writings and ritual teachings spanned the Atlantic so that twenty years after his untimely death he was as well known in America as he was in Britain.

His death itself was the stuff of legend. The story promulgated in the late seventies by Joe Wilson and others was that of a Magister of a powerful witch clan who, wishing to die in the manner of a sacred king, called his clan members to his side, cast a sacred circle and proceeded to drink a ritual chalice filled with a belladonna brew. He gave careful instructions to his people to allow him to die, or failing that calling the authorities only after the chances of reviving him were slim. After his death, his dynasty would live on in his young son who would succeed him as the new Arthur.

However, the actual story was very different -- and very tragic. Having been jilted by a mistress and losing his wife and young son, Bowers ingested a mixture of belladonna and Librium. He lay alone on the couch in his small house, huddled in a sleeping bag until he was found by police. He was rushed to the hospital, stayed in a coma for three days (according to some), and finally died. No ritual, no sacrificial death, no clan at his side: just a lonely, depressed young man who wished to end his life as quietly and painlessly as possible.

Maybe it was his early and tragic death. Maybe it was the fact that he left only a few writings that ever-so-briefly hinted at a kind of witchcraft that was different and more profound than the highly ceremonial form in the works of Gardner and Sanders. Valiente hints at it in her books, yet shies away from the implications. Jones describes it in detail in his earlier books, yet abandons it in his later books for more earthy and colorful forms of magic.

What is the elusive message of Bowers' writings? What does he teach us that Gardner, Valiente, and others do not? Bowers gives us a hint of the craft as a kind of Pagan mystic shamanism – as much a philosophy as a craft. It is the 'why' of the craft rather than the 'how.' It is the devotion to the Goddess as a personal faith rather than merely as a ritual form. Where Gardner gives us the form, Bowers gives us the force. Gardner gives us the outer manifestation. Bowers shows us the inner workings.

Witchcraft isn't just about rituals to honor the changing seasons and the phases of the moon, or spells to acquire love or money. Bowers teaches us something we have forgotten for two millennia – how to be a pagan mystic, tread the inner journey to our ancestral homeland in the kind of vision that a Native American medicine man or a Siberian shaman might have, and return to the ordinary world in order to show others the way.

Tortured artist and poet that he was, Roy Bowers was able to find the gateway to the Otherworld and travel the Sacred Path to the realm of the ancestors. And he remains there as the horned king and blind harper, at the ford of the river that flows between this world and the next, silently conducting the traveler to the Spiral Castle of the Goddess known only as Fate for the purpose of turning us into witches.

It is to him that this book, and the sacred journey that it documents, is dedicated.

Elegy for a Dead Witch

-Written by Doreen Valiente in 1966 after
the death of Roy Bowers

To think that you are gone over the crest of the Hill.
As the Moon passed from her fullness, riding the Sky,
And the White Mare took you with her.
To think that we must wait another life
To drink wine from the Horns and leap the Fire.
Farewell from this world, but not from the Circle.
That place that is between the worlds
Shall hold return in due time. Nothing is lost.
The half of a fruit from the Tree of Avalon
Shall be our reminder among the fallen leaves
This life treads underfoot. Let the rain weep.
Waken in sunlight from the realms of sleep!

Rest in peace, Roy

Chapter 1

The Shamanic Journey

Magic, like its close cousin religion, has two distinct yet complimentary sides: an exoteric and an esoteric side, or a ritual side and a visionary side. The exoteric or ritual side constitutes what most people think of as magic – ceremonies, temples, circles inscribed in chalk on the floor, altars with candles, chalices, and other implements, swords, daggers, wands, and sonorous invocations and elaborate gestures performed in a haze of incense smoke.

This is what the published books describe. Indeed, this is all that a published book *can* describe.

The Western Esoteric Tradition has been dominated for nearly a thousand years by this ceremonial approach to magic. There are a number of reasons for this. First and foremost, it is an intellectual and scholarly approach suited to the classically educated upper and middle classes – the same classes that produced clerics as well as scientists and philosophers. Magicians from these social classes often could write and read a number of different languages. Therefore, their magical lore was transmitted primarily by the written word, in secret manuscripts called grimoires.

The early grimoires from the 15th century (such as the Lesser Key of Solomon from the Sloane collection in the British Museum) consisted mainly of rituals designed to invoke helpful spiritual entities and persuade them to grant magicians something that they wanted. Diagrams illustrated how the ritual space was to be set up, what sigils and other symbols were to be drawn around the circle, on bits of parchment, or ritual tools such as daggers and wands. Invocations were written in script format, presumably to be either memorized or read aloud while performing the ritual. Also included, and perhaps most important – how to banish or get rid of whoever or whatever was invoked before it caused any mischief.

Some notorious grimoires such as Francis Barrett's *The Magus (1801)* helpfully provided detailed descriptions and sketches of the less savory denizens of the spirit world. The would-be magus was told how to recognize such underworld inhabitants if he were to happen to encounter them. More importantly, it listed just what such beings could offer by way of knowledge and power, providing a veritable *Who's Who* of the purveyors of forbidden knowledge.

Other works provided detailed, complex, and extensive categories and classifications of all kinds of spiritual entities: angels, elementals, demons, etc. These listed the name, identifying symbol or sigil, what element they were associated with, what day of the week, time of the day or season of the year they were available to be summoned, and most importantly, what services they could provide for an aspiring magician.

Still, others contained herbal lore as well as a variety of charms used to heal any affliction the flesh was heir to. Some of the herbs have since been found to be effective. Other ingredients of the concoctions were less efficacious, such as the tongue of a dove (carefully dried and pulverized) used in a love potion.

Missing, however, was a description of what was actually supposed to happen after the invocation was completed. Just how did the would-be magician even know that the spirit had heeded his call, much less gain whatever help and advice the spirit was supposed to provide? After all the gesturing and invoking, what was supposed to happen?

Clues were found in later grimoires. In the book *A True & Faithful Relation of What Passed for Many Years Between Dr. John Dee and Some Spirits*[1] written in the mid-17th century, Dee employed a clairvoyant seer named Edward Kelly, who gazed into a polished obsidian disk called a shew stone in order to contact the angels and relate what they said. No ritual is given to enable Kelly's visions. He seems to have simply put himself into a trance by whatever personal means he had, and his visions emerged.

John Dee's original "Shew stone". The obsidian mirror was originally brought to Europe from Mexico in the 16th century and is currently held at the British Museum.
-Photo taken by Dave Finnin

Another reason for the exclusively ceremonial approach was the still-pervasive influence of Christianity on the educated classes. In spite of whatever their prevailing view of the official Church – both Catholic and Protestant – might have been, European magicians were still basically Christian. The Bible still determined their world view. Stories from both Old and New Testaments constituted literal history, and the spirits described in the grimoires were either good (angels) or evil (demons).

Ceremonies and rituals were couched in biblical symbolism. Spirits were invoked in the name of the God of the Bible. References to Jesus Christ and the Holy Spirit abounded. Invocations were annotated at various points with cross marks showing where the magician paused in the invocation to make the sign of the cross upon his breast or in the air in front of him before continuing with his ritual.

Spirits were summoned from either heaven or hell depending upon whether their services were considered moral (i.e., Church-sanctioned)

---

1 *A True & Faithful Relation of What Passed for Many Years Between Dr. John Dee and Some Spirits,* John Dee, published by D.Maxwell for T. Garthwait, London, 1669. (With a Preface Confirming the Reality as to the Point of Spirits) by Meric Casaubon.

or not. Angels could be counted on to deliver knowledge and wisdom. However, for love or money, you had to consult the nether regions. Then they had to be banished when you were done with them on the off chance that they decided they liked the Earth Plane and were reluctant to leave. In any case, the spirits came to you-you didn't go to them.

This utilitarian approach was not only consistent with the Judeo-Christian world view featured in the Bible, but with Muslim and Zoroastrian sources as well. It featured one all-powerful creator God – no matter what name He was called – and various spirits, demons, angels, djinn or what have you. Whatever their capabilities were, they were subject to the will of man by means of the grace of that creator god. God, by definition, was good. Those spirits who obeyed God, and by extension man, were also good. Those who refused to obey God, and in turn did their best to convince man to do likewise, were defined as evil.

Throughout Jewish and Muslim writings, kings and prophets all summoned spirits of various kinds for a variety of reasons. King Saul summoned the shade of the patriarch Samuel using the Witch of Endor as a medium. King Solomon himself trapped 72 spirits in a vessel of brass so he could summon them at will. In some versions of the tale, Solomon could press these 72 spirits into service for the task of building his famous temple. This story would later become famous in the Arabian Nights collection as the story of the genie (djinn) trapped in the lamp or bottle who could only be freed at the magician's command.

So, the problem wasn't whether it was possible to summon spirits. The problem was figuring out how to summon them, how to persuade them to comply with your wishes, and how to get them to leave with no residual problems after your wishes were granted.

This attitude provided a stark contrast to the heathen or pagan view of the spirit world. The Greco-Roman view, which was shared by most of Pagan Europe, was that spirits were either forces of nature or ancestral gods. They were neither good nor evil, but capricious, following their own laws regardless of the wishes of men.

Each entity was capable of either aiding humans or making their lives miserable, quite possibly both at once. They were to be placated and appeased rather than summoned up and ordered about. Furthermore, they would only answer the call of a select few who were members of a certain magical bloodline.

When someone in the tribe was in dire straits, the magician would put himself in a trance state similar to that of Edward Kelly peering into his shew stone. Then, he had to leave his body and go personally to the realm of the spirits (which was neither heaven nor hell, but simply an Otherworld), pay his respects, deliver his offering and make his petition. If his offering was accepted, then his petition would be granted, but he had to make the journey himself to the Otherworld, go where he was supposed to and behave in acceptable ways while he was there. If the spirits met him halfway, he considered himself blessed.

Magical lore was also accumulated by generations of European shamanic magicians. It consisted of elaborate descriptions of the spiritual landscape, the identity and nature of the spirits to be encountered there and what boons they could grant to the magician if he approached them properly, how they were to be appeased, and most importantly, how the magician could return to the mortal world in one piece to deliver his knowledge to the tribe. It also included information on various herbs that not only could heal disease but aid in the achievement of the necessary out-of-body trance state.

This lore was primarily transmitted orally from shaman to apprentice who were usually related to each other. Often families kept the lore as an exclusive family secret to be shared only with those who were born into the family or married into it. Over time, these families provided the tribe with their shamans, priests, and medicine folk and eventually became a priestly caste that guarded their lore and practices like later trade guilds would guard the trade secrets of their craft.

This was the shamanic approach to magic, but since it was practiced by small, illiterate and unabashedly Pagan tribes, the oral traditions were rarely written down. In the famous example of the Celtic Druids, their own laws prohibited their lore from being written down and codified even though they were fluent in not only their own language but Latin and Greek as well. In the case of other tribes, as soon as they learned to write in languages that could be read by outsiders, they came under the control of the Christian church and were forbidden to practice their traditions much less write them down.

With the constant political and social upheaval, which followed the fall of the Roman Empire in the 5th century, tribes constantly migrated from one place to another. With one tribe conquering another only to be eventually conquered itself in its turn, the oral transmission of traditional lore became a hit or miss affair. Eventually, it became so dissipated and diluted that it was unclear which tribe's lore was which.

Soon, the only written sources about shamanic magical lore over the centuries came primarily from the perspective of an authoritarian Church which either sought to figure out a way to convert the shamans from their heathen ways or to warn their parishioners away from taking advantage of their magical services. Much of what we do know about early European shamanic practices consisted of such dire warnings in which heathen practices were described in detail with the admonition to the faithful to avoid such practices and to go to the parish priest rather than the village 'witch' or 'wizard' if spiritual help was desired.

Ironically, the practices were often the same for both the priest and the witch/wizard. Someone who desired spiritual help with an intractable problem such as serious illness or poverty would seek to procure a charm or amulet to ward off any evil influences. That amulet would have to be obtained from the church (often at a price and preferably showing the likeness of an official saint). It had to be blessed with holy water from the church font, not with the water from the sacred well consecrated to the indigenous ancestral spirits of the village, and the accompanying charm must invoke Jesus, Mary, or the Saints, not the local ancestral gods or goddesses.

The Catholic Church, in essence, co-opted the services formerly performed by the shaman just as it built churches on sacred sites and rechristened local gods as saints. Native shamans were condemned and persecuted as witches, sorcerers, and children of the devil. Members of the shamanic or priestly caste (such as the Druids) often became priests themselves and used their ancestral gifts with different trappings.

The Church also had her shamans in the visionaries, and ecstatics who flew into the sky had visions in which they spoke with Christ, the Virgin Mary, and various angels, and exhibited the stigmata or the wounds that Christ suffered on the cross. However, Church officials often took a dim view of such people. Most of them were sequestered away in monasteries and convents, away from ordinary folk. If their visions and experiences were considered orthodox, they were canonized as saints. If they weren't, they were burned as witches, sorcerers, and heretics. In either case, details of how they achieved or nurtured their abilities were scrupulously avoided.

When the Protestant Reformation swept across Europe, one of the first things to be tossed onto the pyre was magic and shamanism in any of its myriad forms. Protestantism was concerned primarily with proper moral behavior as outlined in the Bible, not with visionary experiences. Any and all magical practices were banned either as 'popery' or 'witchcraft.' All spirits (even so-called 'angels') were really demons, and God would not assist anyone in their summoning. If spirits showed up, it was only through the agency of the devil. All magic, even the magic of the Catholic Church was *de facto* evil and anyone who so much as had a revealing dream was subject to torture and death.

Enter the Enlightenment. The late 18th and early 19th centuries saw a resurgence of interest in ancient pagan shamanic practices, but purely as a scholarly and scientific curiosity. Gentlemen naturalists, upper-class amateur anthropologists, scoured the European countryside documenting ancient stone monuments, describing quaint local customs and rituals, and studying ancient poetry and stories – which often included making up several of their own. They reconstructed ancient practices as little more than charming, harmless and invigorating folk customs celebrated in innocent pleasure by hearty peasants before those nasty, backward, and superstitious religious folks got a hold of them.

Some of these practices even functioned as hobbies and amusing pastimes for wealthy gentry who decorated their gardens with statues of ancient gods and held elaborate soirees featuring an abundance of food and drink to celebrate the ancient fire festivals. Some aristocrats even went so far as to erect elaborate temples to various Greek and Roman divinities, nearly always with the emphasis on exalting the earthly pleasures that the Church, both Catholic, and Protestant, had forbidden for the previous seventeen centuries.

For Welsh, Irish, and Breton scholars especially, this newly discovered lore served as effective political propaganda towards the aim of gaining independence (if not politically, at least culturally) from the pervasive English and French dominance. Bits of lore served as badges of ethnic pride. Reconstructions of pre-Christian festivals such as the Eisteddfod in Wales were also celebrated but as rituals of solidarity in which members of a persecuted ethnic minority could demonstrate their unique cultural identity in a positive and life-affirming way. The actual history of the festival and the authenticity of the practices involved were not considered particularly important.

No matter how many statues to Venus or Bacchus a European aristocrat might have in his garden, or how many Beltane festivals he celebrated by dancing around a decorated maypole, he was basically still a Christian. Any religious or spiritual activities such as weddings or burials in which he participated were still performed in a Christian church and under the auspices of Christian clergy. The ancient ancestral gods of his people might be acceptable subjects for paintings or poetry, but they were not to be worshiped, invoked, or God forbid, visited in an entranced visionary journey.

During the Victorian era, such practices were still decried by the Church as being heathen and evil, even though by this time even witchcraft consisted of little more than telling fortunes and charming warts with occasional midnight dances on the heath at Beltane or All Hallows Eve. The worst thing that anybody ever did was have sex with someone else's spouse or get roaring drunk and cast off their restrictive clothing and cause a scandal that might be the subject of gossip or disapproving finger-wagging.

Those of a more intellectual and ceremonial bent recreated ancient ceremonies as part of a secret society or mystical fraternity in which people dressed in elaborate robes or historical costumes, called themselves by strange names, and spouted arcane philosophical concepts. Most of these societies were little more than social clubs in which upper-class people with artistic sensibilities could gather with those of like mind. A few were incarnations of earlier groups who really did study the ancient mysteries, but aside from sonorous rituals or drug-induced visionary experiences, little shamanic magic was ever performed.

With colonial expansion came European contact with a variety of heathen shamanic practices not altogether dissimilar from those still practiced by 'fortune tellers' and 'cunning folk' but with a primitive earthiness that European folk magicians had lost. Horrified clerics and reporters would write lurid stories about rituals involving blood sacrifices, charms and amulets consisting of animal and sometimes human body parts, tattooing and ritual scarring, and of course, sexual practices of the most salacious kind.

How much the lurid tales accurately depicted indigenous shamanic rituals is a matter of some debate. An increasing market for exotic adventure stories encouraged writers to be as dramatic as possible, and exaggeration of an innocuous practice into something more colorful is not only possible but extremely likely.

Native shamans quickly learned that Europeans were not only secretly superstitious but squeamish and sexually repressed as well. It wouldn't take much to intimidate a European governor or landowner by judicious use of psychoactive plants, bloody animal bits, and naked human bodies by making him (or his wife) think that the wrath of some unknown and horrible god was being called down upon him. What the natives did among their own people might have been totally different and a great deal less colorful and dramatic, but few Europeans were even permitted to witness them much less write about them.

These indigenous ritual practices were also being studied from a scholarly perspective, minus the Christian moral outrage, but also with no clue as to what they meant or how they were truly performed. Shamanic journeys were almost always described from a proper scientific and therefore materialistic mindset, and often descriptions of subjective experiences were taken literally.

Many an anthropologist would sit beside the entranced body of the shaman hoping it would rise and fly away to realms strange and distant and when it never left the fur rug upon which it lay, would feel irked and cheated. When the shaman described his elaborate experiences while journeying through the spirit world, the clueless scholar would sniff in derision and protest that the shaman never really went anywhere and wrote the entire journey off as a drug-induced delusion. Consequently, the experiences were described in the anthropological literature with a condescending attitude that indicated that highly educated and civilized people not only shouldn't do such things, but in reality couldn't since the practices were too primitive, and modern minds just didn't work that way anymore.

The writings of Freud and later Jung warned that such practices might also serve to arouse certain atavistic instincts and desires that, if given free rein, could result in 'improper' behavior and possibly imperil the magician's social standing and ability to make a living in a civilized society. Sexual indiscretions and drug taking were bad enough but finding ritually murdered bodies in London slums or encountering shrieking patients in cells in a mad house was a great deal more disturbing.

Eventually, shamanic abilities and psychic experiences became medicalized. The seers of visions and the hearers of voices were considered to be mentally ill, and more often than not were hospitalized. There, they could be cured by psychoanalysis, electroshock, lobotomies, and later by strong psychoactive medications.

It was expected that the visions and the voices would eventually go away and the patient could assume his or her role as a rational, productive member of society. The fact that these treatments only worked in a limited number of cases did little to change the assumption that such experiences were an aberration and that eliminating them would return the patient to normalcy.

The 1960s saw another resurgence of interest in indigenous shamanic practices, with the advantage of being freed from concerns of both Christian morality and Victorian propriety. Researchers noticed that shamanic journeying began with a technique to induce out of body experiences that yielded the intense experience of a lucid dream.

Induction of such trance states was pivotal to this research, and much of the psychology of the 1960s and 1970s consisted of studying the methods for inducing such states, rather than working to prevent them. Consequently, psychoactive drugs were used not to prevent altered states of consciousness, but specifically to produce them – provided that the results were controlled and did not render the subject unable to return to the real world.

By the end of the 1980s, there were entire books that detailed how such trance states could be achieved, often using psychoactive substances both legal and illegal. Humanistic psychology came into prominence and took a more anthropological approach to shamanism. The visions and voices in and of themselves were not signs of illness. They were natural occurrences in many cultures, and they could be used for healing not only clinical mental problems but also emotional issues such as feelings of alienation and relationship problems.

There were a few researchers, mostly in the neuroscience fields, that discovered that journeys taken in the imagination could be just as meaningful as those taken in the physical world. Guided imagery involving emotionally arousing situations could literally produce the same physiological changes (i.e., increased heart and respiratory rate) as the physical experiences. Furthermore, such imaginary journeys could be induced by the proper techniques, many of which did not require the use of illegal psychoactive drugs, such as hypnosis or neuro-linguistic programming.

They also discovered that such imaginary journeys could be dangerous. The imaginary Otherworld was very real and could be dangerous if visited without proper supervision. In his 1913 journal *The Red Book*[2], Carl Jung reported that he had not only suffered a mental breakdown but was,

---

2 *The Red Book* by Carl Jung, W. W. Norton & Company, 2009.

as he put it, living in an insane asylum of his own making which threatened his professional life as well as his personal life.

People could become possessed by unnamed entities and develop obsessive/compulsive behavior patterns that could ruin what lives they had. They might suffer psychotic breakdowns, and in rare cases suicidal tendencies, without ever having ingested so much as a sugar cube full of LSD. Jung reported that he "went about with all these fantastic figures: centaurs, nymphs, satyrs, gods, and goddesses, as though they were patients and I was analyzing them." This presented many unexpected practical, ethical, and legal ramifications.

Consequently, the questionable practices were watered down, sanitized, packaged attractively and sold to soul-starved westerners in the form of lectures, books, and 'shamanic' workshops and retreats. Participants could lie down on a carpeted floor for a few minutes in some warm, comfortable hotel ballroom, drift off into a reverie accompanied by the soothing voice of the facilitator, maybe some formless new-age electronic music, or the soft, rhythmic thumping of a self-styled shaman's drum.

They might be directed to meet their power animal, an Aztec god, a Celtic goddess, or a Sioux medicine man who would counsel them on how to do their next business deal or to make their teenage children do better in school, or to maintain good health, or get through a divorce, and so on. After an hour or so, they would get up, stretch, hug the leader, and get in their expensive cars and go home – only to find that the issues remained unsolved.

The problem wasn't so much the journey itself, but the destination. Even if one had a reliable technique for out of body travel, where exactly did one go? There isn't a monolithic, centralized, homogenized shamanism that anybody with a drum and an hour to kill can practice.

In the case of European immigrants to America, Australia, or South Africa, the shamanic practices that they encountered were from the native indigenous culture with a unique mythos, a collection of lore of symbols, gods, spirits, and cosmology. These images gave the shaman a framework, a road map, and a guidebook of where to go and who he or she was likely to meet there, including possible pitfalls, wrong turns to avoid, protocol to observe, and so on. This culture was closely guarded by ancestral spirits of a particular tribal bloodline from which most European immigrants were barred from participating.

This was where the anthropology student-turned-weekend-shaman often ran into trouble. He had no idea where he was going or why. He didn't know the passwords or the signposts which would signal acceptance by the denizens of the Otherworld who, in his heart of hearts, he couldn't accept as real and autonomous. In the end, he just ended up journeying into the murky depths of his own subconscious, and all the demons from his own id crawled out of the abyss and gobbled him up for lunch.

As the neo-shamanic movement progressed in the 1980s, members of Native American tribes often voiced outrage that their most sacred practices and symbols had been co-opted by new-age therapy practitioners as just one more expensive fad that promised to solve the problems of affluent westerners. Europeans had let their own shamanic traditions become lost, so they wanted to co-opt the traditions of other cultures and sell them for profit. It wasn't right, and it wasn't fair – and it wasn't necessary.

In 1951, the last of the English laws against the practice of witchcraft were repealed. Suddenly the religion of Witchcraft (or as it was called then Wicca) emerged as a possible source of the lost European shamanism that had been hidden underground from the authoritarian Church for nearly eighteen centuries. Gloriously, it reemerged from its hiding place – complete with rituals, spells, chants, charms, descriptions of ancient Celtic and Norse gods and goddesses, and scripts for seasonal ceremonies. Finally, European Neo-pagans felt as though they had rediscovered their shamanic birthright.

However, what we know now as Wicca wasn't dug up intact from a peat bog. It was an early twentieth-century reconstruction. The bulk of the rituals and practices were taken from the same Western Esoteric writings that Western magicians of a century earlier had done. Gone was the Christian worldview and biblical cosmology, but the rituals were often taken verbatim from the earlier works of ceremonial magic written to summon demons.

Serious researchers did what they could to uncover the ancient practices, but by the middle of the 20th century, just about the only access to serious magical training of any sort was from books -- often a century or more old. A few practitioners of genuine family traditions still existed, but they were secretive and difficult to find. Even when they were found, many of their practices were fragmented and sketchy, and like the Musgrave Ritual in the Arthur Conan Doyle story, the reasons for them had long been forgotten.

Consequently, someone like G. B. Gardner could only glean information from the writings of an earlier era and try to put together as best he could instructions on how to perform certain rituals, run a coven to perform said rituals and pass them on to a subsequent generation. Sometimes they worked, and sometimes they didn't. So, witchcraft or Wicca ended up as little more than paganized ceremonial magic, minus the Judeo-Christian world view, but retaining the emphasis on rituals and spells rather than visionary experiences.

There were reasons for this. For one thing, trance state induction is a touchy business. Research into traditional witchcraft practices involving trance work usually revealed recipes for herbal concoctions, such as flying ointment, which involved ingredients that could be dangerous even if they were formulated correctly, and lethal if they were not.

Other, less dangerous hallucinogens were illegal and could net the coven leaders jail time if they were caught. Occasionally, some individuals took the chance and used such herbal concoctions for 'traveling' anyway and recorded their experiences. However, that led to another problem: How did one travel together as a coven?

Trancework is difficult to do as a group. When people go into a trance, they tend to go inside their own minds, effectively tuning out everyone else in the room. A coven meeting where everybody is meditating often ends up with everyone being physically together but spiritually and mentally going on their own personal journey – no different from a new age shamanic workshop. There had to be a common journey that everyone could go on together. A guided meditation could help, but it's not quite the same thing as having everyone go to the same place on their own guided only by forces from the Other Side.

In the late 1960s, the writings of one Robert Cochrane hinted that there were indeed remnants of a Western European shamanic tradition that had been hidden and nurtured for centuries by certain witch families. Instead of spells, charms, and scripts for seasonal rituals, his writings told of a visionary journey to a spirit realm where a group of people could encounter a variety of ancient god forms and symbolic images, and it could be performed by purely natural means, without the use of dangerous or illegal herbal preparations.

In an article entitled *A Witches Esbat* published in *New Dimensions Red Book*[3] in 1968, Cochrane wrote:

> "This article deals with an actual witch meeting and is a combination of fiction and fact since the full ritual cannot be described, but basically the forms used are correct for the witches of Warwickshire. Also, there is no overstatement of phenomena, the writer has tried to describe accurately the actual feeling of working this type of ritual, which is not that type usually presented to the public as witchcraft yet is nonetheless of a pattern practiced by certain families for many centuries."

The article goes on to describe a ritual in a cave in which a group of people travel in a shamanic vision to another place and contact what appears to have been an otherworld guide.

> "We began to pace the compass round holding the ring in the air, then finally lowering it upon the skull. Turning, we place our staffs upon the ground fashioning the pattern of the ritual and begin to tread the mill. Round and round in absolute silence, fingers following the pattern that the seven knots make in the cord. ... I am no longer walking the floor of the cave, but treading on air. My body is in many different places at once, an incredible sense of disorientation fills me and I am no longer conscious of my body. Darkness rolls in upon my consciousness and I float

---

3 *New Dimensions Red Book: A Symposium of Practical Occultism*, Basil Wilby (editor) Toddington, UK: Helios Book Service Ltd., 1968

in a void around the circle, my body stumbling mechanically on and on. ... I become aware of everyone else in the Clan as if they were in me. I can feel them all. A strong feeling that someone is standing where the skull is impinges my mind. . . . A feeling of exhilaration erases our tiredness, he exudes strength and wisdom. We greet him."

Finally, we have a sense that this is a journey could be undertaken as a group, a clan which shared a common spiritual history and a common bond. This was indeed a fragment of a kind of shamanic journey that European paganism had lost, but it was only a fragment. Where did one find the entrance to the Otherworld, the realm of the Western Ancestral spirits, the Sacred Clan? Where was the beginning of the path that led to the Pale Faced Goddess in her mysterious castle?

We found it at the Rollrights.

Chapter 2

The Sacred Circle

The Rollright Stones, West Oxfordshire, England.
-Photo taken by Dave Finnin

The moon is full. Mist swirls around the distorted shapes of a circle of ancient stones. Somewhere, an owl hoots in a tree, breaking the expectant silence. You stand outside the perimeter of stone feeling that you are facing a boundary like that between the worlds, between dream and waking, between life and death. Shadowy figures in cloaks with hoods thrown up over their heads stand silently in a circle around a small fire. Their faces appear blank beneath their hoods. There is no way of telling who they are, whether they are young or old, men or women. It doesn't matter.

"Who be ye?" There is no way of telling which figure has spoken. That doesn't matter either.

"I am me."

"Would ye be one with we?"

"If I may be."

"Who are we?"

"My Friends and Family."

"What brings ye to we?"

"Another as we will."

"If we receive ye, how believe ye?"

"By fellowfaith and this, its token." You hand your token over to the outstretched hand before you.

The hand closes over the token.

"Taken, turned and tendered."

"Thanks be to ye."

So goes the Rollright Ritual by William G. Gray, reprinted in *'By Elder Tree and Standing Stone'*[4] by Llewellyn Publications, 1990.

The Rollright Ritual had always posed something of a mystery to us. We knew Bill Gray primarily as a cabbalist and ceremonial magician. We had been trained in Ceremonial Magic, Cabala, and Goetia and cut our teeth on *Magical Ritual Methods*[5] and *Ladder of Lights*[6] but, this was different. No Cabala, no Archangels, none of the trappings of a ceremonial lodge. Just an ancient stone circle at the boundary of time, a shadowy hidden company, a challenge to a seeker using no hoodwink, no sword pointed at the breast, no dire oaths. Merely the asking of three questions:

---

4 *Ritual and the Unconscious*, Llewellyn's New World Magic Series, 1990.

5 *Magical Ritual Methods* by William Gray, Helios Book Service, 1969.

6 *Ladder of Lights* by William Gray. Originally published by Helios, 1975.

Who are you? Do you want to join us? Do you have the key? Then, welcome.

Simple. Evocative. Alluring.

It's difficult to describe the effect such a ritual had on us as opposed to people actually living in places with standing stones. Growing up as I did in Southern California, where nothing of human making is more than 250 years old, standing stones of the kind described in the Rollright Ritual had an unreal almost mythic quality to them.

Yes, we knew on an intellectual level that stone circles do exist and were indeed historic, but they weren't part of our history. They were more like a backdrop to a Dungeons and Dragons game, a Disney film, or a Tolkien novel. Reading about them in books, even seeing photographs of them, did not prepare us for the experience of actually standing in the middle of these ancient stones, awed by their incredible age and being able to say little more than, "I am … me."

The Rollrights, then, served as the first key in our quest. I have related the story in *The Forge of Tubal Cain*[7] how, in 1971, Joe Wilson was given a fragment of stone by Norman Giles who claimed that it came from the Rollrights, particularly the ruins of the Cromlech called the Whispering Knights. Norman informed Joe that possession of the stone empowered him to bring Roy's tradition, which he called '1734,' to America. Norman, apparently, even went so far as to claim that Roy himself, in one of his letters, had appointed Joe to be his successor.

Years later, in his cups and despondent over his wife and priestess Mara leaving him, Joe handed the stone over to us along with whatever claim he had to the tradition. He had decided to pursue other paths, particularly Native American, and no longer wanted anything to do with the tradition that he and Mara had worked on together.

We had our doubts about whether the stone truly conferred any kind of authority. After all, we weren't the first ones to have received this

---

7 *The Forge of Tubal Cain*, Ann Finnin, Pendraig Publishing, 2008

anointing, and we wouldn't be the last. We even had our doubts as to whether the stone was really from the Rollrights, but it was all we had to work with at the time, so we used it as a focal point for our magical workings. As it turned out, it was enough.

Our first visit to England in June of 1982 just happened to coincide with the Ley Hunter's Moot held in Cambridge. It featured such experts in the field as Nigel Pennick and Paul Devereaux and included actually visiting a number of sacred sites in the Cambridge area, including a seven-church ley line. Intrigued, we decided to attend.

We were already familiar with the concept of ley lines. In our early years in the Southern California pagan community, we attended several rituals held by pagan artist Frederick Adams. Adams, also a student of the work of Robert Graves, had mapped out many of the ley lines along the California coast. He had even launched an expedition to plant crystals at the various sites along the ley line and link them up psychically by means of ritual. What did ley lines have to do with our journey? Quite a lot, as it turned out.

Back in 1966, Robert Cochrane wrote to Joe Wilson that the ley paths originally were drover's roads, used by the Neolithic herdsmen to drive sheep and cattle. They were designed to go from one part of a country to another in an absolutely straight line. Cochrane claimed that these ley paths were very strongly connected to the religion of the wise, since the sheep-herders who carved out the hills also made the stone circles such as Stonehenge, Avebury, the Rollrights, and so on.

The Herme post was a solitary altar stone often found upon these ancient roads. If these are approached correctly, they may serve as places to gain whatever one might desire by means of prayer and magic. They are sites of ancient power that still function as places where more than one world meets.

For two days, we immersed ourselves in every manner of ley line lore. Following literally at the heels of Nigel Pennick and Paul Devereaux, we walked the ley line up and down the Cambridgeshire countryside. We learned that medieval churches were often situated on sites that originally held a stone circle, cairn, or sacred spring. While it is true that putting a church on a site that the people of the area held sacred anyway was a relatively painless way of transitioning a population from paganism to Christianity, there may have been a deeper reason.

The church, as I have noted in Chapter 1, not only wanted to appropriate the exoteric worship of the ordinary people but also the magical power of the shamans. The local clergy, who were often drawn from the same shamanic families, knew that certain sites emitted a mysterious power that their ancestors had used for generations in their magical rituals.

So, they built a church on what was left of a sacred site, sometimes using the very stones from the cairn or circle to construct the church walls, or incorporating a standing stone or a spring into the design. If the ley line ran through the church, it was only reasonable to construct a special window or chink in the wall to accommodate it. And the altar was situated in the east where it was sometimes illumined by a shaft of light from the rising sun shining through a specially aligned window on a certain day of the year.

After examining the Cambridge churches, we tramped along the ley line between Thriplow and Fowlmere, noting how the church spires line up on the horizon and admiring the Sheela-na-Gig figure on the church wall in Whittlesford. Finally, we watched people dowsing along the edge of the road, noting how the rods would turn and whirl, finally crossing firmly over the notch in the hedgerow where the line was supposed to run.

Photos taken by Dave Finnin 1982

At the time, there were two competing theories about just what the ley lines were. The first theory was purely physical as described by Alfred

Watkins in 1925 in his seminal book *The Old Straight Track*[8]. Watkins coined the term ley lines, using the Saxon word "ley" meaning "a cleared glade" to describe these alignments, a word also closely linked to "lea" meaning "a track of open land."

Watkins was a surveyor by trade. His ley lines were little more than deliberate alignments of ancient stone circles and earthworks which allowed prehistoric people to navigate their way around the countryside. Evidence for this theory was provided by the fact that old Roman roads often followed these tracks, providing a convenient way of going from place to place by the shortest possible route, but there was also a metaphysical theory.

In his 1969 book *The View Over Atlantis*[9], John Michell postulated that the ley lines were part of a grid of invisible psychic energy that crisscrossed the earth. These energy lines were similar to the Chinese concept of Lung Mei lines in Feng Shui and were marked by stone circles and other Neolithic monuments. Sensitive people could locate them using dowsing rods, which would detect them in the same way that they could detect water or oil.

Esoterically, they marked the signposts of the psychic landscape. They provided the spirits of our ancestors a straight and direct path enabling them to travel from this world to the Otherworld. The newly dead, particularly if they had been condemned for witchcraft, could be prevented from going to heaven by burying their bodies along the lines in the wrong direction, thereby confusing them as to the right path to the spirit realms.

The predominance of folklore surrounding the ley lines led many researchers to dismiss them as superstition, noting correctly that a straight line could be drawn to connect any prehistoric sites that dot the landscape and that finding three or more in a straight line could be only a statistical coincidence. Of course, the assertion that the ley lines serve

---

[8] *The Old Straight Track,* Alfred Watkins, Methuen & Co., London (1925)

[9] *The View Over Atlantis,* John Mitchell. First published, Sago Press, London (1969).

as runways for prehistoric UFOs does not contribute to the scientific credibility of the existence of such lines. Michell addresses this as follows:

> "From the human point of view, there appear to be two forms of truth, poetic and scientific, and the two cannot always be made strictly compatible. Scientific facts emerge in the first instance as revelations from the unconscious mind. Where these revelations can be shown to accord with what has already been established, they are accepted. Where they stand alone, they tend to be dismissed as fantasies, even though to certain people they are more real than the system which they appear to contradict."

By the 1980s, the ley lines were postulated to be electromagnetic fields that crisscross the earth, unseen but still entirely physical like electricity or radio waves. Birds, it appears, can follow them, allowing flocks to migrate across long distances with surprising accuracy. This is because the brains of migratory and non-migratory birds and mammals such as bats contain a small amount of magnetite (Fe_3O_4), a compound containing iron that serves as a kind of organic compass enabling them to detect magnetism and navigate by it.

There is also evidence that this organic compass dwells in our own brains as well. By using an ultrasensitive superconducting magnetometer in a clean-lab environment, researchers have been able to detect the presence of similar ferromagnetic material in a variety of tissues from the human brain. This means that theoretically at least, humans are also able to detect and navigate by the magnetic field of the earth. Modern-day dowsers might be people in whom this organic compass is genetically strong, hence their ability to sense the existence of the lines. Often, they will use rods and pendulums, but many dowsers and sensitives claim to be able to sense the lines without the need for such aids. The existence of the ley lines as electromagnetic emanations from the earth seemed the logical explanation for this phenomenon.

In 1977, the Dragon Project Trust (or DPT) was founded by ley hunter Paul Devereaux in order to mount an interdisciplinary investigation into the possibility that certain prehistoric sites had unusual forces or energies associated with them. The DPT conducted many years of physical monitoring at sites in the UK and other countries. Devereaux and his team set up sensitive equipment in the midst of stone circles and other sacred sites to try to measure this electromagnetic energy and somehow prove their existence to the satisfaction of materialistic scientists. They failed. The experiments showed no conclusive evidence of a grid of electromagnetic energy linking sacred sites. The materialists scoffed, but the true believers continued to experience strange psychic and out of body experiences in the vicinity of ancient sites. Even though the DPT showed no organized grid, it did often measure magnetic and radiation anomalies at some sites, and some evidence of infrared and ultrasonic effects also.

In addition, they discovered that the kind of locations favored by megalith builders tended to have a higher than average incidence of unusual light-ball phenomena or "earth lights." Did this electromagnetic field cause the visions or were they caused by the strong power of suggestion that wandering around at night amid a circle of ancient stones can cause?

By the time Paul Devereaux's book *Shamanism and the Mystery Lines*[10] was published in 1992, the concept of ley lines had morphed into a less of a physical phenomenon and more of a psychological phenomenon. It is well known that the human brain, under certain forms of stimulation, will produce sensory impressions that come from the brain itself rather than from the outside world. Again, in *View Over Atlantis,* John Michell writes:

> "The human eye has a natural inclination to detect patterns, and specialists trained to detect and embellish one particular pattern can become so attached to it that they resent the suggestion that there may be others. The ley system may be invisible to those whose previous knowledge tells them that it cannot exist. Until a few years ago, when the amazing prehistoric civilization in Britain first became known, no one anxious to preserve a reputation for sanity and objectivity dared to admit the evidence for its existence which the ley system presents."

---

10 *Shamanism and the Mystery Lines* by Paul Devereaux, 1992, W Foulsham & Co Ltd

The psychological establishment tends to dismiss these impressions hallucinations and considers them symptoms of mental illness. However, as discussed in Chapter 1, it is these visions that make up the world of the shaman.

A shaman goes into a trance, either with the aid of dance, drumming, sensory deprivation or with the use of hallucinogenic plants. He will see strange shapes, even straight lines of light stretched out over the familiar landscape of his homeland. He will see spirits of the ancestors, the newly dead or totem animals residing in the various distinctive features of that landscape. When he awakens from his trance, he will transfer those visions to the physical landscape in the form of rock paintings, earthwork mounds, and circles of stone.

Devereaux writes,

> "Landscape lines, leys, alignments, are traces. They may have become physical tracks, ritual pathways, avenues of the dead or whatever, but they are in essence simply traces of an effect of the human central nervous system transferred to the land."

Ley lines then are a physical construct designed to mimic the psychological and physiological results of the practice of shamanism. Often enhanced by psychotropic drugs, there is an inner landscape hardwired in the brain that is common to all cultures. The ley lines are in the brain, and the stone circles and alignments of the outer landscape have been constructed to correspond to the inner landscape of the mind.

So, can we really follow the ley lines physically across the uncharted wilderness like migrating animals? Or can we only follow the spirit lines out of the body in a shaman's vision? Or can we do both? Are the ley lines physical realities or merely the product of the patterns made by the firing of neurons in the brain? There is evidence for both. Which view is real? The answer depends entirely on whether or not you are the sort of person who insists that physical reality is the only reality.

For our ancestors, there was no dichotomy between spirit and matter, between traveling the landscape physically and traveling it in spiritual vision. Both modes of experience were equally real and equally valid. This view is the only way that ley lines, and so much else in psychic and religious experience, can make sense.

Each realm follows rules according to its nature. The two realms coexist, but the shaman's journey is only possible if certain rules are followed. The gateways between the realms are only open in certain places and swing open or closed only at certain times. They are no more subject to human whim than a bus schedule. If you are waiting at the designated station when the bus arrives, you may board (providing, of course, you pay your fare). If you are waiting at the wrong place or at the wrong time, you miss the bus.

The stone circles and standing stones, then, serve as markers and signposts for our *Journey to the Castle.* They not only mark the borderlines between physical and psychic realities but also serve as gateways to the other realms. Furthermore, these gates only open at certain times of the day, certain days of the month, at set points in the timeless dance between the sun, the moon, and the stars.

In the pivotal work, *Stonehenge Decoded*[11] published in 1965, astronomer Gerald Hawkins demonstrated to a skeptical scientific establishment that the stones which make up Stonehenge were placed not at random but in a precise pattern by which the positions of the sun, moon and certain of the fixed stars, as they had been in 1500 BC, could be traced. Stonehenge wasn't a temple, as orthodox archaeologists had claimed. It was an observatory.

Hawkins' book was quickly followed in 1969 by the book entitled *Megalithic Sites in Britain*[12] by a Scottish professor of engineering named Alexander Thom. Amid a plethora of hard to refute graphs, numbers, and statistics, Thom was able to state that not only were the stones of ancient monuments aligned to celestial signposts; they formed precise geometric figures related to that which was taught by the school of Pythagoras.

---

[11] *Stonehenge Decoded*, Gerald Hawkins, Doubleday Books, 1965

[12] *Megalithic Sites in Britain*, Alexander Thom, Oxford: Clarendon Press, 1967

For the next several decades, researchers at other stone monuments as far-flung as Newgrange, Chichen Itza, Callanish and Chaco Canyon have also found such alignments. More orthodox archaeologists still dismissed their existence as merely part of the emerging cult of believers in extraterrestrial visitors influencing ancient cultures, but the evidence continued to mount until it seemed rather silly to continue to refute it.

So, what was the purpose of tracking these alignments? Why was it so important for ancient peoples to know with precision what time of year or what phase of the moon it was? The obvious anthropological explanation would be that it could be used to determine when the best time for planting various crops would begin or where the herds of game animals would likely be located during their seasonal migrations.

This is plausible, certainly, but aligning a circle of huge stones to celestial signposts seems to be a great deal of work in order to be able to predict the optimal time for planting or hunting. Indeed, such tracking data has also been found inscribed upon bits of animal bone, presumably to provide a more portable version of the same information.

The question remains, why construct a stone circle with such alignments? Was it really an observatory used by prehistoric astronomers to track the movements of the stars and planets, or was it merely a stone temple in which a primitive, barbaric people conducted blood-spattered rituals? Or, was it both?

What was supposed to happen within that circle when the sun, moon, and stars rose over certain marking stones? Like a vast cosmic padlock, when all the tumblers within it lined up correctly did something click open? And if so, what was it?

Determined to find out, we set about in 1982 visiting every stone circle and standing stone that we could, using an ordinance survey map for reference. We examined every stone monument, cairn, and hillfort we could find with that map, a rented car, a tent and three weeks' worth of vacation time.

In Cornwall, we visited Lanyon Quoit or the Giant's Table and the

Man-an-Tol or the Devil's Eye. On the wild plane of Bodmin Moor, we stood in the center of the Hurlers and watched the shaggy long-horned cows regard us balefully out of the corners of their eyes. We stood at the foot of Silbury Hill and had tea in a pub inside the confines of the massive stone ring at Avebury.

Stonehenge Photo by Dave Finnin

We were first in line on a dewy Thursday morning waiting for the gates of Stonehenge to open so we could feel the ancient brooding of the stones before the rest of the tourists arrived.

On the Isle of Anglesey, we stood at the mouth of the chambered cairns at Bryn-Celli-Dhu, the Mound in the Dark Grove and Barclodiad-y-Gawres, the Giantess's Apronful. We crawled inside the Trefignath burial chamber on Holyhead and stood at the feet of the two standing stones at Penrhos-Feliw.

But it wasn't until we stood in the Gros Fawr stone circle in Dyfed deep in the Preselli mountains where the bluestones of Stonehenge came from that we could catch a glimpse of what actually does happen when the cosmic forces align and the portal between the worlds opens.

We had managed to visit the circle on the night of a full moon, escorted by a couple of kind friends we had met along the way. We had seen it the previous afternoon, but in the moonlight, the entire circle positively glowed. We had no ritual tools with us, so all we could do was stand in the center and announce our presence.

Then, from out of the west came three white horses, galloping in tight formation. It never occurred to us to get out of their way. All we could do was stand there and stare. They galloped past us and vanished…

just like that. They weren't imagination, nor part of a personal vision since all four of us saw them. They could have been physical, although it would have been extremely unlikely for horses to be galloping around the moorland in the middle of the night.

They didn't feel physical. We didn't hear them, we only saw them. Their hooves made no noise on the grassy turf. We didn't see where they came from or where they went. No one had any rational explanation for their presence. We only knew that we had succeeded in experiencing some kind of opening of the gate between the worlds; but what did it mean?

Eventually, we ended up at the Rollrights.

The landscape was everything that William Gray had described in The Rollright Ritual, including the car park and the tourist buses. We arrived about mid-morning, on a weekday, half hoping that we might get a little privacy, but it was summer, and there were several people already at the site. We parked our rented car along with the others in the car park and began exploring.

The Kingstone (left) and The Whispering Knights (right).
Photos by Dave Finnin 1982.

Even in broad daylight with the tourists all around us, the energy in the stones was palpable. We found the King Stone, imprisoned in his wrought iron fence. The Whispering Knights too were familiar from the photographs we had seen. The fallen capstone from what had been the Cromlech lay in pieces. We examined the stone fragments carefully, satisfied that our stone had indeed been one of the fragments that littered the ground on the other side of the fence.

We found the stone circle itself some ways away near the house. The scene was like that which we experienced at other stone circles. A few people were wandering around examining the stones with varying degrees of interest. Children ran around, oblivious to the aura of antiquity that surrounded them. A woman knelt on the ground changing a baby's diaper near the center of the circle where the fire would have been.

We waited around for a couple of hours, hoping against hope that the people would clear out and leave us alone in the circle for just a little while. Finally, late in the afternoon, we suddenly found ourselves alone with no one else in sight. At last, this was our chance. The portal was open. We entered the circle.

Ann in the Rollright Circle. 1982

"Who be ye?"

We could almost hear the question whispered in the breeze rustling in the leaves of the trees overhead.

Speaking softly but aloud, we introduced ourselves to the unseen powers.

"Would ye be one with we?"

We declared that we had paid our fare to travel across both a continent and an ocean to stand in this circle to petition that very thing.

"If we receive ye, how believe ye?"

We answered, "By fellowfaith and this its token."

We planted a specially consecrated coin that we had brought with us all the way from California in the center of the circle, a small representative of the shield from Bill Gray's ritual. We stepped back and waited.

The only response was the insistent roar of a tour bus containing a bunch of Italian tourists. The bus had been blocked at the entrance by the Guardian of the Portal – who, in this case, was the woman who owned the property and lived in a small cottage on the edge of the circle. She had noticed that we were doing a ritual in the midst of the stones and had single-handedly held the Italian tourists at bay until we had finished.

However, as much as we appreciated her efforts, the moment had passed, and it was clear that the portal had closed. Disappointed, we got into our car and drove off. Obviously, whatever was going to happen wasn't going to happen immediately, or even on the physical plane the way it did in Bill Gray's ritual. Something else was needed.

We had found the lock to something strange, ancient and immensely powerful, but we didn't have the key. Once the gate to the Otherworld was discovered, how did one open it?

Chapter 3

The Reluctant Guru

Be careful what you ask for.

The original intent of our trip across the pond was not to try to inherit Roy's tradition or even to join Roy's old group. We had no idea if Roy's old group even still existed. We had heard that after Roy's suicide the members of his coven had scattered in the wake of the resulting investigation. At this point in time, we still believed Norman's account of Roy's death as being a ritual suicide with his coven in attendance, so it would stand to reason that they would have taken great pains to avoid having their involvement discovered. So, we had no idea who they were or where to find them. And even if we were to find them, would they even talk to us?

However, while preparing for our trip, we had written a letter to Bill Gray asking if we could see him with the intention of asking him about the Rollright Ritual. His reply was very prompt, friendly and encouraging. He invited us to visit him at his home in Cheltenham.

Finding his house was a challenge. He had sent us directions, but we got lost anyway. The streets in Cheltenham were poorly marked, and some of them only went one way – like the road that led to Bill's house. The main road took you to the road, but you had to turn right at the intersection since it was a one-way street. The problem was that Bill's house was in the other direction, but we couldn't find the tiny road that opened onto that road further down. So, we took a chance, turned left at the intersection anyway and hightailed it the wrong way a half a block or so until we got to Bill's house.

He welcomed us like long lost kindred. He told us that he had been watching out his window waiting for us to arrive. When he saw a little car racing up the street the wrong way like a bat out of hell, he knew it just had to be us.

During the conversation, we told Bill about Joe Wilson's ad in *Pentagram*[13] which Cochrane answered, and produced copies of the letters he had written to Joe – which apparently, he had never seen before. We explained that something in those letters had sparked a passion within us to know more about the tradition, but with Joe's marital troubles and the lack of additional information available to us, we were at a loss.

After listening patiently to our story, Bill told us that he had worked with Cochrane for some years, attending his rituals and carrying on an extensive correspondence with him on a variety of topics, part of which appears in the chapter entitled "Paganistic Principles" in his book *Western Inner Workings*[14], the first volume of his Sangreal series. Since the book was finally finished, he had intended to toss them out but hadn't done so yet. Would we like copies?

We said that we certainly would like copies, and we followed him into town to the one place that had a copier and made copies of all of them. When we returned to his home, he asked us to promise that we would not publish them until after he was gone since they contained some personal material about his family. We could, however, give them to the

---

13 Pentagram was a private newsletter/magazine published in England from 1964-1965. It was published under the auspices of the Witchcraft Research Association, an organization started by Doreen Valiente and Gerald Noel. Valiente was listed as editor. Copies of the newsletter can be found online.

14 *Western Inner Workings* (The Sangreal Sodality Series Volume 1) by William Gray. First published, 1983 by Weiser Books

members of our group. We duly promised him, and kept that promise until his death in 1992.

Then, he reached into a drawer in his desk and produced a red silk cord. It had a loop on one end and an elaborate knot on the other. It was, he told us, Roy's cord. It originally had eight knots in it, but he had untied the knots to release Roy's troubled spirit. He put it into Dave's hands. We inspected it reverently, but when Dave tried to give it back, Bill shook his head and smiled mysteriously. The cord now belonged to Dave.

Taken, turned and tendered.

It has taken nearly thirty years for us to fully appreciate Bill's role in our quest in the summer of 1982. We had no idea that he even knew Roy much less worked with him. So, our visit to him had to have been the result of the forces we had contacted taking us where we needed to go. We needed a genuine contact and that contact ended up being Bill.

Still, he insisted that he wasn't the one we should talk to regarding Roy's tradition. He told us that he would write a letter to the man who had been the *Man in Black* for Roy's old group, recommending that he talk to us. We were to give him a couple of days to receive the letter, then we were to call him and arrange to meet him. He would be able to answer all our questions. The man's name was Evan John Jones.

John was a short, powerfully built man with flaming red hair and a square, pugnacious jaw. His west country accent was so thick, it took us a little while to get used to it so we could understand what he was saying. He constantly smoked cigarettes which he would roll himself with tobacco stored in a tin, and had a fondness for dark beer, particularly Guinness.

John and his wife Val welcomed us hospitably, but we sensed that John was less willing than Bill had been to talk about his experiences with Roy. For John, our visit must have seemed like a bolt out of the blue. After all, nearly fifteen years had passed since Roy's tragic and senseless death. John still maintained contact with Bill and Doreen, but in the meantime, he and Val had gone on with their lives. They had three young children and Val was active in local politics. John had retired from his profession as a civil engineer and was already suffering from emphysema. It seemed as though the last thing he wanted to do was relive that emotional pain, but he did.

He told us the story of how Roy really died, not the fanciful legend that we had heard, but the human and tragic story how he ingested belladonna and prescription drugs while sitting alone in his living room. John had seen him the previous weekend. He even still had the tie that Roy had taken off and left behind that night.

We also discovered that John hadn't known Roy very long. He had been acquainted with Roy's wife Jane and had worked with her in the same company for some years. How and where he joined Roy's group he didn't explain, but he hadn't been a member for longer than two years. Still, Roy had made quite an impression upon him, and with his friendship with Jane, Roy's separation from Jane and his subsequent death was personally troubling.

He was particularly critical of the young actress who had seduced Roy and broken up his marriage. The problem was that the group had at the time a shortage of women. Jane was apparently the only permanent member. Several women were associated with the group, including Doreen Valiente, but few had shown up regularly for rituals. An attractive young woman was a welcome addition -- until she seduced Roy. Why?

John felt that the problem was that he believed his own myth. The myth? That he was, as magister of his clan, a sacred king that had to die for his people.

Newtimber
Photo by Dave Finnin
1982

John finally warmed to his story. He took us up to Newtimber, a hill dotted with oak trees. One specific oak tree was special. This was the oak under which Roy and the group did the magic. Every year, John and Bill had made the trek up the hill on the anniversary of Roy's death to burn a candle in remembrance and place it on the base of the oak tree.

As we approached, we noticed there was a strange thing about that oak tree. John examined the trunk where two large branches formed a fork. He pointed something out to us. There between the forked branches was a tiny sprig of mistletoe. John explained that mistletoe usually didn't grow on oak trees. It normally grew on apple trees, which was why mistletoe on an oak tree was so special.

John apparently took the presence of the mistletoe on the oak tree as a kind of omen. He took us back to his house and announced that we would be going up to a nearby hill at midnight. If we wanted to discover how Roy worked, he would show us. We would 'tread the mill' and 'cross the river to the castle' just as they had done when Roy was alive. It would be a kind of vision quest. After the ritual, he would question us and see if we received the 'keys.' If we did, he would teach us what Roy had taught him.

We waited until midnight, drinking bottle after bottle of Guinness until we were quite tipsy. John assembled his tools. He explained that he had few of them left after Roy died. All he had was a Solinger bowie hunting knife and a cup made of cow horn. Those implements in hand, plus a small candle and another bottle of Guinness, he led the way up to an old Roman age hill fort within walking distance from his housing tract.

He cut a circle in the turf with his knife and led us into it. We set the things down in the center of the circle, lit the candle and paced around the edge of the circle, first slowly then faster concentrating on the candle in the center. Then, he started a chant that sounded like eeeayeeeeohhahh.

Around and around we went, I had no idea how many times. In the dark, with much too much Guinness and only a candle to concentrate on, it was easy to become disoriented and lose track of where you were in the circle. Suddenly, he ordered us to drop. We dropped like rocks, lying sprawled in the grass, panting and wheezing.

He then instructed us to leave the circle. We were to go past the oak tree to the edge of a river. Then, go across the river.

I remember very little of the vision. All I remember was that I was met at the other side of the river by a hooded figure that had no face. He led me up a winding path past a desolate landscape. In the distance was a castle surrounded by roses.

The next thing I knew, I heard John's voice calling for me to come back across the river. I opened my eyes and got to my feet. Without a word, he led us quickly out of the circle and down the hill. Back at his house, he served us tea and queried me about what I had seen. None of it made rational sense to me, but I told him about the figure without a face. To my surprise, he nodded. I had seen the blind harper, the figure that served as a conductor of souls across the river between the quick and the dead. I told him about the castle and the roses. He paused for a moment and asked what color the roses were.

I answered that they were red

He explained that the river was the boundary between the living and the dead. In order to cross it in this life required a guide from the Other Side to take you where you needed to go. Without a guide, one might wander around alone and possibly never return. The castle was the abode of the nameless goddess that Roy had called *Fate* – the goddess that Joe, and we, had known as the goddess whose secret name lay hidden in the code '1734.'

He explained about what he called the *Objective Astral*. Where I went in my vision was a real place in the other world, not just a place in my imagination or in my personal unconscious. It was a place that had been made real by the Clan. The fact that we had been taken there meant we were accepted by the *Hidden Company,* or the ancestors who had gone on before us.

We had passed the test. He would teach us.

Over the next three days, he talked nonstop about how Roy and the clan had worked, how they had set up the circle, how to tread the mill, what implements to use and so on. It seemed to pour out of him in a torrent. Frantically, I tried to take notes, but eventually just gave up and concentrated on soaking it all in.

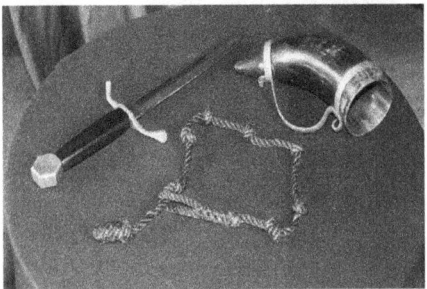

The knife and the cord.
Photo by Dave Finnin

We learned about the four implements that the group had used in their rituals:

1. **The Knife** was the male implement of courage and will. It didn't need to be a dagger, it could be an ordinary hunting knife like the one he still used.

2. **The Cord** was the female implement. It had eight knots, a loop at one end and a 'monkey's paw' or elaborate knot at the other. This was identical to the cord that Bill Gray had given us that he said had belonged to Roy. It was worn around the neck like a noose.

3. **The Stang** was the altar, or world tree. It was to be made of ash with two prongs at one end and a 'shoe' of iron at the base. It stood at the north to serve as a gateway to the otherworld. It was to be adorned with a circular garland with two arrows thrust into it, points upward, one going from left to right and the other from right to left.

4. **The Cloak**, preferably of some dark color with a hood, represented secrecy. When worn with the hood covering the head, it was possible for the wearer to literally vanish into the shadows on a dark night.

The stang and cloak.
Photo by Dave Finnin

He explained that there were several keys that indicated that we had been guided to the Castle. It was those key images that we would have to see, certain archetypical figures that we would have to encounter in order for him to conclude that we had indeed made the "Journey." If we were to take our students on the same journey, we were to question them to see if they had seen the same key images that we had. If they did, then they had been accepted by the Clan. If they didn't, then all they did was go on an imaginary journey, maybe personally significant, but not relevant to the Clan – and that was that.

No mention was made during that visit about adoption or initiation, or indeed anything to do with joining Roy's old group. We didn't ask. We didn't even think it was possible. There was no group for us to join. There were a few scattered old timers like Bill and Doreen who had gone on to other things. Roy's old coven had been disbanded for years and John had no intention of reviving it. And we had a group of our own: The Roebuck.

We told him the history of the group, how we had been inspired by what little we knew of Roy's teachings and described some of the people we had working with us.

John seemed relieved that we had a group of our own and didn't expect to join any other. We were to use what he would teach us to enhance the Roebuck and bring it more into line with what Roy had actually done, and that was the assumption that we went away with. However, he was adamant that we not make the same mistakes that Roy had – mistakes that cost Roy his life. We solemnly agreed, thanked him profusely, bid him farewell, and went back across the pond. Adoption into the Clan of Tubal Cain wouldn't come until much later.

By the time we returned to Los Angeles, we had been gone nearly eight weeks. Many of the people we had been working with had drifted away. Only three or four remained, but that was enough to begin doing the work that we learned from John and discovered to our consternation that the results were very disturbing. For one thing, we noticed that there was an edge to the work that wasn't there when we were working Roebuck rituals. We didn't want to call it sinister, but it felt strangely chaotic as though we had something by the tail that could turn and tear us apart if it wanted to. The rituals themselves were simple enough to perform, but it took a tremendous effort of will to get up the energy to do them in the first place, and once we were finished, we felt emotionally and physically drained.

Still, we persevered. Due to our Summoner's National Guard schedule, we were only able to meet for the Sabbats every six weeks or so. But we faithfully wrote to John after every ritual, explaining what we did, what happened and to whom. He would answer promptly, telling us what he thought the significance of our ritual was and what else we could do for the next ritual. This process went on for nearly two years. In his frequent letters, he told us more about how Roy worked, the structure of the group, and so on. Still, there was no mention of any formal initiation or adoption into the Clan of Tubal Cain. We were trying to make the rituals work within the confines of the Roebuck structure – and they didn't work very well. Something was missing – something important.

Ultimately, it wasn't the rituals that caused the problem that prompted our adoption into the Clan. The results of our visit had hardly been well received on this side of the pond. For one thing, we had learned from the few Gardnerians who would actually talk to us that Roy had actually been initiated into one of the Gardnerian covens, probably around 1961 or 1962 before Doreen Valiente had met him. This was roundly denied by many in the Gardnerian establishment, particularly Jack Bracelin, who hadn't liked Roy in the first place and had been horrified by his suicide, but since Doreen had her falling out with Gerald and founded her own group, there were some Gardnerians who had liked Roy and had worked with him. One couple had actually initiated him into their coven.

In her talk at the Wiccan Conference in Canberra in 1991, Julia Phillips states that Roy had been initiated by C.S. and her husband D.S. This confirmed what we had learned from D.S. himself who had visited us in the late 1980s and had described the ritual to us in some detail. Still, the Gardnerian establishment on this side of the Atlantic who had traced their lineage from Monique and Scotty Wilson through the Bucklands insisted on keeping to the official story.

Most vocal critics came from among those who called themselves "1734". By this time, Joe Wilson had become a pillar of the local community and was the head of a large and diverse group called the Temple of the Elder Gods. What caused the most controversy was the stark contrast between Joe's version of Roy's death and the version that we had learned from John and Bill.

Joe's version, which he had obtained from Norman, had been accepted without question for over fifteen years by everybody who had any connection with 1734. Everybody knew that he was the one who had corresponded with Roy and brought his tradition to America and he was considered the uncontested expert on Roy's tradition and the one who was anointed by Norman to carry it on. Nobody knew just who this John Jones was and why anybody should believe him, or us for that matter.

John was horrified at the current story being circulated about Roy's death. It was not only wrong but glorified and romanticized what was in reality a tragic and sordid end to a brilliant man's life. We agreed and told everyone we encountered what the real story was.

Joe, however, predictably stuck to his version of the story as told to him by Norman since to question that would mean to question everything else Norman had told him. We were accused of spreading lies and casting aspersions not only on Joe but Roy as well who, by this time, was approaching legendary status.

Finally, in 1984, I wrote to John complaining about this state of affairs. Even though the true version of Roy's death was less than flattering, it was still the truth, and to deify Roy and what he did might serve to justify the things he had done which led to his suicide. However, in order to be believed we had to have some credibility, and we had none. John promptly wrote back suggesting that we join the Clan of Tubal Cain. Even though Roy was no longer alive, any member of his group can start a group of his own.

What? Join the Clan of Tubal Cain? Until that moment, we had no idea that such a thing was even possible. Us? Join Roy's Clan? John's membership in Roy's group had apparently given him the authority to pass Clan membership along to us and this authority had existed when we had visited him two years previously, but we hadn't asked for it, and he hadn't offered it to us until now.

After much thought, we decided to take him up on his offer. There were several reasons for our decision: some of them noble, others not so much. The first and most noble reason was that if we were working Clan rituals, then having an initiatory connection to Roy's Clan to be able to pass along to our people was a good thing. It validated our work and allowed us to feel as though we were carrying on an old and legitimate tradition rather than just our own personal fantasy game. It made us all feel as though we had come into alignment with something far bigger than ourselves and were performing a service by preserving it rather than allowing it to be lost.

However, the temptation to pull a Gardnerian-like ego trip on the other so-called "1734" covens was overwhelming. Joe might have letters from Roy, but he didn't have the adoption into the Clan by a member of Roy's group. We did. After years of being *not acceptable* to the Gardnerian hierarchy, we finally had a legitimate lineage that didn't depend upon their approval.

So, we sent John a letter accepting his offer. He sent us instructions how to perform the ritual. We were to perform it to each other, then to the rest of our group. Then, David would in fact be the Magister of the group, and I would in fact be the Maid. The words "in fact" were duly underlined.

The ritual itself was fairly simple. Once we were in the circle, we would each light a candle and kneel at the other's feet. We would renounce our baptism and all other faiths we may hold and swear to serve Our Lady the Goddess in all her forms. We would swear to hold true to the Clan of Tubal Cain and regard all others in the clan as brothers and sisters in the faith, to aid them in time of need, protect them in time of danger, and hold true to the Clan laws and secrets.

We had some grave misgivings about taking such an oath. We had not required oaths in the Roebuck like the Gardnerians did, nor had we required the renunciation of baptism that had traditionally been a part of old witch covens. The Roebuck was more egalitarian than that. After all, we felt that any oaths of fealty should be made to the gods, not to us.

Besides, there was no evidence that Roy had taken any sort of oath. Instead, he wrote, "I was taught by an old woman who remembered the great meetings - and she took no terrible oath from me, but just an understanding that I would be discreet." This approach seemed more sensible than the taking of dire oaths that are broken all the time with no dire consequences.

Many of the oaths sworn in various secret and occult societies exist for the purpose of weeding out those who are not serious and sincere in their purpose. The newly minted Mason, for example, swears an oath to have "my throat cut across, my tongue torn out by its roots, and my body buried in the rough sands of the sea, at low-water mark, where the tide ebbs and flows twice in twenty-four hours, should I ever knowingly violate this my Entered Apprentice Obligation."

These dire consequences, of course, consist of the three ways that Hiram Abiff was murdered and are meant to be taken symbolically rather than literally. However, all such oaths come from a time when it was very dangerous to join such a secret magical society.

We of the twentieth century tend to be very blasé about such things as oaths. The worst that can happen if one is discovered to be a witch, at least since the repeal of the Witchcraft Act in 1951, is that one could get a reputation for being strange and be barred from certain social and professional circles. Occasionally, one could lose a job or a child in a custody battle, but neither in England nor America has anyone been tortured or killed for being a member of a witch coven, and in America, at any rate, membership in a witch coven is a 1st Amendment right.

Three hundred years ago, however, it was a different story. The persecution was real and often fatal. Whether it was from a local magistrate or by royal decree, people of both sexes were condemned to torture or death for practicing things that seem so innocent and banal to us now. The fact that we would casually attend a witch meeting on a Saturday night, often in a public or semi-public place, without a fear of legal reprisals much less hanging, says a lot about the evolution of our civilization. However, it also tends to render us a bit more cavalier about taking oaths, especially since there are no real consequences to breaking them, but aside from that, there didn't seem to be anything specific in the oath that we hadn't heard before, or that we would have any difficulty in keeping.

However, there wasn't just the oath. There were also laws. By swearing the oath, we were also supposed to swear the following:

1. That you hold true to the Clan in word, thought, and deed.

2. That you offer hospitality to any Clan member when it is demanded.

3. That nothing is published or told without the consent of the rest of the Clan.

4. That whatever goes on within the circle will not be carried outside of it and used against any member of the group.

5. That should a member of the group wish to use a name within the Clan he shall be known by this name only.

6. Any two members who feel that they have an affinity to each other in ritual working may if they so wish be married within the circle and will be treated as so, but this marriage must not be allowed to carry on outside the circle if it can damage others by doing so.

7. That any member who forms his own group must realize that you David and you Ann are heads of the Clan and will need your permission to do so and that any group so formed owe allegiance to you through the leader of that group.

8. That any member has the right to call for the Clan sword to be brought to the circle if he or she feels as though they have been harmed by any other member of the Clan.

9. No member can be expelled from the group or Clan without a formal hearing in the circle.

We had no idea where these laws came from, since nothing of the kind was ever mentioned in any of Roy's writings. They had the same kind of faux-medieval feel to them that Gardner's 'ardaned of olde' laws had. They, like the oath, were supposed to come from a time when belonging to a witch coven constituted a hanging offense. Doreen mentions them in her books. Indeed, coven laws were included in the American Tradition Book of Shadows that we had originally received from Bill and Helen's original American Trad coven that met a few miles east of Los Angeles.

Some of them seemed obvious. There is, in any group, a need for discretion about what goes on in meetings. This has less to do with outsiders finding out sacred ritual secrets and more to do with providing fodder for gossip and promises of mutual support and hospitality feature in the by-laws of many organizations, as do procedures for redress of grievances or resolution of disputes.

The warning against revealing the identity of the members to outsiders and the option of using a special 'coven name' within the circle, presumably to hide one's real name, seemed to harken back to a time when the discovery that one was a member of a witch coven could have unpleasant social and economic consequences. Occult writers have used pseudonyms for years for the same reason.

There was also the law that stated in no uncertain terms that any group that would 'spin off' of ours would continue to owe allegiance to Dave and me as heads of the Clan. This effectively established the Clan lineage or lines of descent, what the Gardnerians call their "upline".

There was, of course, one law that we found decidedly suspicious and consequently never actually used it. That was Number 6 which allowed for the "coven marriage" of two people who were presumably not married outside the coven, and who quite possibly were both married to someone else entirely.

The only reason we could see for having such a provision was that in a society where marriages were arranged, one's legal spouse would likely not share one's interest in the craft and might even be opposed to it, and since up until very recently, divorce was costly and difficult to obtain, the only way to have a working partner of the opposite sex in the circle was to form an attachment to someone other than the legal spouse.

Of course, a great deal of discipline and discretion would be required to keep from carrying on this relationship outside the circle as well. As Dion Fortune warned, such relationships will tend to be more intense and emotional – not to mention sexual – than the ones that people would have with their lawful spouses.

In *Esoteric Philosophy of Love and Marriage*[15], Fortune talks about the problems of being unmated in esoteric work. Ordinary people could be mated on the physical and emotional levels and that was generally good enough for them, but when people got involved in esoteric work, they wanted to be mated on mental (shared interests) and spiritual (shared aspirations) levels as well. If their spouses couldn't provide such mating, it was expected that they would seek mates on those levels elsewhere, perhaps within the coven itself.

---

15 *Esoteric Philosophy of Love and Marriage* by Dion Fortune. First published: London : Rider, 1924.

If there was no physical infidelity involved, such a practice was considered acceptable. Most people during that period, especially women, married young and tended to marry someone deemed suitable by their families. So, it wasn't unusual for people to reach the age of thirty or forty, begin studying the occult and realize that their spouse of fifteen or so years, with whom they have children, not only is not interested in their studies but might be actively hostile. Considering the difficulty of getting a divorce in pre-1960s England, the practice of having a magical spouse in the coven or lodge would make a certain amount of sense.

However, the problem arises in our present culture, particularly in California, where the majority of people choose their own spouses on the basis of personal preference, sexual attraction, and shared interests, and get married of their own free will. Divorce, if child custody and property issues can be resolved, is easy to obtain and carries no social stigma. People can, and do, eventually find a way to legally marry, or at least openly cohabit with their magical partner. After all, Dave and I did just that back in 1974.

So, we suspected that this particular law could open a nasty can of worms whereby coveners who didn't want to go through the expense or inconvenience of a divorce could have their cake and eat it too by carrying on an affair with another covener and calling it a 'coven marriage.' Not to mention that this practice was starting to sound uncomfortably like what Roy himself had tried to do during the final months before his death, so we decided to dispense with it and never allowed it for any of our members.

Despite our misgivings, we decided to go ahead with the ritual. We felt that we had come too far and were already in it too deep to back out. Besides, we sensed that it would help take our work to a new level, and we were touched and humbled by the fact that we had been chosen to do our bit to carry on Roy's work in the States. So, we gathered everyone at our house and took them up to a hill behind our house to tread the mill and conduct the ritual, just as John had instructed us to do.

By this time, it was Beltaine of 1984. I administered the oath to Dave, he administered to me, and we administered it to the others in our group.

There was a total of six of us. We were now the American branch of the Clan of Tubal Cain.

We continued working Clan material under John's tutelage until the summer of 1986 when we returned to England for a second time. We went to Brighton in the company of a young Gardnerian named Peter Larkworthy. Peter had been corresponding with us for some time regarding the Cochrane material. In 1984, just after we had performed the Clan ritual, he visited us. We initiated him into the Roebuck, then into our Clan and referred him to John for further Clan work.

There, on the same hillfort where we had done our first ritual, I took the Clan oath to John in person. After that, Dave took the oath to me as did Peter. The ritual was the same one that John had originally sent us only instead of my taking the oath to Dave as Magister of our Clan, I took the oath directly to John.

Did it make a difference? Absolutely. There is a phenomenon in traditional religious practice which the Catholics call the laying on of hands. This consists of an in-person ritual in which a religious authority physically transfers power and lineage to someone by means of some kind of physical contact, as when a Catholic Bishop consecrates a new priest by laying his hands on the crown of the new priest's head. The ritual can be simple or elaborate. It doesn't matter. What seems to matter is the actual physical contact, what Dion Fortune calls an exchange of "personal magnetism".

In any case, whatever had been passed from John to us allowed us to finally make that final and crucial connection to Roy's tradition. We returned to the states and continued for the next several years to work Clan rituals under John's tutelage while Peter began making regular trips down to Brighton from his home in London. The quality of the work improved, the energy began to flow more easily, and we soon discovered that we were finally able to make the rituals work.

We also repeated the oath taking ritual with the members of our original Clan as well as administered it to several other candidates. We all felt as though we had finally plugged into the cosmic wall socket. We were now psychically as well as officially part of Roy's tradition and it showed. We continued our correspondence with John as we had done before, reporting on our progress and receiving advice and instructions for future work.

Then, in 1987, John dropped another bomb on us – a far bigger one. We were now to be the heads of the Clan and he would owe fealty to us. He stated that no group or coven would be able to call themselves part of the Clan of Tubal Cain unless they have taken an oath recognizing our position as titular head of the Clan.

This was not open to negotiation, arbitration, civil liberties, uncivil liberties or anything else. In addition, any group starting up in England in the Clan ways would be in the same position as the groups in the States, they would owe their oath to us and our group and to no one else. Even if John himself started a group of his own, he would have to take an oath recognizing us as head of the Clan of Tubal Cain before they could claim to be part of the Clan.

Wow.

In 1990, John's book, *Witchcraft: A Tradition Renewed*[16] came out. It was dedicated as follows:

> *In Memory of Robert Cochrane*
> *And to Doreen, Jane, Bill*
> *Mike, Peter, Ann, Dave*
> *and The Roebuck*
> *And Valerie for all her help.*

John even managed to get Doreen to autograph a copy for us.

John and Doreen's book, *Witchcraft: A Tradition Renewed,* consisted of the tradition as he had laid it out for us from 1982 to 1990. The only thing that we found different was that the Magister in the circle had been

---

16 *Witchcraft: A Tradition Renewed* by Doreen Valiente and Evan John Jones. Published August 1st 1990 by Phoenix Publishing (WA).

replaced by the stang rather than an actual man. When we inquired why, John told us that Doreen had wanted it to be that way in print. She didn't want another man abusing his magisterial role in the circle the way Roy had.

According to John, this was deliberate. The book gave enough info for anyone reading it to be able to set up working along kindred lines to what the Clan was doing. Too much information would result in carbon copies rather than a like development, which was the one thing that he wanted to avoid. Any carbon copy could then claim that they were the only true inheritors of the tradition of Tubal Cain whereas in reality only the Roebuck could claim this. This was what he had in mind when he mentioned the Roebuck in the dedication and coupled with our names.

In John's book, we discovered that there were two initiations. The first initiation, which included much of the ritual we had originally received from John via letter, made the initiate a member of the group. The oath was similar to the one we had taken in 1984 including the renunciation of all other faiths, but not the promise to aid and protect the other members. It also included the dire consequences of breaking the oath where the Dark Gods of the Underworld would "extinguish the very light of my existence." This initiation was valid for a year and a day. At the end of that time, if all were agreed, the candidate would be eligible to take the Oath of Full Admission. This involved, as John and Doreen wrote, "not so much an oath of membership as a reaffirmation by the person taking it in the aims, ideals and tenets of the faith as practiced by the Clan." Furthermore, it was also a recognition by the member that, by the taking of this oath, he or she is willing to accept the responsibilities that are part and parcel of the running of a coven. It is this reaffirmation that we made to John in 1986. The oath was the same, the intention was the same. The only thing missing was the sword, and that was only because John didn't own one. So, as far as we knew, it was official. We were the inheritors of Roy's tradition, whether we wanted to be or not.

We tippy-toed around this at first. We didn't want to be heads of the entire Clan. We didn't even know what that meant, yet. So, despite John's letter, we never fully assumed the authority that he gave us. We may be Magister and Maid in name, but we always considered John sort of a Magister Emeritus, not actively running the group, but functioning as a guru and senior advisor. We did nothing without consulting him. We still reported in great deal the results of our rituals. We told him all about the members of the group and encouraged them to write to him on their own.

In addition, while we continued to work Roebuck rituals for training purposes, we decided to set up another group called the Clan of Tubal Cain. It was comprised primarily of Roebuck initiates, but it was to be run as a completely separate group to explore John's teachings within the framework of the Clan without involving the other members of the Roebuck. The Clan would function differently, with different lines of authority than the Roebuck even though at first it consisted of the same people.

As the Roebuck grew and new members came into the group, we did the best we could to keep the Clan as much under wraps as possible. Only Roebuck initiates knew the Clan even existed, and they were told that it was an independent group with a completely different initiation process. In a Roebuck circle, all initiates, Clan or not, were equals. The last thing we wanted was to have Clan members consider their Clan membership to be the equivalent of a sort of Roebuck third degree and decide that they somehow outranked those who were not Clan.

We continued this uneasy arrangement for seven years. We considered people for Clan membership only after they had received a Roebuck initiation (itself the end of a year-long process) and had been active with the circle for a year and a day. During that year, we watched them for signs that they were tuning in to the Clan vibrations. Often, by the end of their maiden year in the Roebuck, they would have been told about the Clan and would have expressed some kind of interest in it. If their experiences in the circle or if their personal dreams and visions were full of Clan key symbolism, we would approach them for Clan membership. If they were agreeable, they were taken into the circle and taught how to tread the mill. Then, they would be taken on the same journey I had undertaken with John on that hillfort in Brighton and asked what they saw in their vision. If they saw most of the symbols in the Journey to the Castle, they were adopted into the Clan.

Roebuck initiation didn't automatically lead to Clan adoption, and after several years there were a number of people in the Roebuck who had been there as long as Clan members but who had either failed their test or for some other reason never took Clan adoption. This made for strained relations within the group, particularly from newcomers who were put off by what they perceived as the ruling clique of Clan members who they felt were given special consideration even though they had no official rank within the Roebuck.

However, the Clan continued to meet independently of the Roebuck on the Saturday night closest to the greater and lesser Sabbats and as close to midnight as possible. Sometimes, we would go up to the hills behind our house and perform the ritual there. Other times we would meet in the temple. We kept track of the visions and experiences everyone had and soon it was clear we had tapped into something old and very powerful. The first thing to appear was the presence of the Hidden Company or, as one member called them, the Unseen Crew. These were shadowy presences that would show up whenever we were performing a particularly intense ritual. During our post-ritual debrief sessions, members would report the distinct sense of someone standing behind them, even though they knew that there was no one there. Sometimes, there was just one or two, other times there were many, as though they had decided to converge on us for some reason.

Most of them were indistinct and were felt rather than seen. However, one or two were actually seen by various people over the course of the years. One in particular, a tall woman with long fair hair apparently was named Jennet. Another was a young man in a great kilt who carried pipes and, occasionally, a harp, but who they really were and why they were there we never could discover.

Then, there was Stuart.

John had hinted in one of his letters that sometimes circle guardians could be summoned to inhabit skulls that were buried on the edge of the circle. Mostly these were sheep or horse skulls, but occasionally a human skull could be used. This intrigued us for a number of reasons.

In Celtic lore, the head was the seat of the soul. Celtic warriors would lop off the heads of their enemies as trophies and bring them back to their camp. Skulls of dead chieftains were often tucked into niches in the walls of meeting houses. They were consulted during discussions of policy issues as though they were still alive and given food and drink as offerings during feasts and revelries.

In the second branch of the Welsh saga, The Mabinogian, Bran (which means raven) and his company of warriors have gone to Ireland to rescue Bran's sister, Branwen, who has been captured by the Irish king. They succeed, but Bran is mortally wounded in the process. As he lies dying, he instructs his men to cut off his head, and bear it with them in their journey back to Britain.

They comply, and for seven years, they remain in Harlech[17] where Bran's head continues to laugh and jest with them just as it did in life. However, one of the men eventually opens the door of the hall which faces Cornwall, and the memory of their trials return to them. Bran's head falls silent, and the survivors bury it on a hill overlooking the sea as a guardian against invasion.

So, we decided that we needed to get ourselves a human skull in order to have our own guardian. Sure enough, we managed to acquire one soon after that. The skull itself was a present, of a sort. One of our members had a friend who worked for the city morgue. The medical specimens that the morgue kept for training purposes were periodically cleared out to make way for new ones.

During the next clearing out process, this friend liberated the skull of a homeless man who had no family and had donated his body to science. It had what looked like a massive hematoma on one side (which had probably resulted from a blow which caused the man's death) and had been prepared as a specimen with the crown sawed off and reattached with hooks and the jaw attached to the skull with springs. The cranium was filled with hazelnuts and gleefully presented to us in a plain cardboard box.

---

17 Harlech, a magnificent stone castle in Wales

Now that we had our skull, the first thing we had to do, according to John, was to purge it of the vibrations and influence of its former owner. This was important because the intended guardian was not the spirit of the person who had inhabited the skull, but the spirit of a Clan guardian who would be invoked into it. So, we were instructed to perform the cleansing ritual with four people, two men and two women, representing the four elements. The ritual goes as follows:

> *Air carries the skull into the circle, Fire kindles a sacred flame and sets the skull beside it. A widdershins mill is trod, then Air picks up the skull with the right hand, using the left as though drawing air from the nostril cavities and says, "As I draw the breath of life from your nostrils so shall the very breath of life be drawn from you." This is done three times.*
>
> *Then Earth chants three times "Lo ... I am your mother, the womb from whence you came and in death you must return." The skull is passed through the flames three times by Fire who says, "Thus from the grave to the fire of purification you shall pass where both good and evil are cleansed." Water says, "With the waters of life, time and for forgetfulness I wash both past and present away until re-birth."*
>
> *After this, the skull is named. The Maid takes the skull and says. "Through our Lady and for our Lady I breathe the life of the Clan into you." Then, she blows into the nostrils three times. Strands of colored wool are placed on top of the skull: red for re-birth, black for knowledge, and finally, white for death. If a name occurs to everyone, then sprinkle a little wine on the skull in baptism and name it.*

When we performed this ritual with our skull, the name we received was Stuart. Henceforth, the skull was addressed as Stuart, and was treated like another member of the Clan. At first, working with Stuart was something of a game. The skull resided in a silk-lined bag made of Stewart tartan. It was brought out for every ritual and set out on a table or a pillar if we were in the temple, or sat on the ground beside us if we were outdoors. When cakes and ale went around, Stuart always got his share. He was greeted by name when the skull was taken from the bag, and talked to freely during the course of the ritual.

Gradually, Stuart began to take on a personality all his own. People would hear him speak. When you scried on the skull, a man's face would appear, leer at you (that is, if you were female) and make suggestive comments and bawdy observations. We wondered if this might have been due to the power of suggestion. We all talked about his eccentric behavior, and so everybody, perhaps unconsciously, came to expect to experience it.

So, we decided to see if this was indeed the case. We made Stuart's existence a deep, dark, initiatory secret. The skull was only brought out for initiates-only rituals and was not talked about in front of students or visitors. At some point after a student had completed the pathworkings, he or she was taken into the temple for an 'ancestral working.' After a short ritual, Stuart was taken out of his bag and placed in the students' hands. The student was told to meditate on the skull and report any impressions or messages.

One of three reactions tended to occur. The first one was a general freaking-out over the fact that the object was obviously a real human skull. Another unnerving reaction occurred when students received impressions of deceased relatives along with emotional reactions to unresolved issues surrounding their deaths. Several others 'picked up' impressions of the previous owner of the skull, which we had thought we had banished by the naming ritual. The fact that such impressions still existed led to an interesting conclusion.

Stuart was not actually imprisoned, so to speak, in the skull. The physical skull functioned as a vehicle for his manifestation if he wanted to appear to someone, but he was not confined to it, and proved to be quite selective to whom he deigned to appear. When we introduced students to him, he would show up or not as it suited him. If he chose to manifest to a student, it was obvious to everyone. The student would react to him the same way we had, with surprise at his strong personality, delight and embarrassment at his bawdy remarks, and wonderment at how real he seemed. We would validate the student's impressions by relating our own experiences with him, and because Stuart had chosen to appear to the student, it meant that the student belonged with us and their work towards Roebuck initiation proceeded.

However, it was the Clan who began working extensively with Stuart. During our meditations and rituals with him, we kept getting impressions of just who he had been and, more importantly, who he was to us. Stuart, apparently, was not his name but his title. He was a clan chieftain from the Scottish borders who practiced the old faith, much like the North Berwick witches had, and had suffered persecution from the English authorities.

As the years went on, many of the members of the Clan discovered that they had a personal past-life relationship with Stuart. We had all been together before, and he had been our Clan chieftain. So, he had been related to all of us in various ways, as lover, brother, son, father, grandfather and so on. It bound all the Clan members together in strange -- and not always friendly -- ways as old karmic patterns started to surface and cause disputes and ill feelings that didn't seem to have any rational, here-and-now reasons for existing.

Gradually, the Roebuck began taking on a distinctly Celtic flavor. The men dressed in kilts and the women in green gowns with tartan sashes for formal occasions such as spierings (commonly called inquisitions) and initiations. This Celtic bent had started, of course, back when we were putting together the Roebuck pantheon. The gods and goddesses at the quarters were called by their Celtic names since our research led us to believe that the gods that Roy had written about had Celtic roots.

Indeed, Roy's entire approach to magic, as evidenced by his use of the *White Goddess*[18] as an inspiration, seemed to have a mystical, bardic character to it. The riddles he posed in his letters to Joe Wilson could have been posed by Taliesin himself. He spent a great deal of time dissecting the Song of Amergin and described the mystical journey to the castle in a poem similar to the Predui Annwyn. He spoke of the three treasures of Annwyn, particularly the Roebuck in the Thicket, which directly inspired the name of our coven.

John would later disparage this Celtic influence, insisting that the Clan was purely Anglo-Saxon which was strange, considering that John

---

18 *The White Goddess,* by Robert Graves. First published, 1948, Faber & Faber, Ltd

himself was a Welshman, and it proved to be ironic that the falling-out we would later have with him mirrored on a spiritual level the kind of dispute that a Scottish chieftain would have had with his English overlords and their sympathizers in the 16th century.

Whether or not our work with Stuart was the cause, our visions during Clan workings became full of intimations of the sacrificial king and how they revolved around the person of the magister, to the point where it was starting to make us nervous. It constituted the myth that Roy had believed in and that John had insisted had led to his suicide. It was no wonder that Doreen had chosen to leave it out of the book.

John had been very specific about the duties of the Magister – in our case, Dave. He was the representative of the Horned God in the circle and was, as such, a sacrificial victim. After every circle, the summoner would present Dave with a coin before Dave cut the circle. The summoner would lead everyone out and Dave would follow, tossing the coin over his shoulder as he went. This was called "paying the coin" for the site and it was a substitute for the ultimate payment that the Magister might be called upon to make for the sake of his people. In fact, traditionally the Magister could only reign for seven years unless he either paid the coin in some way or found some substitute to do it for him.

Later that year, we returned to England a third time with two other Clan members in tow and visited John. We videotaped a two-hour interview in which he discussed some of the traditions he learned from Roy and where they might have come from, but he was also working on another book. This one involved animal masks.

In 1992, Bill Gray passed away. With Bill gone, John no longer made his yearly trek up to Newtimber to light the candle at the foot of the oak tree in Roy's memory. We mourned Bill and performed a memorial ritual in his honor, but we had no idea at the time that something else had passed away with him, but something had, and it soon made itself evident.

****

By 1994 the Roebuck had grown too big to be one group. It eventually splintered into five daughter covens, each with its own high priest and priestess, coven-stead, initiations and ritual practices. However, the Clan continued to meet at the sabbats with the original members just as it had done for the previous ten years, and with the same authoritarian structure as it originally had.

The problem was that most of the Clan members had become leaders of their own Roebuck daughter covens. A number of them already had initiates of their own and performed their own separate rituals. However, they were still expected to honor their fealty oath to Dave and me as though they were still in the Roebuck. This was becoming increasingly more awkward and difficult to do as the years went by.

Then, the inevitable happened. A couple of members wanted to break off from the original Clan and form their own Clan. Under other circumstances, we would not have had a problem with this. People hived off of the Roebuck all the time, either forming their own groups or working on their own, but we had a problem with this particular hive-off proposal. For one thing, Roebuck wasn't Clan. The rules for forming a new Clan group were different than forming a Roebuck daughter coven. There were still oaths to be kept to the original Magister and Maid. John's writings in 1987 had made that very clear.

It was also becoming increasingly clear to us that this situation wasn't merely a hive-off. It seemed as though our legitimacy to run the Clan at all was being questioned. Even though we were not accused of any wrong doing and nobody called for the sword against us, we were effectively, albeit discreetly, being deposed as Magister and Maid. The new Clan group apparently was being formed mainly because the leaders wanted to exclude certain existing members that they didn't like and include new members that would take a fealty oath to them, and not to Dave and me. This had never happened before, and we didn't understand why it was happening now.

We knew that the other Clan members were corresponding with John on their own. In fact, we had encouraged it, but it was becoming clear that there was something he was telling them that he wasn't telling us – something that made them want to do an end run around us and establish another Clan without acknowledging our authority.

All the while this was going on, John continued to write conciliatory letters to me. He suggested that it might be time for Dave and me to retire from being heads of the Clan and go off to work on our own. He even mentioned at one point that Roy and Jane had been considering doing this. Apparently, they had felt that running a group was holding them back from developing their own magical abilities and they felt they could go further on their own.

Okay, maybe so, but that still didn't explain why the members of the Clan were acting the way that they were. Finally, I called John on the phone in the winter of 1997, asking him what was going on. All he would say to me was that I couldn't hold onto them. I had to let them go.

I asked another member of the group who wasn't involved with the hive-off if he knew anything that could shed some light on the issue. He said that the letters I had received weren't anything like the letters that he had seen that had been sent to other members of the group. In them, John claimed that he had never made us Magister and Maid of the Clan, that our adoption into the Clan was a farce and a sham and that he never gave us the authority that we claimed he had.

The problem wasn't that we weren't letting another Clan hive off. This was nothing less than completely reversing what he had said fifteen years previously -- that he had never adopted us into the Clan at all, much less given us the authority to run it. He was, essentially, accusing us of misrepresenting what our role in the Clan was and claiming some kind of authority that we didn't, in fact, have.

So, Dave and I called a special Clan meeting. We spread all the letters we had received in the last eighteen years out on the living room carpet. We picked up one and said that this was the letter where he told us we were members of the Clan of Tubal Cain. We picked up another and said this was the letter where he names us Magister and Maid. We picked up a third and said this was the letter where he declares the Roebuck to be the only inheritors of Roy's tradition. If John had changed his mind about us and our role in the Clan, then it was certainly news to us.

The members were flabbergasted. They had never seen the original letters we had received from John and had no idea what was in them. One of the members involved in the hive-off dispute produced one of her letters and showed it to us. In her letter, John wrote that I was never ever given any sort of authority at the Samhain ritual and that it wasn't all that much of a ritual to start with. All Dave and I did was to take an oath to follow the strictures of the Clan of Tubal Cain which was something any member could do when dealing with people who wish to follow his way without being members of the Clan. My power extended only to the members of my immediate group and the leader of the daughter group pledges themselves to me in the name of the others, but that was it. Strange what a difference ten years made. But there was more:

John wrote that he could not have passed absolute power in the Clan sense over to me because he didn't have the authority. The ones above Roy who he referred to in one of his letters were the only ones who could do that. As they had never met Dave and me, nor have the slightest intention of doing so, the chances of me being granted absolute Clan authority is limited.

As for the Roebuck? John's answer was that I was brought into the Clan through him with the idea that I would found a branch of his workings in America which meant moving people away from the Roebuck and into the Clan. Now, if I wanted to continue working Roebuck, that was fine. But to continue working the Roebuck and calling it Clan was wrong. The Roebuck was the Roebuck and the Clan was the Clan and never the twain would meet.

So much for the Roebuck being the only true inheritors of the tradition of Tubal Cain.

After we discussed the matter with the group, our Summoner carefully drafted a letter to John referring to the letters he had sent us. He made it clear that this wasn't about Dave and me. This was about eight people who had accepted everything he had taught us without question for fifteen years and had believed themselves to be members of the Clan of Tubal Cain even as Dave and I had. Were we legitimate members of the Clan of Tubal Cain, or weren't we? The letter was then signed by every single member of the Clan, including those who had originally wanted to form their own Clan. We sent it off special delivery and waited.

Our summoner soon received an answer. In it, John insisted that he was still following Roy's tradition. All he did was to develop what was there. Did that include the mask workings? Apparently, yes. If I had truly been following the Clan tradition, then I, too, would have arrived at the concept of the masked workings within the coven structure.

So, were we Clan, or weren't we? He wrote only that we had our American Clan of Tubal Cain and no one in England could strip anyone of membership in that even if they wanted to, which they don't. All he would say is that he and we had grown so far apart that we have nothing left in common. The best we could do would be to disassociate ourselves from each other and go our own separate ways -- thus putting a formal ending to what had been happening for years.

So, yes. We were still members of the Clan. We were just not members of **HIS** Clan. He had been inundated with letters from our members complaining about us, but now they were siding with us against him. Still, with all the letters he had received complaining about the other members, nobody had ever expressed the least bit of interest in what he and his group were doing. How dare we involve him in our internal squabbles. He never wanted to hear from us again. So be it. With that letter in February of 1998, our association with John was over.

Chapter 4

The Aftermath

After the dust had settled on our severance from John, we carefully examined the information we had received in 1982 versus what he was claiming he had in 1998. We originally had no intention of keeping to the tradition rigidly. John hadn't wanted us to. He himself hadn't done so. He had done just as he had claimed to have done in his last letter. He had gone on and tried to develop Roy's tradition in areas that he thought Roy would have done had he lived. He was understandably irked that we weren't interested in what he had done in the intervening years and incensed that we were critical of it on the basis that it wasn't what he had originally taught us in 1982.

Fair enough, but that wasn't what his early letters had said. Between 1982 and 1987, he had presented the Clan of Tubal Cain to us as a secret, unbroken family tradition from antiquity, and had solemnly made us the heirs to it, charging us with oaths to keep to it no matter what, and this is what we had attempted to do. However, in 1998, he would criticize us for doing what he had told us to do in 1987, and he was angry when we called him on it, sending him copies of his previous letters and demanding to know why his story had changed so radically. It should have come as no surprise that he would eventually tell us to get lost.

We would eventually learn that John had appointed at least three Maids and Magisters between his 1987 letter to us and his death in 2003. He would find a suitable and knowledgeable couple, work with them for a little while, and then make them Magister and Maid of the Clan while he stayed in the background, did his research and wrote his books. When the group fell apart or if the couple declined the position, he would find another couple and repeat the process.

That was totally fine with us. We never expected to be the one and only Clan. John even stated that there was not just one but many branches of the Clan, all with the same root, like the branches of a tree, and we would have been happy to acknowledge as kinfolk other Clans on both sides of the Atlantic.

But that wasn't what the issue was. He wasn't just taking away our exclusivity. He was disavowing us entirely. Something had happened sometime after 1992 that had caused him to change his mind about us, strip us of whatever authority and legitimacy he had bestowed upon us and label us frauds and usurpers who were claiming to be something we never were. Why?

Part of the problem seemed to be that we were Americans. Somewhere along the line, he had decided that the Clan should rightfully be kept as a purely British tradition and that any money to be made from it should stay in British hands. In 2001, we received a note from Chas Clifton, the writer and professor who had co-authored *Sacred Masks, Sacred Dance*[19]. He had been collaborating with John on another book dealing with Roy's legacy to be called *The Cave and the Castle* under a contract from Llewellyn publications, the same publisher who published *Sacred Masks, Sacred Dance*.

However, all of a sudden, John had decided to break his contract with Llewellyn in order to give the book to a British publisher instead. He eventually did just that and a book entitled *The Roebuck in the Thicket*[20]

---

[19] *Sacred Mask, Sacred Dance,* Evan John Jones and Chas Clifton, 1997, Llewellyn Publication

[20] *The Roebuck in the Thicket*, Evan John Jones, Robert Cochrane, Michael Howard (editor), Capall Bann Pub, 2002

came out in 2002 from Capall Bann Publishing, coauthored by British craft writer and editor of *The Cauldron*, Michael Howard. Clifton was left totally in the lurch. John didn't want the manuscript that Clifton had prepared, and Clifton couldn't sell it anywhere else. So, he sent the manuscript to us to do what we wanted with it. We discovered that the book that was eventually released from Capall Bann bore little or no resemblance to the manuscript that Clifton had written.

Another part of the problem was that John still insisted that the mask workings constituted an integral part of the Clan, was annoyed that we didn't do them, and had told Clifton as much. We protested that there had been nothing in any of his previous teachings, or in any of Roy's letters or articles, about using animal masks in ritual. The rituals that he described in *Sacred Masks, Sacred Dance* were so totally unlike anything that we had previously learned or that were described in *A Tradition Reviewed* that I wondered if this was indeed the same tradition.

There was something about the mask workings themselves that I took a visceral dislike to. John insisted that it was "shamanism", but it bore no resemblance to the kind of shamanism that we had studied about from other sources. It seemed too much like the fantasy role playing games that we had been involved with; middle class urbanites dressing up in animal masks and dancing around pretending to be primitive shamans. It was the same kind of craft that Roy had derided in his articles.

In *The Faith of the Wise*, published in Pentagram Magazine, August 1965, Roy writes:

> It is said by various "authorities" that the Faith of the Wise, when they do believe in its existence, is a simple matter: a pre-Christian religion based upon whatever Gods and Goddesses are the current vogue--full of simple, hearty peasants doing simple, hearty peasant-like things ... things that in some cases complex, nervous sophisticates also enjoy doing in urban parlours. Consequently, we have an interesting phenomenon: civilized sophisticates running round behaving like simple peasants--and simple peasants who have never heard of such things!

In the article, Cochrane was describing Gardnerian Witchcraft, but was a ritual consisting of running around wearing animal masks a whole lot different? Gone was the mystical journey, the poetic imagery, the spiritual devotion and personal connection with divinity that had formed such a large part of Roy's work. Whatever this was, it didn't come from Roy.

John disagreed. He claimed that the mask workings were a part of the traditional craft that Roy had practiced, even though he had not mentioned it in any of his letters – even those to Bill Gray. He referred to it as an inner tradition, one that was worked exclusively by the Clan elders and not taught to the rank and file members, and that if we wanted to be part of that inner tradition, it would mean performing the mask rituals.

I tried to explain to John that the mask workings weren't shamanism and had nothing to do with what made Roy's work special. But John insisted that he knew very well what Roy's work consisted of: he was the one who had worked with Roy, not us, the mask work was part of it, and how dare we question him?

It left me wondering where on earth had this imperious attitude come from? Why had John, who had made such a big deal out of claiming that he didn't think groups should be carbon copies of each other, now appointed himself the one and only arbiter of the Clan? It constituted a complete reversal of what he had told us back in 1982. It was disturbing precisely because it didn't make sense.

In trying to figure out this abrupt change in attitude, we went back and revisited the events that had occurred between the mask book in 1994 and our final break with him in 1998. What had caused John to discard Roy's approach to the Craft and take up the mask workings in the first place? And where did the mask work really come from?

I had known that John had been involved with author Nigel Jackson. John had expressed an admiration for his artwork in one of his letters and mentioned that they were collaborating on some research. Indeed, we ended up purchasing a copy of Jackson's book, *The Call of the Horned*

Piper[21] and were very impressed. In it, Jackson writes, "In modern workings, spirit masks open up fertile possibilities for dramatic rites based on sacred myth, shape-shifting magic and votive ritual. The value of such masks lies in the fact that they help us to transcend the personality and enter into the nature of the Old Ones; they enable us to enter the magical reality of Elphame." This was nothing new. Roy himself had used the symbolism of the mask. In *Western Inner Workings*, Bill Gray describes something called a Leaf Mask: a seven-pointed leaf which was imagined overlying the face as though it were being viewed through a screen of foliage. With it, the human face merged with that of the Green Man and various parts of it were touched in sequence while reciting a Leaf Mask prayer.

Actual Leaf Mask.
Photo taken by Dave Finnin

The Leaf Mask wasn't an animal mask though. It wasn't even a mask, *per se*, although it could be used as such. We did make one and use it on a couple of occasions. It functioned as a kind of mandala, a meditation device in which the parts of the masks are symbolic of the greater mystery of the sacrificial king. It wasn't the kind of mask that was to be used in the rituals that John had described in *Sacred Masks, Sacred Dance*, and it still didn't explain the complete sea-change in tone that John's letters exhibited. Something else had happened, something larger than just dancing around wearing animal masks. In his next book, *Masks of Misrule*[22], Jackson wrote:

> "This mystical self-reversion or initiatic regression to the root of the *All* is synonymous with the Horned God's law of Misrule. It provides the

---

21 The Call of the Horned Piper, Nigel Jackson, Capall Bann Pub, 1994.

22 *Masks of Misrule*, Nigel Jackson, Capall Bann Pub, 1996.

inner metaphysic of ritual reversal, symbolized by the Backwards Prayer, the Widdershins Dance and the black tapers and ceremonial inversions characteristic of the Sabbat-Rite. All these infer the way of infinite return and self-reversal to the ground and matrix of primeval unity which is the true state of Sabbatic ecstasy."

Now, the Horned God was many things, and the Lord of Misrule was certainly one of them, but where did this Backwards Ritual, black tapers and so on, the classic signs of Satanism, come from? There was no indication in any of Roy's letters that described anything like this.

Masks of Misrule also contained a curious dedication: "To Andrew D. Chumbley, for revealing the Black Light…" In 1997, we had received a letter from Andrew Chumbley wanting to know about the Roebuck and how we worked. Hailing me as Maid and Dave as Magister, he included a copy of a booklet proposing a structure for a new traditional Witchcraft alliance called the Cultus Sabbati -- a Sabbatic Tradition made up of initiates descended from the Elder Gods through Cain, the perfected sorcerer.

The prospectus didn't sound like anything we had encountered before in the work of Bill Gray, Doreen Valiente, John, or even Roy. It almost had a Crowley-esque feel to it with illustrations that reminded me of the works of Austin Spare. It stated that the primary work of the Cultus was the reification of the Quintessential Magical Current through the sorcery of the Crooked Path. In addition, the general foundation for this work was a Grimoire entitled *Azoetia*[23] as formulated through the vision of the present Magister of the Cultus, Alogos Dhu'l-quarnen Khidir, whomever that might be (Chumbley himself, perhaps?).

Empowerment was directed from an autonomous circle of adepts, the Synomosia Draco-ta'us or the Sworn Brotherhood of the Peacock-Dragon but initiates from "certain affiliated bodies and circles of magical work" could apply. However, only those bodies of comparative lineal integrity

---

23 *The Azoetia: A Grimoire of the Sabbatic Craft,* Andrew D. Chumbley, Xoanon Publishing Ltd, 1992

or of suitable initiatic provenance would be considered for collective affiliation.

After some thought, I decided not to pursue the correspondence with Chumbley or take him up on his offer. It wasn't until much later that I would learn that the Cultus Sabbati was a group that practiced something called the Luciferian craft -- an odd mixture of traditional Cunning Craft coupled with the elaborate ritual of the Typhonian OTO, a Thelemic offshoot founded by British occultist Kenneth Grant.

The grimoire *Azoetia*, aside from having a lot of Spare-like illustrations and names reminiscent of the mixture of Egyptian and middle-eastern terms that Crowley was fond of, seemed to be little more than a means for inducing visionary experiences and not with traditional witch magic *per se*. There were elements that looked like they were taken from the Gardnerian tradition, including the invocations to the elemental watchtowers and the consecration of salt and water, along with the descriptions of a variety of magical implements -- some that seemed to come from the Key of Solomon and some from various hereditary traditions including the stang. The rest consisted of poetic invocations to the spirits with whom one was supposed to have "congress" and elaborate and erotic descriptions of that congress.

What Chumbley appeared to have done with the Cultus Sabbati was attempt to merge this kind of Typhonic magic with the elements of ordinary Cunning Craft (with its visionary experiences, herbal lore, and charms) under the aegis of the figure of Cain as the archetypal magician. This was the most apparent from his book *One: The Grimoire of the Golden Toad*.[24]

When we were in Wales, we tried to visit a stone cairn that was pictured on an ordinance survey map. We couldn't find it and inquired at a farmhouse as to its whereabouts. We were told that unfortunately the farmer who had lived there previously had dismantled it as the stones had blocked his plow. But the woman was intrigued as to why we were

---

24 *One: The Grimoire of the Golden Toad*, Andrew D. Chumbley, Xoanan Publishing, Ltd, 2000.

looking for it. When we told her, we discovered that although she was originally English, she had lived in Wales for some time and had studied the local customs.

One such custom was the making of something that the locals called Toad Wine or just Toad. What one did was take a toad of the genus Bufo, plop him into a bucket of wine and make him swim around for a while. Then, the toad was fished out of the bucket and set free. The wine then had hallucinogenic properties. This wasn't surprising, since the unhappy toad would excrete a psychoactive toxin called bufotenin, which is a chemical similar to that found in Amanita Muscaria.

The Toad of course, is the quintessential witch animal, even more so than the black cat. During the various witch trials, a witch was often accused of suckling a toad at her breast. Owen Davies in his book *Cunning Folk*[25] describes a practitioner called a Toad doctor. Toad doctors were charmers who healed by touch – mostly scrofula, but other ailments as well. They didn't do divination and incantations. They healed by laying on of hands, like a faith healer. They used the leg of a toad in a muslin bag as a charm which was placed around the sick person's neck.

In *The Golden Toad*, Chumbley tells how to isolate a charm called the 'Toad Bone' which is used to command man, beast and spirit alike. It can also be used to call the Devil who will answer questions and a black horse that can be ridden over all the *Face of the World*. The name of this horse was 'Man'. And his master's name? 'Cain'.

We later heard that Chumbley had been associated with John's group

---

25 *Cunning-Folk*, Owen Davies, Hambledon and London, 2003

during the time that we were having our problems with him. A couple of his newer members apparently had embraced the Luciferian craft and had decided to become part of the Cultus Sabbati. Had John actually adopted Chumbley's Luciferian Witchcraft as part of the Clan?

Jackson's Luciferian connection soon became clear with his next book called *The Pillars of Tubal Cain*[26]. Jackson co-authored it with Michael Howard who had co-authored *The Roebuck in the Thicket*. In it, Jackson writes, "It reveals the symbolism and meaning of the previously forbidden Luciferian occult tradition concerning the Watchers, or fallen angels, and the so-called 'Prince of Darkness' who is revealed to be really the Lord of Light." Apparently, by refusing to accept the mask workings and the rest of the Cultus Sabbati trappings, we had rejected that Luciferian influence, which had been decreed to constitute the only true Clan of Tubal Cain, and we had been summarily excommunicated and branded as heretics.

Eventually even Nigel Jackson reconsidered his involvement with the Luciferian Craft. In an Amazon UK review of *Pillars of Tubal Cain* in January of 2009, he writes a refutation of his previous work with regards to Luciferian witchcraft: "… by the beginning of the millennium, I had already come to regard 'luciferien' occultism as little more than a facile confabulation of distorted themes deriving wholly from metaphysical error and sustained misreading and subversion of symbolism from a non-traditional (or even anti-traditional) perspective." So much for the genuine shamanic roots of the Clan.

Roy's craft was intensely personal and devotional. It consisted of a spiritual/religious method of gaining an individualized connection with a divine power that he visualized as the Goddess. His rituals seemed to consist of a journey in a trance state to commune with the Goddess and to discover Her will, not only in his own life but in his outer work. The purpose was to gain the power of the Goddess through personal sacrifice in order to become the Sacred King, and to use that power to serve others.

---

26 *The Pillars of Tubal Cain*, Jackson Howard, Michael Howard, and Nigel Jackson. Capall Ban Pub, 2000.

Roy had written to Joe that some groups seek fulfillment in mystic experience. However, one must not forget the duty of 'involvement' which was the prime duty of the wise. It was not enough to see the Lady, it was better to serve Her and Her will by being involved in humanity, primarily by participation in the process of Fate. This is Shamanism in its purest form. No costumes, no masks, no complicated authoritarian structures are necessary. Just a visionary mystic traveling to an ancestral otherworld to commune with the divine mother of his people, to worship her and to discover what she wants him to do with himself, and the function of the Horned God is to guard the sacred portal against the unprepared, guide the mystic shaman into the realm of the Goddess, and protect him while he is there. It doesn't have to be any more complicated than that. And it isn't.

In 1963, Roy wrote in an article for the *Psychic News*[27]: "The genuine witch is a mystic at heart." The closest that we found to Roy's dedication to the Goddess was the devotion of the poet to his muse, the White Goddess as portrayed with such enraptured poignancy in the poems of Robert Graves. For Roy, as for Graves, shamanism was the magic of the enraptured bard who would speak the "secret and holy name of God" and was able thereby to command the elements themselves into physical manifestation.

John for some reason did not seem to be able to relate to that devotional mindset. Unlike Roy, John was not a mystic. There is nothing in John's letters over the entire twenty-year period that came anywhere close to the kind of personal devotion and selfless service to the Goddess that permeated everything that Roy wrote. For John, shamanism consisted of ritual practices that you did to gain power, not what you saw or experienced in a personal way that helped you grow spiritually. It was all about raising energy as an end itself rather than a means to access the divine. If anything, the gods were to be placated in case someone might put the "mockers" or a curse upon you, and the gods would drive you mad out of spite.

---

27 *Psychic News* was a weekly spiritualist newspaper founded in 1932 by Maurice Barbanell

In 2007, we were contacted by yet another of John's former coveners. It seems that in 1998, just about the time we were having our disagreement with John, there had been a schism brewing within John's own Clan. A fierce rivalry had broken out between two Maids, each in the running to be named John's heir apparent. One maid had been with John longer than the other and practiced the original version of the tradition the way John had taught us, which included the influence of Bill Gray. The other Maid was a devotee of the Luciferian craft as developed by Andrew Chumbley, Nigel Jackson and Michael Howard. John, for reasons of his own, had chosen the Luciferian maid as his heir, but after his death, the two branches separated and formed two rival Clans, each with its own Maid and Magister.

Both branches had known about our existence. However, it was the Luciferian branch that dismissed us in such scathing terms. The more traditional branch was willing to acknowledge us as equals. It was this branch that we became associated with and worked with for several years to attempt to fill the gaps that were missing in both our versions of what we recognized as our shared tradition.

After much back and forth correspondence and a couple of trans-Atlantic visits with this British branch of the Clan, we discovered something interesting and profound. Despite all of his books and letters to the contrary, John essentially had continued to practice Roy's craft just the way he had taught us in 1982 and written in his first book in 1991 until his death in 2003. In fact, when we circled with the traditional Clan in 2010, we could only see one or two small things that they did that we did not. The rest was identical to how we were taught almost thirty years earlier.

What had happened to the mask workings? According to what we were told, John had tried to work them back in 1994 with a couple he had attempted to groom into taking over the Clan. The couple in question apparently didn't like the workings, and left John soon after that. That was, apparently, when the Luciferian influence began to creep into the Clan, becoming more and more prominent until the schism that happened just before John's death.

There were other confirmations as well that indicated to us that we had been on the right track all along. The mysteries that John had alluded to so long ago – the mysteries that he had described as being from Norfolk – had been fleshed out and reconstructed by the British Clan in their extensive book of rituals. In it, there was no mention of equating Tubal Cain with Lucifer or Quayn as there had been in Jackson's or Chumbley's works. Instead, there were frequent references to Bill Gray as the true spiritual seed bearer of Roy's legacy. Bill Gray had not just been a frequent visitor to Roy's rituals. He was a member of full admission in the Clan of Tubal Cain, just as John had been, and, it appeared, just as empowered to bring new members into the Clan as John was.

We also had further confirmation that Roy had been initiated into a Gardnerian coven after we were given a Gardnerian initiation of our own, into the same lineage as Roy. After that, the cork came out of the bottle, and we were given information about the early Gardnerians and Roy's influence on them that we could have never acquired any other way.

Finally, we actually trod the Peddar's Way in person. Our kind hosts in Norfolk initiated us into the Whitecroft line of the Gardnarian tradition and took us to the sacred places described by John: The Castle of the Four Winds, the Rose from the Grave, the Stone Style, the Cave and the Cauldron, and the Mound and the Skull.

Finally, our journey to the castle was complete. It took almost forty years and four trips across the ocean, but we felt as though we were standing at long last in the midst of the circle surrounded by the Ancestors and hearing them say to us:

COME IN AND BE

AT HOME WITH WE.

To which, we could only reply,

"Gramercy."

Chapter 5

The Art of Cunning

So, what was this *Cunning Art* that Chumbley and his associates sought to incorporate into the Luciferian Craft? The Cunning Craft tradition consists primarily of folk magic of the sort that was practiced by various families all over Europe and America for the purposes of healing ailments, cursing enemies, divination, channeling, and unfortunately often playing hoaxes on the local gentry if they got too uppity, and poisoning their well with nasty herbs if they didn't get the message.

This is the *Craft* side of Witchcraft. It is a science and an art rather than a religion. It involves not only of the knowledge of herbs, plants, animals, and astronomical cycles, but also basic psychology of alternate states of consciousness, techniques of suggestion, and creative visualization. Using this knowledge, a cunning man or woman offered herbal treatments for common ailments, advice on love, money, and personal relationships based on tarot card or palm readings and provided spiritual solace in the form of banishing evil influences for people whom often had no recourse to any other help.

None of this is intrinsically evil, of course, any more than any other sophisticated technology is evil in and of itself. They are merely traditional ways of harnessing natural forces to produce effects in the material world. It also involves the knowledge of the powerful symbols of the particular culture, its gods and myths, and how to weave those symbols into poems and stories, rituals, spells and charms that will stimulate the innate powers of the ordinary person into making positive changes in his or her world.

This is priest-craft in its purest form. It makes no difference whether it is a shaman in feathers and body paint or a priest in an embroidered surplice and mantle. If it inspires people to believe in their own blessedness and give them the motivation and encouragement to work out their own problems, then it is a sacred art. One becomes a mediator, and according to Bill Gray, acts as an agent between other humans and the spiritual source of influence or intelligence with which he or she has established contact.

When the Catholic church took over, it appropriated the art of priest-craft and claimed exclusive control of it. However, for a number of centuries after the fall of Rome, Christianity remained primarily an upper-class religion. In early centuries, the Church tagged along with an invading force and served their needs, such as England after the Norman Conquest. Even though they were expected to be Christian, the poor natives in their villages often didn't have recourse to the priesthood even if they wanted it.

The priests tended to speak a different language. Churches tended to be located inside the keep of the local warlord and did little except sanctify marriages and baptize babies. If a peasant needed an herbal potion to heal an ailment, a midwife to deliver a baby, or a talisman or blessing for the well-being of their livestock, they wouldn't go to the priest. They would go to the local cunning man or woman who spoke their language and, as often was the case in villages, was related to them by blood or at least ethnicity. They would get what they needed in exchange for a chicken, calf, a cooking pot or other useful item.

However, as the centuries progressed, villages turned into towns. The local lord was able to ensure relative peace, and commerce flourished. Townspeople were able to support their own priests and churches.

Material prosperity also meant doctors (such as they were) and other professionals which served the needs of the increasingly prosperous, newly minted middle class. After awhile, the only people who would go to the cunning man were those who wanted something that the church or other official professionals couldn't – or wouldn't – provide.

Some of these, of course, were last-ditch attempts at healing an ailment that the doctors of the day couldn't cure, no matter how much money was tendered. Herbal remedies had long been more effective than the purges and blood lettings employed by university-trained medieval physicians, and in many periods of history the nobility were less healthy than the peasants they ruled for precisely that reason. So, when the doctors gave up or proved to be ineffective, a wealthy townsman might venture out into the countryside and consult the cunning man.

However, there were other things that people went to the local cunning man for. These were often things that were deemed sinful by the church: love charms, curses to exact revenge, incantations to lift curses from less benevolent witches or wizards, herbal preparations to induce an abortion, or render a man impotent. A young woman who wanted to compel a lover to marry her or a young man who wished to hex a rival would go to the cunning man for a spell or charm which would presumably do the job.

Often these spells would involve distasteful activities, such as killing small animals or collecting body parts and fluids. A young woman who wanted a man to love her might bake strands of her hair or drops of her menstrual blood into a cake and trick him into eating it. Or, if he spurned her and married another, she might procure a lock of her rival's hair or a piece of clothing and put it into a wax doll to melt over the fire along with incantations that the rival should waste away just like the doll.

Were these elaborate steps necessary to procure the effect? Probably not. However, a wise cunning man would know that if a young woman was willing to go through all that trouble and unpleasantness to win a man or kill a rival, then she would be even more determined that the spell or charm would work, and the more effort she put into it, the more it worked not because of the charm itself, or the power of the cunning man, but because she wanted it to so desperately.

The *Oxford English Dictionary* defines cunning as 'having or showing skill in achieving one's ends by deceit or evasion.' So, the cunning art has always involved a certain element of deception – for the simple reason that most charms and spells only work if the person performing them believes that they will. This is the classic placebo effect. If the doctor can convince you that the sugar pill is a powerful medicine that can make you well, then it will. "Thy faith," said Jesus in the gospel of Luke, "has made thee whole."

Many stage magicians will admit that a great deal of the art of prestidigitation or sleight of hand tricks originally came from tribal shamans who would employ such techniques in order to reassure the members of their tribe that they indeed did have the magical power they claimed to have in order to heal their ailments and ensure their prosperity.

Similarly, a magician also employs much the same unusual props, impressive costumes, grand gestures and incomprehensible words that a shaman might use to convince his clients that he possesses secret knowledge that they do not. It is due to this secret knowledge that he is able to perform his magic. He might also claim to have a special relationship with unseen beings or spiritual forces that will come to his aid if called upon in the proper manner.

Trickery? Maybe. But if the health and wellbeing of the tribe depended on their belief in the divine power of the shaman, then the trickery had a useful purpose. After all, if people figured out that it was the power of their own minds and wills that was performing the desired magic and not the spell itself, they would be cunning folk themselves.

However, the temptation for practitioners to trick their clientele into spending money on spurious services or snake oil nostrums is undeniable. On both sides of the Atlantic, there arose gypsy laws and laws against fraudulent mediums which tried to prevent practitioners from preying on frightened and ignorant people, for example, by telling them that a neighbor has placed a curse on them, and that it can only be removed by the practitioner – for a hefty fee, of course.

Even so-called sophisticated people in our modern day fall for this scam. Most people don't realize just how much their own minds and expectations can influence their perception of events that happen to them. A job loss, a troubled marriage, a run of bad luck will cause a lot of people to seek some cause outside themselves – something that is done to them by somebody else rather than as a result of their own actions or lack thereof.

So, such a person goes to someone who is out of the ordinary, not part of mainstream society, slightly dangerous, and not approved of by the establishment for answers. Sometimes, he will do this after the establishment doctors, lawyers, and psychologists have proven unable to fix the problem. Other times, it will involve a problem, such as lifting a curse, that establishment authorities either believe is evil (in the case of the clergy) or believe is not real (in the case of mainstream psychology).

Unconscious beliefs, often from childhood, will convince him that, like they did his ancestors, that the power that is forbidden by the establishment – either science or religion – is the only power that will actually work for him. So, he will find an impressively attired practitioner who will tell him exactly what he wants to hear; that it isn't his fault, that some powerful magical force is at work against him. And only magic, and money, will stop it.

The practitioner, of course, could do a reading or divination of some sort and tell the client that he has been either a nitwit or an asshole and has earned the enmity of his neighbor, and, "What goes around, comes around. Change your attitude and your life will change accordingly." However, more likely, the practitioner will say, "your neighbor is jealous of your success and has gone to an evil witch or sorcerer to put a curse on you. I can lift that curse – but it will cost you a hundred dollars."

The grateful client hands over the hundred dollars and watches the practitioner perform an impressive ritual, complete with costumes, props, chanting and clouds of incense smoke. If the situation doesn't change, and it likely won't, the client will return to hand over another hundred dollars and witness another impressive ritual, and on and on.

There are many self-proclaimed witches, hoodoo practitioners, Santeros, curanderos, brujos, and medicine men and women who have clients who come to them regularly for years on end for readings, psychic healing, and exorcisms that never seem to resolve anything for very long. They can make quite a good living off these clients, even if the fees are considered as donations.

So, just what are these unfortunate people really paying for? You could say that they're getting harmless entertainment. They're paying money for a front row seat to watch their own personalized magic show which is being staged just for them. It makes them feel good, so they want it repeated often, and if the practitioner is talented and theatrically inclined, he'll put on a good performance, and earn his money thereby.

But is it really harmless? After all, he doesn't motivate his clients to make any changes in their lives that might resolve their problems. They're still encouraged to think that the problem is outside themselves and can only be solved by someone else other than them, and the magical practitioner, no matter how skilled, is giving them what they want rather than what they need. He is giving them feel-good delusions rather than the unpleasant truth. In other words, he is enabling their problem not alleviating it.

To be fair, often the practitioner himself will be convinced that he has special knowledge to heal someone that the mainstream medical establishment doesn't, and that may be absolutely true in a lot of cases. He may have herbal preparations that will alleviate the symptoms of an ailment more effectively and more gently than a drug made by a pharmaceutical company. He might also be able to provide the patient with an affirmation or mental exercise such as a chant or charm that will provide positive suggestions for healing and encourage the person to make certain lifestyle changes that will truly help them.

He can also delude himself into thinking that he actually has the magical power that he has convinced his clients he has. This might be a product of his ideology, his disgust with materialistic science or ignorant doctors or greedy drug companies, or authoritarian religion. He may go so far as to convince his clients that only he has the power to heal them and that they must not go to anyone else.

Deliberately bilking gullible people out of their money is bad enough. Often, the worst that happens is that the magician uses the money and power to support self-destructive habits such as alcohol and drug abuse or sexual excess. When this powerful art is placed in the hands of an angry and petulant practitioner who succumbs to the temptation to wreak vengeance upon a personal enemy or worse, a rival practitioner, it can cause a great amount of harm to innocent people.

It is amazing to the extent that even an experienced and otherwise intelligent magician can convince himself that a magical attack against another magician or group is justified. He may convince himself that the rival group is out to get him, and he must protect himself against their attack. This is surprisingly easy if there is a sexual component to the rivalry, that is, if an ex-lover or spouse is involved.

A spurned husband might be able to tell himself that the group that his ex-wife has joined may be launching psychic attacks against him and that he is justified in defending himself. Or he is sure that they are planning to do so at some point in the near future and that he must stage a pre-emptive attack to discourage their efforts.

He could also convince himself that the rival group is practicing black magic on innocent people. If a favorite student or protégé leaves him and joins that rival group, he may decide that the group is exercising some kind of undue influence over that student, and he must step in and rescue the victim, and prevent the group from doing the same to someone else.

Or he could use a political ideology to justifying getting rid of a rival. If the rival group belongs to an opposing political party, engages in behavior that he deems dangerous or holds opinions that are contrary to what he thinks is right and proper, then they are evil and must be destroyed for the good of the community, and possibly humanity as a whole. This is the stuff that witch wars are made on.

Chapter 6

The Clan of the Cave Bear

What was it about the animal mask workings that bothered us so much – enough so that we were willing to jeopardize our relationship with a beloved mentor and friend in order to avoid working them?

It wasn't the masks so much. Masks were often worn in the mysteries. In *The Wicker Man*[28], masks were worn by the people portraying particular roles in a mummer's play. They serve a valuable purpose to depersonalize the actor, as in the case of the Greek plays, where an actor would wear a mask to portray a god, goddess or other celestial being. The identity of the person wearing the mask ceases to be important. What is important is the power that he is portraying in the ritual.

It wasn't even the animals themselves that were the problem. The gods often took the form of animals in order to appear to people in dreams and visions. Doreen, in her notes about the Clan, describes the animal powers in a kind of totemic relationship to the group. We had our totem animals as well – the Stag, of course, but also the Raven, the Salmon, and the Eagle, all traditionally symbolic of the four elements of earth, air, water, and fire.

However, treading the mill in animal masks, concentrating on assuming

---

28 The Wicker Man, (movie) 1973, British Lion Films.

the animal nature corresponding to the mask one wore, or even summoning animal powers rubbed me the wrong way. The first problem I voiced to John was that there was no reason for summoning animal powers in a civilized society. We aren't primitive people anymore. Our task, difficult as it is, is to become more human, not regress into a more animal nature. Besides, what would we use these animal powers for, and why would we think that we would even have the right or the knowledge to summon animal powers in the first place?

It sounded less like shamanism and more like one more fantasy role playing game where dull, ordinary, middle class people put on fancy costumes and spend an evening pretending to be something they're not. Yes, animal masks were certainly used at one time by shamans. However, an animal mask does not a shaman make. Nor does it automatically confer upon the wearer true totem animal powers no matter how long one dances around a circle.

"The Sorcerer"
From the Cave of Les Trois Freres
c. 12,000 B.C.E..

This is why, 10,000 years ago, the shaman put on his deer hide and antlered headdress that either he or someone in his tribe had killed and skinned, the meat of which he had consumed. He then went into his cave, took his bone implement which he fashioned from the same deer, danced himself into exhaustion, went into a trance for three days and received a vision from the gods of his tribe telling him where the herds would be this winter.

Recovering from his trance, he told the hunters where to find the herd and assured them that the gods would grant them a good hunt with no deaths. The hunters found the herd where it was supposed to be, killed a number of them with only a few injuries to the hunters, and returned triumphantly to the tribe which would have food for the winter.

Fast forward 10,000 years. A wannabe shaman puts on a deer hide, antlers and bone implement that he has fashioned from things that someone else killed which he bought at a store for money. He goes to a gathering on a Saturday night, which is the only time he can get off from work. He puts on the costume, dances for an hour or two, gets drunk, has feelings of arousal and energy which make him feel good, then drives home to sleep it off in a soft, warm bed.

The next day, he buys meat wrapped in plastic at the supermarket. Monday morning, he goes back to the real world and goes back to his real job, the job which feeds, clothes and shelters him and those who depend upon him. He works at his job but looks forward to the next convenient time when he can perform the ritual again.

Maybe there are superficial similarities between the two. Certainly, the wannabe shaman might go to great lengths to do the research to ensure that his costume and his chant is as authentic as possible, but there is something that has vanished during the course of the millennia between these two antlered dancers: consequences.

Our modern would-be shaman could spend his Saturday night watching television. It wouldn't matter – to him or anyone else. No tribe would starve, no hunters would return empty handed trying to find a herd, or having found the herd, would make no kill, and maybe lose a hunter to injury or death. Nothing was accomplished by his actions. His dancing and drumming were a game, mere entertainment. It possibly stirred up primal energies in his repressed, 21st century, techno-geek self, which felt good for a while until he had to return to his day job, but ultimately no one was served. Not even him.

Ultimately, the energy that he raised which caused all the good feelings becomes the end in itself rather than the means to an end. So, he returns time and time again to the gathering to go through the whole thing again, but like an opiate causing artificial euphoria, it isn't real. It is a sham. The real energy that our ancestors stirred up that was vital to their survival now has no purpose, no outlet other than his own personal gratification.

Once the energy is stirred up, it needs a purpose. 10,000 years ago, it had a very important purpose: the survival of the tribe. Now, all it does is entertain, and eventually feed an addiction for a level of excitement and intensity that our modern world has lost.

It hasn't been that long in the cosmic scheme of things since our world was turned from an agrarian one to an industrial one, when we as a culture traded in our subsistence farming with its dependence on the vagaries of natural cycles for the more predicable income that a factory could provide.

In America, in particular, it has only been a hundred years or so since our muddy streets were paved with asphalt, our horses and mules replaced by cars and trucks, our houses and office buildings turned into hermetically sealed fortresses against wind, rain and insects, and our diseases cured by antibiotics and other modern medicines. Very few people, even Pagans, are able to endure life without these comforts even for the length of a weekend camp out.

Consequently, in the process of conquering nature and its attendant problems, most modern adherents of the Craft are drawn to the worship of the gods of nature with absolutely no idea of what kind of nature they are gods of. They know they have lost something, a vital and visceral part of themselves. However, they don't know what that part is or how to get back in touch with it. In *The Craft Today*, published in *Pentagram Magazine*[29] in 1964, Robert Cochrane wrote:

> "…the Craft has rapidly become an escape hatch for all those who wish to return to a more simple form of life and escape from the ever-increasing burden of contemporary society. In many cases the Craft has become a funkhole, in which those who have not been successful in solving various personal problems hide, while the storm of technology, H-bombs, and all the other goodies of civilization pass by harmlessly overhead. Modern Witchcraft could be described as an attempt by twentieth-century man to deny the responsibilities of the twentieth century."

---

29 *Pentagram Magazine* (Issue #2), BM/Elusis, London, W.C.I, 1064, D. Valiente editor

In a desperate and sincere attempt to regain our connection with nature, we have instead reconstructed a plastic diorama of nature, an illusion of being in nature without actually having to deal with the unpleasant natural things that propelled our grandfathers and great grandfathers into building our antiseptic industrial society in the first place. We want the beautiful, fun, and exciting bits of nature but none of the hard, unpleasant, and dangerous bits, and in the process, we have lost both.

Many years ago, we had a friend who lived on a farm in Wales. Every year, he would watch hordes of Londoners move to Wales and he would try to predict how long they would last with none of the creature comforts of the city. Most of them didn't even last the winter. As soon as they felt the bitter cold in their bones with no furnace to turn on, felt the ache in their muscles after chopping wood and hauling it into the fireplace, felt the emptiness in their stomachs when the available food didn't fill it, they bailed and went back to civilized society.

After all, it wasn't as though there wasn't a civilized society for them to go back to. Unlike their ancestors, who had no choice but to make do with whatever circumstances they found themselves in, the would-be back-to-naturists had a choice to remain or leave, and they chose to leave.

There is nothing wrong with creature comforts. In fact, our ancestors worked very hard to devise ways to keep the more uncomfortable and dangerous aspects of nature at bay long enough to develop what we know as culture: art, music, literature, poetry and religious ritual. Once we are no longer in danger of being killed and eaten by predators or dying from hunger, disease or infection, or being incapacitated by natural disasters, we can turn our attention to other matters less concerned with bodily or tribal survival.

We can draw pictures on the walls of our caves. We can tell stories and sing songs of our ancestors and eventually write them down for future generations to read. We can track the motion of the stars and navigate our way across oceans. We can spend time and effort making jewelry, ornaments and things of beauty. We can develop codes of law and government. We can sow seeds and reap them and turn them into bread. We can selectively breed herds of animals with increased capabilities for nourishment and labor. We can develop medicines that cure illness. We can build cities. We can invent machines that will do our labor for us, that will convey us from one end of the continent to the other, that will fly through the air, that will perform complex calculations almost instantly. We can go to the moon.

However, this freedom from nature's dangers has led to nature becoming romanticized. Over the last hundred years, an entire film genre has grown up dedicated to anthropomorphizing animals, particularly dangerous animals. This goes beyond the occasional heartwarming story of devoted domestic animals such as cats, dogs or horses doing heroic, lifesaving deeds.

Cartoons such as those produced by Disney gave animals, especially wild animals, human characteristics and emotions, making them kind, sweet, innocent and fun loving instead of fierce and bloodthirsty. They talk, sing, dance and get along with each other and share like well-behaved kindergarteners.

This admittedly is standard children's fare and has been for many centuries. However, in the past, children would balance out the tales of talking animals with interaction with actual animals. They would eventually discover that the horse that drew the milk cart, the cow in the field across the road, the mice that lived in the roof thatch and the cat that caught the mice, and even the wolf that lurked on the edge of the forest not only didn't talk or sing, but didn't like humans and actually harmed them if provoked.

They also didn't get along with each other very well. The cat that chased the mice didn't dance and sing with them. It eventually caught, killed and ate them often leaving blood and mouse parts all over the floor. As they grew up, such children learned the difference between the story and the real world.

However, many children in our modern era don't learn that lesson quite so well. They not only hear stories about friendly talking animals, they see the cartoons on television and in the movies, and there are few real animals in the everyday life of most modern children to counteract the cartoon message.

After a certain age, most children will know the difference between a cartoon and real life, at least on a conscious level. On an unconscious level, however, not so much. Increasingly for most people what constitutes the real life of animals is what they see in zoos and on television in carefully filmed and edited documentaries which portrayed wild animals just like they were in the cartoons as tame and friendly to humans – just like dogs or cats.

This was particularly true for the kinds of animals which used to be considered enemies of humanity. Once, they were creatures that inspired terror. If a large predator could jump out of the bushes at any time and snare us, we were concerned only with staying out of its clutches. It was only when we had learned to live in caves and tamed the awesome power of fire that we were able to ensure our own safety and draw pictures of them instead.

The less and less we were subject to their predation, the more pictures we could draw and the more stories we could tell about them. They became remote, distant. Their threat was minimized until finally we saw them in person only behind bars or glass in a zoo or in an animal park, and we had the luxury of admiring them, of choosing to care for them or exterminate them as it suited us. We became the predator and they the prey, and they inspired terror no longer.

Take the lion: King of the Jungle and predator par excellence. Even today in parts of Africa, hunting and killing a lion which is ravaging a village and killing and eating the most vulnerable members of that village constituted a test of courage for the local warriors. At the risk of life and limb, a warrior will defeat the lion, kill it, then dress himself in its skin and claws as a kind of blood right. Through the control and discipline of his own predatory nature, he has defeated the lion and is now entitled to command its power to aid him in his next battle.

Travel to a large urban area in Europe or America. A would-be warrior fashions a mask of a lion (inspired by images taken from photographs) and puts it on. In a ritual on a Saturday night in between work weeks, he summons the spirit of the lion and attempts to identify with it. Since he has never even seen a lion in the wild, much less killed one, all he can do is pretend to be a lion for a while.

The problem is that he has no idea how a lion really behaves. The closest he has come to this kind of feline predatory energy is to keep a house cat. The predatory energy of the lion is foreign to him and is something he has no legitimate use for. At best, nothing happens, and he plays an entertaining and ego gratifying game for a few hours or years. At worse, it unleashes a power within him that he has not learned to control, and he causes others harm. This is particularly the case if the person wearing the animal mask is exercising some kind of authority over others, such as John describes. What does wearing an animal mask and the power it presumably carries confer upon the wearer that he can't achieve as a human?

In the case of the African warrior who has summoned and controlled his own predator instinct, assuming the power of the lion is advantageous since he belongs to a culture that dictates that he must hunt and kill to eat and provide for his tribe.

The process of hunting is dangerous. The hunter could, and often does, get injured and then turns into prey himself. The power of the lion carries a price. The hunter must acknowledge that his encounter with the lion could have just as likely resulted in his death rather than the lion's, and the next encounter might very well turn out that way. He and the lion are equals; today, the lion lost, and the hunter wears his hide. Tomorrow, it might be the other way around.

The 21st century urban shaman has not earned the right to command the power of the animal. He has risked nothing, sacrificed nothing to obtain the power so the power commands him. He might actually become a channel for predatory power, but since he has no prey animals to use the energy on, he turns on members of his own species who have something that he wants or that he considers a threat to him, and herein lies the problem.

Perhaps there is nothing so iconic in the popular imagination regarding witches as their ability to turn themselves into animals and fly off and do a lot of things that they couldn't do in human form. Legends from all cultures abound in shamans taking on animal form and traveling abroad, usually at night. Sometimes the shaman would take the form of predators – wolves, foxes, hawks, eagles. Other times, they were everyday animals that would be able to come and go without anyone really noticing them – ravens, hares, cats or dogs.

It isn't difficult to see where this legendary ability comes from. It comes from the folk memories of shamans dressing up in often elaborate animal costumes. The dancing and drumming served to put the shaman into a trance, and the costume he wore served to add the hypnotic suggestion that he should act like the animal he was portraying. So, he does – to the point where he convinces not only himself but others as well.

In my early days of studying magic, I attended a performance of a stage hypnotist. At one point in the performance, the hypnotist called a few people up onto the stage, gave them a hypnotic induction and told them that they were chickens. Immediately, they started clucking, crowing, flapping their arms and scratching the floor of the stage with their feet.

I noticed that, rather than being embarrassed by the ridiculous spectacle they were making of themselves, they seemed to be having a whale of a good time, like children playing a game of make-believe. The audience picked up on their fun and started laughing at their antics, which seemed to encourage them all the more. Then, the hypnotist reversed the suggestion and snapped his fingers. The spell was broken. The chickens became human again and returned to the audience where they were gleefully received by their companions as having put on an entertaining show.

Did they really think that they had been turned into chickens? Even if they didn't, they certainly put on a convincing performance, and these were just ordinary people. What if they had been shamans who lived in a culture that believed that people could turn themselves into animals at will?

Isabel Gowdie was a Scottish witch who lived in Auldearne in the 17th century. In 1662, she was reported to have confessed to the inquisition that she used a special incantation to turn herself into an animal "in the devil's name" and roamed about at night until she came home again.

> *I shall go into a hare,*
> *With sorrow and sych and meickle care;*
> *And I shall go in the Devil's name,*
> *Ay while I come home again.*

The witches in Staffordshire had another part of this ritual, detailing what would happen to the 'hare' in question.

> *And we shall follow as black tom-cats*
> *And chase thee through the corn and vats*
> *But we shall go in Our Master's name*
> *Aye to fetch thee home again!*

So, what's actually going on, here? The entire poem, called the Allansford Pursuit by Robert Graves, can be found in a footnote on page 402 of the *White Goddess*[30]. It was, he claimed, a restoration of the fragmentary seventeenth-century text, "as danced by North-country witches at their Sabbaths".

> *Cunning and art he did not lack*
> *But aye her whistle would fetch him back.*
> *o, I shall go into a hare*
> *With sorrow and sighing and mickle care,*
> *And I shall go in the Devil's name*
> *Aye, till I he fetched home.*
> *—Hare, take heed of a bitch greyhound*
> *Will harry thee all these fells around,*
> *For here come I in Our Lady's name*
> *All hut for to fetch thee hame.*
> *Cunning and art, he did not lack*
> *But aye her whistle would fetch him back.*
> *Yet I shall go into a trout*
> *With sorrow and sighing and mickle doubt,*

---

30 *The White Goddess*, Robert Graves, Faber & Faber (UK), 1948

> *And show thee many a merry game*
> *Ere that I be fetched hame.*
> *—Trout, take heed of an otter lank*
> *Will harry thee close from bank to bank,*
> *For here come I in Our Lady's name*
> *All but for to fetch thee hame.*
> *Cunning and art he did not lack*
> *But aye her whistle would fetch him back.*
> *Yet I shall go into a bee*
> *With mickle horror and dread of thee,*
> *And flit to hive in the Devil's name*
> *Ere that I be fetched home.*
> *—Bee, take heed of a swallow hen*
> *Will harry thee close, both butt and ben,*
> *For here cornel in Our Lady's name*
> *All but for to fetch thee hame.*
> *Cunning and art he did not lack*
> *But aye her whistle would fetch him back.*
> *Yet I shall go into a mouse*
> *And haste me unto the miller's house,*
> *There in his corn to have good game*
> *Ere that I be fetched hame.*
>
> *—Mouse, take heed of a white tib-cat*
> *That never was baulked of mouse or rat,*
> *For I'll crack thy bones in Our Lady's name:*
> *Thus shalt thou be fetched hame.*

Assuming for the moment that Graves hasn't added additional verses of his own to this poem, it indicates that Isobel's invocation is less of a shape shifting spell and more of a poetic description of a transformational vision wherein a would-be shaman is chased by vengeful gods from which he can only escape by turning himself into various animals. The pursuing god will turn himself into the shape of an animal which normally preys on the animal whose form the shaman has taken. The shaman takes another shape, the god takes the shape of the natural predator, and it goes on and on until the shaman is fetched home again.

In the tale of the famous Welsh bard Taliesin, Taliesin begins life as an ordinary boy named Gwion Bach. Gwion is employed by a powerful sorceress named Cerridwen to tend a cauldron containing a magical brew formulated to confer wisdom on her ugly son. While performing his duties, Gwion accidentally swallows three drops from this cauldron. He receives the wisdom meant for Cerridwen's son and realizes that once she discovers what has happened, she will try to kill him.

He turns into a hare on the land, but she turns herself into a hound in order to catch him. He turns into a salmon in the river, but she turns into an otter. He turns into a sparrow in the air and she into a hawk. Finally, he turns himself into a grain of wheat on the threshing floor and she into a black hen and gobbles him up. When she returns to her human form again, she discovers that she is pregnant. When she gives birth to the child that was Gwion, she finds him so beautiful that she can't bring herself to kill him. So, she puts him into a bag and casts him into the water, where he is eventually found by the king's son and given his name Taliesin, which means *shining brow*.

As bardic poetry, this tale describes an initiatory shamanic vision in which an ordinary person must learn to use shape-shifting wiles to elude a guardian god long enough to be reborn as a shaman-bard. In this story, Taliesin is reborn as the son of the goddess Cerridwen who appears in other Welsh tales as a white sow who eats her own young and as an old woman who stirs the cauldron of rebirth. After his rebirth from the womb of the goddess of death and rebirth, Taliesin becomes a sacred king, and mediates the power of the gods for his people by means of his inspired poetry. Unfortunately, this isn't the only reason for shapeshifting.

In the book *The Compleat Vampyre*[31], by Nigel Jackson we learn that the shape shifting shaman is the forerunner of the legend of the werewolf. The witch or shaman shape shifts into wolf form under the light of the full moon and goes forth to traverse the sacred landscape of the night.

However, what does the shapeshifter actually do in these legends? Does

---

31 *The Compleat Vampyre,* Nigel Jackson, Capall Bann Pub, 1995.

he travel in animal form to the realms of the gods for the purpose of wisdom and knowledge? Does he assume animal powers in order to benefit the tribe by serving as an intercessory with the natural forces that surround it? No.

In the legends surrounding them, shapeshifters turn into predators who feed off the blood (or, more accurately, the vital energy) of their fellow humans. They become figures of terror and dread whom the intended victims must guard against by magical charms and spells to keep from being the "Blue Plate Special" on that particular full moon night.

In a common tale, a witch turns herself into an animal shape in order to go forth at night and do mischief to one of her neighbors, or to her neighbor's livestock, such as suckling at the udder of a neighbor's cow or hag riding a neighbor's horse. She is eventually caught in the act and wounded in some way, either by a bullet or by having a paw severed by a knife or sword. She miraculously escapes and returns to her human form the next morning, but she is found suffering from the very wound which the animal suffered, which serves to incriminate her. This mirrors the legend of the werewolf, which can only be killed while in wolf form by a silver bullet. When he returns to his human form, the bullet wound remains.

Dion Fortune explains this phenomenon in *Psychic Self Defense*[32]. When the witch goes into her trance, her astral body or etheric double emerges, changes shape and goes forth to do whatever it desires, and since the etheric double is what animates the physical body, any harm done to it will transfer to the physical form when it merges with it again, much in the way that the medieval saints manifested the stigmata or wounds of Jesus in the hands and feet. In this way, a bullet or a sword wound that injures the etheric double would appear in the physical body when the witch came out of her trance.

So, if shapeshifting is a real phenomenon, then it is performed on the astral plane rather than the physical. The witch in question might have done nothing by way of dressing up in a mask or animal skins to affect

---

32 *Psychic Self Defense,* Dion Fortune, First published by Rider, London, UK (1930)

her transformation. All she would need to do was place herself in a trance state - perhaps by applying hallucinogenic herbal ointments to her bare skin - and lie down next to a warm fire. Her trained mind would perform the spell, and her astral body would separate from her physical body and change its shape accordingly.

After all, she wasn't performing in front of an audience, like a costumed shaman performing his dances in front of the tribe and acting like whatever animal he was portraying. The former is an actual rite of magic; the latter is a stage show designed to play to the gallery of the shaman's tribesmen like modern-day stage magicians do. Why don't we know the difference?

This is a perennial problem with both religions and fantasy games alike. Material reality is confused with the astral reality, the physical with the metaphor, the individual person with the persona or archetype. We often think that the material item, such as the lion mask or the deer antlers has the power when in fact what carries the power is our relationship with it. The lion skin gives power to a hunter shaman because he has done the work and taken the risk of developing a relationship with the lion. The wannabe has developed no such relationship, and therefore, the skin or the mask holds no real power.

In this case, the material reality is the shamanic trappings, the deer hide, the antlers, the bone handled implement. They are fun for children or childlike adults who want to entertain themselves by playing a game, so long as they understood that it is only a game. The trappings can be useful for getting untrained people in the mood for the ritual and to provide a bridge for the real work which is done on the astral, not on the physical, but they are not necessary. They are a metaphor, not a reality. At best, they are a pretend game. At worse, they are a distraction, and they are not necessary for getting in touch with the ancestral powers.

What is ultimately missing is a sense of responsibility both to oneself and to one's tribe. The energy that is raised by such methods is a means to an end, the end being accomplishing something that somehow, some way, brings the power of the ancestral gods into some kind of physical manifestation that helps the members of the tribe in their own journey towards the stars. If the shaman has done this, then the trappings are no longer necessary. If he has not, then the trappings are all he has.

John didn't agree. For the next seven years, he continued to insist that the animal mask workings formed the inner circle of the Clan. This disagreement formed the first line of fissure between him and us that would only grow wider until 1998 when it finally shattered.

However, we don't regret our association with John. We had learned something from him that proved to be far more profound than running about wearing animal masks. What the Clan of Tubal Cain turned out to be, whatever else it had been, was a vehicle for the preservation of many interesting and profound ideas and practices of shamanic witchcraft, most of which had been lost in the Crowley-Golden Dawn-Ceremonial Magical approach of Gardner. Eventually, we were able to strip away the romantic and pretentious trappings and explore the techniques and concepts hidden therein. One of the most significant was called *Treading the Mill*. It proved to be the key to gate as we embarked on the Journey to the Castle.

Chapter 7

The Moat and the Mill

Air breathe, air blow.
Make the mill of magic go
Work the will for which we pray.

Io Deo Evohe!

Fire flame, fire burn.
Make the mill of magic turn.
Work the will for which we pray.

Io Deo Evohe!

Water heat, water boil.
Make the mill of magic toil.
Work the will for which we pray.

Io Deo Evohe!

Earth without, Earth within.
Make the mill of magic spin
Work the will for which we pray.
Io Deo Evohe!

-attributed to Bill Gray

Picture a huge stone wheel, completely circular with only a hole in the center. Some people buy them in antique shops and make tabletops out of them, or put them in a garden to plant flowers in. Most modern people don't even know what they are or what they were used for or how indispensable to daily life they once were.

A millstone is a round stone either cut in one piece or in several slices and bolted together. A central pole of some hard wood was thrust through the hole in the center. Around and around the millstone turned inside a stone chamber, powered by a stream that ran beside it. Some kind of grain, such as wheat or barley was dumped into the chamber. The friction between the millstone and the walls of the chamber ground the grain into flour, to be baked into bread, the staple of civilized life.

To our ancestors, there was no difference between the sacred and the profane, between the spiritual and the mundane. Everything had both a mystical dimension and an ordinary one. The mystical dimension was reflected in the ordinary and the ordinary served as a symbol of the mystical. By partaking in the ordinary function, they could access the mystical. As above, so below. As within, so without. The millstone was no different.

In a strange and largely ignored work entitled *Hamlet's Mill: An Essay on Myth and the Frame of Time*[33], historian Giorgio de Santillana and ethnologist Hertha von Deschend tell the story of Amlodhi, the

---

33 *Hamlet's Mill: An Essay on Myth and the Frame of Time,* Giorgio de Santillana and Hertha von Dechend, Published by Gambit, Incorporated (1969)

Scandanavian counterpart of Hamlet, the dour Danish prince immortalized by Shakespeare. Amlodhi was the proud owner of a fabulous Mill which originally ground out peace and plenty, but due to greed, was debased to grinding out salt. Eventually, it sank to the bottom of the sea where it ground rock and sand and created a vast Maelstrom or whirlpool which led to the land of the dead.

As the story unfolds, Amlodhi himself is revealed to be Kullervo and Krishna, Quetzalcouatl and Odyssius, Samson and Gilgamesh, Avalokiteshvara and Jesus Christ. Thus, he is an incarnation of the Demiurge or Craftsman god, a figure of supernatural strength, a figure who was, "a speaker of cryptic but inescapable truths, an elusive carrier of fate who must yield once his mission is accomplished and sink once more into concealment in the depths of time to which he belongs: Lord of the Gold Age, the Once and Future King."

Furthermore, Amlodhi's Mill is none other than the mighty wheel of the ecliptic, of which our earth is the center. The center pole is the axis of the earth which points to the north star around which the sun turns in its yearly journey past the equinox and solstice points against the vast backdrop of the constellations of the zodiac.

But the mill is flawed; the center-pole, the axis or *World Tree* is not perpendicular to the mill. It is tilted at a 23 1/2-degree angle causing an irregularity in the earth's rotational motion. This tilt causes the sun to appear to shift ever so slightly in its path, returning to a slightly different part of the zodiac at the vernal equinox from year to year. This Precession of the Equinoxes causes the rise and fall of the World Age, a Twilight of the Gods, occurring every 2,600 years, in which all worldly structures collapse and sink back into the primordial sea of time, only to rise again in a new form at the beginning of the next world age.

Consequently, all the great myths of the world have a common origin. The geography is the same for all of them, because the places described are not on the earth: they are located in the heavens. The figures in the myths are not people, nor are they even gods. They are celestial bodies and the journeys upon which they travel are the cyclical motions of these bodies as seen from the 'midrealm' of the earth. They describe a cosmology, a world view that is at once childishly simple and philosophically sophisticated. They describe a hero's journey through the vastness of the starry realm, and that hero is as much human as he is divine -- the Sacred King.

This cosmology also charts the psychic landscape for an ecstatic journey of the shaman to commune with the various denizens the spirit world. In order to fulfill his duties to his tribe, he must ascend the center-pole of the mill, aided by the measured pulse beats of his drum, to the highest sky to get the information he needs to fetch a lost soul, defeat hostile spirits which cause disease, discover where the herds have gone, or escort the recently deceased to the realms of the dead.

Ultimately, according to the authors of *Hamlet's Mill*, it describes the supreme gnosis, or knowledge of the way, "which leads outwards-upwards through the planetary spheres, past the threatening 'watchtowers' of the zodiac to the desired timeless Light beyond the sphere of fixed stars, above the Pole star; beyond and above everything, where the unknown god resides eternally."

The mill of earth, the humble round stone wheel which transformed the grain into flour, was the mirror of the Mill of Heaven, the vast circle of stars that turned around and around overhead on a central axis grinding out the fate of both gods and mortals.

The old adage that the mill of the gods grinds slowly, but exceedingly fine is a way of saying that the wheel of fate, although it takes a long time in human estimation, eventually transforms human endeavors into something useful. A situation in which things appear to be intractably wrong, say, someone has done something hurtful and has seemingly gotten away with it and indeed has prospered, will be resolved eventually. The truth behind a lie will eventually be revealed, and the wrong-doer will reap what he has sown.

While this does little to meet the need for justice or vengeance of the people who allowed themselves to be victimized, it does reassure everyone else that eventually, perhaps beyond the lifetimes of those involved, cosmic justice will be done, and the situation will be transformed into something of use to future generations.

It is all, as another old saying goes, grist for the mill. Grist is any grain that has been separated from the chaff. Sometimes, it isn't the kind of grain that the customer prefers and may not be of the best quality. But it is tossed into the mill chamber anyway in hopes that something good will come out of it.

People, by their actions, provide the grist for the mill of magic. Some provide good grist which produces good flour. Others, not so much. But everyone contributes grist for the mill and the Cosmic Miller will do the best with what he has. And, if he performs his magic well, he will turn questionable grist into useful flour.

If we choose, we can participate in this process. We can grind the mill and make magic happen, but once the wheel is in motion, the people and situations which provide the less-than-favorable grist will appear and we must deal with them the best we can.

So, how does one grind the mill in a magical ritual? Cochrane wrote that there was a practice in the East known as 'Kundeline' which consisted of shifting the sexual power from its basic source to the spine and then to the mind. Cattle use this principle extensively which can be noted if a person creeps silently up to a deer or cow. There is always one beast that will turn its back to the person and then twist its neck until it regards the person out of its left or right eye alone. It is interpreting the person by what is usually called 'psi' power.

And that is how an altar is used. You turn your back to it with your head turned right or left. But before you do, it is necessary to offer devotions and prayers by bowing three times to the altar, with arms crossed upon on the chest. Then, you turn about the altar for the number of times appropriate to the deity you are invoking or praying to.

Circumambulation is an ancient religious practice that is supposed to represent the soul's journey from the world of mortals to the world of the gods. Vedic circumambulation, from India, consists of walking around a sacred place as a sign of veneration and piety. One treads a circular path, around and around, following an established pathway which symbolizes the transition from ordinary life to the world of the gods. One begins at the temple door, then moves in a clockwise direction around and around towards the inner sanctum where the deity is enshrined. During the journey, a worshiper will pass through stages which mark the journey from the mundane to the spiritual. One Walks the Way from the world of mortals to the world of the gods.

Circumambulation around the altar also constitutes one of the oldest ceremonies of Freemasonry. In his *History of Freemasonry*[34], Albert Mackey writes:

> The essence of the ancient rite consisted in making the circumambulation around the altar, from the east to the south, from the south to the west, thence to the north, and to the east again. In this the masonic rite of circumambulation strictly agrees with the ancient one. This circuit by the right hand was done as a representation of the sun's motion. It was a symbol of the sun's apparent course around the earth. As the circumambulation is made around the lodge, just as the sun was supposed to move around the earth, we are brought back to the original symbolism with which we commenced that the lodge is a symbol of the world.

Note that the path of worship in both the above examples is deosil, that is, sunwise or clockwise. It mirrors the orderly pattern of the earth around the sun, following the hands of a traditional clock. By keeping the fire on the right side, we walk from left to right, rightward, the right-hand path of devotion, worship and celebration.

There is however, another way to approach the altar, and that is widdershins, moonwise or counterclockwise. One keeps the fire on the left side and walks from right to left, traversing the circle counter to its orderly progression, against the flow of time itself. This method of circumambulation constitutes a left-hand path, a sinister path, a counterclockwise path. If clockwise motion imitates the journey of the sun

---

34 *History of Freemasonry*, Albert Mackey, First published by Masonic History Company, USA, 1898

across the sky, it begins in the east at the dawn, and travels across the midheaven at noon to the fall in the West. Counterclockwise motion does something else. It travels to the North, the place of darkness and the underworld before ending up at its destination back in the East.

This kind of circumambulation is avoided by most magical systems, to the point where many temples will not permit their members to walk from point A to point B, even if it is only a few steps, if doing so necessitates traveling in a counterclockwise direction. Members are instructed to walk all the way around the circle to arrive at their destination, thereby keeping the flow of energy always in the clockwise direction.

So, what is so bad about going widdershins around the circle? Why would someone want to take the sinister path, the counterclockwise path? The answer that is usually given is that widdershins goes against the right and proper order of things. Where the deosil path is one of devotion and piety, a good path, the widdershins path is one of rebellion and revolt, a path of evil. When a magician travels widdershins around the circle, he does so only to work harm, to curse instead of bless, to hurt, rather than heal, to exact revenge or to impose his will on others rather than honor the gods and seek to become one with them.

Traveling widdershins will certainly do all of that, if the magician desires it, but it does something else. It constitutes a path of magic rather than worship. Deosil is celebratory; widdershins, on the other hand, is evocative. It causes friction. It creates energy. It focuses will. It makes things happen. It breaks things down. It grinds the mill.

In her classic book *The Cosmic Doctrine*[35], Dion Fortune discusses so-called "Positive Evil". Evil is that which runs counter to the prime current of evolution. It serves as a thrust-block against which action in any direction is possible. "You will always get your push-off from evil," she wrote. "Every advance to a higher plane is a reaction to evil. If there were no evil, there would be no point in improvement; therefore, there would be no growth, no evolution."

---

35 *The Cosmic Doctrine*, Dion Fortune, first published by The Society of The Inner Light, 1949

Positive Evil, then, is what turns the mill of magic.

Philosophically, this concept functions as a kind of metaphor for an approach to magic in general. Going with the flow, the tides and the natural rhythms of the earth, feels good. It celebrates the cycles of life, the seasons of the year, and the path of the planets around the sun. It worships deity. It is effortless and entails no risk. It generates no energy. It does no work.

Going against the natural energy of the earth, going against the grain, the tides, even time itself takes effort. It creates conflict and friction. It feels wrong. It generates energy and heat. It entails risk. It wears down. It grinds. It requires work.

It is the path of magic, of invocation, of bringing down the fire from the realm of the gods into manifestation on the earth. Instead of following the sun to the point of its greatest blessing and fulfillment, we follow it down to the greatest depths of darkness of the underworld where it dies and is reborn. And it never happens without discomfort and risk.

Magic is not celebration, prayer and worship. It is hard work. It is unnatural. It goes against the natural tides of life. To primitive humans, the natural tide of life was to grow, eat, mate and die, and to do so as comfortably and securely as possible.

But, this isn't the way of the magician, the shaman, the walker between the worlds. The way of magic entails risk, discomfort to the point of pain, coming out of one's comfort zone and accepting the grinding process. Grinding the mill takes effort, produces friction, and wears out the wheel. But it produces flour, which is baked into bread, which nourishes the body and preserves life.

Soon, the great wheel in the sky will turn again, and the point of the elliptic will enter the sign of Aquarius. There will be another millstone, another harvest, and another pile of flour.

And another magician will appear to turn the mill of magic.

Midnight, no moon. Only the stars overhead, glowing in their eternal mosaic. It's so dark, that the stones are little more than a dim silhouette. In the center of the circle, the only light is a flickering fire, the flames dancing above the glowing embers.

You face to the left, standing straight, body facing forward with only your head turned to the dancing fire. Slowly, you put one foot before the other and walk forward in a measured pace around the fire, to the left, sinister, moonwise, widdershins.

It's strangely difficult to do. It feels wrong. It feels as though you are pushing something uphill, against gravity.

You chant. Vowels, the five primal sounds of every human language. Take a deep breath. Eeee. Eyeee. Ahhh, Ohhhh, Ooooo. Then, another breath. Over and over. Together. The sounds mean nothing. They aren't meant to. They are meant to excite the part of your brain that doesn't care about meaning, only what the vocalizations sound like. What they feel like. In your stomach. In your head.

Ee ... Eye ... Ah ... Oh ... Oo. The pitch doesn't matter. For greater effect, the women can chant one pitch with the men chanting a fifth lower.

Why vowels?

"The English peasantry" wrote Cochrane to Bill Gray, "shouted "E.O.I.AU., EOIAU – poor neddies work is done, "EOIAU."

In *The Secret Doctrine*[36], Blavatsky claims that the whole process of creation was carried on by the means of sound or speech or the word. Every letter has its occult meaning and rationale. These letters or sounds could

---

36 *The Secret Doctrine,* Helena Blavatsky. First published 1898 by Theosophy Company.

be combined to form a secret word which, when uttered, caused material reality to conform to will.

Most of the secret names of the gods were vowel combinations. The unpronounceable name "IHVH" was the vowel combination IAOUE, chanted without closing the mouth.

In one of Rudolf Steiner's lectures[37], he states:

> "If one wishes to describe what is in this higher world adequately in words, one can say that it consists entirely of vowels. Lacking the bodily instrument, one enters a tonal world colored in a variety of ways with vowels. Here, all the earth's consonants are dissolved in vowels. This is why you will find in languages that were closer to the primeval languages that the words for things of the supersensible world were actually vowel-like. The Hebrew word "Jahve" for example, did not have the J and the V; it actually consisted only of vowels and was rhythmically half-sung. Using mostly vowels, the words naturally were sung."

In *The White Goddess*, Graves quotes Demetrius, the first-century B.C. Alexandrian philosopher, as saying, "In Egypt the priests sing hymns to the gods by uttering the seven vowels in succession, the sound of which produces as strong a musical impression on their hearers as if flute and lyre were used."

The Gnostics are reputed to have also experimented with these magical formulas. For them, Christ was The Logos, The Word Made Flesh who had shown the way to triumph and rule over the lower elemental powers of the world. In *The Gospel of the Egyptians,* part of the Nag Hammadi collection discovered in 1945, there are chants which represent Gnostic holy names for Christ like IAO or IEOU. Other chants are simply spontaneous, seemingly random combinations of vowels. Catholic apologists consider the Gnostic vowel chants to be an attempt to control the material realm via sorcery. What if that's precisely what they are?

---

37 *The Inner Nature of Music,* Rudolph Steiner, Lecture: S-5087: 2nd December, 1922

Cochrane wrote that the Jewish orthodoxy believe that whosoever knows the Holy and Unspeakable Name of God has absolute power over the world of form. The name of God spoken as tetragrammaton ("I am that I am") breaks down in Hebrew to the letters IHVH, or the Adom Kadmon (the heavenly man). Adom Kadomon is a composite of all archangels, that is, a poetic statement of the names of the Elements. So, what the Jew and the Witch believe alike is that the man who discovers the secret of the Elements controls the physical world.

In the story of the *Golem of Prague*, the inhabitants of a 14th century Jewish ghetto in what is now the Czech Republic appealed to a Rabbi to defend themselves from the abuse they were suffering at the hands of the Christian authorities. The Rabbi fashioned a figure of mud and clay in the form of a huge, burly man, called a Golem, but the figure lay inert until he inscribed the secret name of God on a piece of parchment and thrust it inside the figure's mouth. Immediately, the Golem came to life and laid waste to the abusers. Soon, however, it began to turn on the very people that it was designed to protect. After much effort and danger, the Rabbi captured the Golem and removed the parchment from its mouth. Immediately, the Golem crumbled into a pile of earth.

So, how does it work? In his book, *Cymatics*[38], Dr. Hans Jenny found that intoning pure sounds, such as vowels, will leave complex geometric patterns in a plate of sand. Jenny claims that by the process of harmonic resonance, the sounds of vowels will also produce changes in the structure and function of organic molecules -- like those which make up the human body.

According to the Rosicrucians, the vowel sounds are similarly used to affect a change in the vibratory rate of the psychic centers (chakras), physical glands, and the human aura. The higher the rate of vibration, the more in tune it is with the emanations from the Divine Mind or the Cosmic. Thus, the intonation of certain sounds can assist in raising the vibrations of the body above those of disease also raising consciousness to a higher level.

---

38 *Cynatics*, Dr Hans Jenny, Basilius Presse Basel, Switzerland (1967)

The frontal chakra is developed with the intonation of the vowel I, pronounced like "ee", as in "bee".

The laryngeal chakra is developed when chanting the vowel E, pronounced like "eh", as in "egg".

The cardiac chakra is developed while vocalizing the vowel O, pronounced like "oe", as in "toe".

The umbilical chakra is developed by intoning the vowel U, pronounced like "ou" as in "you".

The pulmonary chakra is developed by singing the vowel A, pronounced like "ah" as in "tall".

In William G. Gray's *Magical Ritual Methods,* vowel sounds are associated with the five elements: earth, air, fire, water, and spirit or unity.

E (pronounced "eh" or "ay") for earth

I (pronounced "ee") for air

A (pronounced "ah") for fire

O (pronounced "oh") for water

U (pronounced "oo") for Spirit or Unity

However, chanting the vowels out loud does something else. It regulates the breathing. In the practice of Pranayama, various exercises are performed which involve deepening and slowing the breath. Inhaling from the diaphragm, exhaling through the nose, and so on, have as their purpose teaching the conscious control of the breath. This is because the ancients knew something that modern science is just now rediscovering, that is, breathing can alter consciousness in several predictable ways.

By intoning a simple vowel chant in unison, we are plugging into something very old – and very powerful. Combine that with the simplicity of circumambulation around a fire, with the head turned to the left so that the blood flow to the brain is altered slightly, as well as an absence of sensory clues to location, we have a simple technique that can pack a wallop when performed correctly.

Focusing on a bright object produces a hypnotic state. That, along with changes in blood flow to the brain, specifically the left hemisphere, can lead to an altered state of awareness. Add the suggestion to go on a journey and you will go on that journey.

******

Around and around the circle you go. The energy rises, the mill turns faster, easier. You walk faster, chant faster until you are trotting around the fire like horses in a ring. You don't know how many times you have gone around the circle. You no longer even know at what point in the circle you began. It doesn't matter.

The fire in the center flickers and dances, flooding your retinas with light. The stars turn overhead around and around. The vowel sounds emerge from your throat in a sigh, a grunt, a pant. Your knees begin to feel wobbly.

Drop!

The authoritative male voice of the Magister breaks through your tortured breathing. You fall on the ground wherever in the circle you happen to be, you lie motionless, panting, gasping, exhausted, your head still spinning around the circle even though your body is now motionless. You shut your eyes, but you still see the flickering flames from the fire in the center of the circle on the surface of your eyelids.

The boundary between the worlds has dissolved. You don't know where you are in relation to your surroundings. You imagine yourself at a particular place in the circle. When you return from your journey, you find that you are in a different place altogether, but that doesn't matter, now.

You feel the rush of the river in your ears. You have crossed one symbolic river, the moat, in order to reach the circle. You are ready to journey across that river again, this time to the realm of the Great Goddess.

The gateway opens. A figure appears, beckoning you.

Chapter 8

The Ancestors

In 1982, a strange book was published by three British researchers, Michael Baigent, Richard Leigh and Henry Lincoln, entitled *Holy Blood, Holy Grail*[39]. It proposed the radical notion that Jesus, the Son of God and the second person of the Holy Trinity, sired a child or children upon Mary Magdalene, to whom he was married according to Jewish law. After his crucifixion, his uncle Joseph of Arimathea took Mary Magdalene and her children to Britain, where there was a Jewish colony. Eventually, the family emigrated to southern France where one of her descendants married into the French Royal family, making the Merovingian kings literally sacred kings, the descendants of God himself.

'Jesus Appearing to Mary Magdalene'
Fra Angelico (Guido di Pietro) (1400-1455), Convent of San Marco, Florence

The story goes on to tell how an emerging church expunged all mention

---

39 *Holy Blood, Holy Grail,* Michael Baigent, Richard Leigh and Henry Lincoln, Johnathan Cape Books, 1982.

of the marriage of Jesus and Mary – insisting on Jesus' celibacy despite the fact that Rabbis were supposed to be married -- in order to cement their claim to be Jesus' spiritual successors through St. Peter. A blood descendant of Jesus would, of course, supersede that claim. So, the story goes, the church set out to murder the Merovingian king, thereby committing both deicide and regicide. However, they couldn't eliminate the bloodline entirely and the existence of the descendants of Jesus became a secret guarded by esoteric societies for the next fifteen hundred years.

Thus, was born the legend of the Holy Grail, or in French, Sangreal. The official story from the Church was that the Grail was the cup containing the blood of Jesus that Joseph had obtained and taken to Britain for safe keeping. Stories of the quest for the Holy Grail included visions of a chalice of the kind used in the celebration of the mass in which the priest proclaims that the chalice of wine is Christ's blood.

However, this was just a cover story for the fact that the Grail was none other than Mary Magdalene herself who contained the blood of Jesus in the person of his child. The word 'Sangreal' can be read as San Greal or Holy Grail. It can also be read Sang Real, or Holy (or Royal) Blood, i.e., the bloodline or sacred lineage of Jesus, the Son of God.

Even though the convoluted 'evidence' behind *Holy Blood, Holy Grail* has proven to be a fabrication, the story of a sacred royal lineage for Jesus is hardly new. In a novel entitled *King Jesus*[40], Robert Graves postulates that Jesus was a member of a royal bloodline through his mother, Mary, who was a legitimate heir to the Jewish throne. She was secretly married to Antipater, a son of Herod the Great in order to secure the throne, but he was killed before Jesus's birth by collusion between Herod and the Roman authorities in order to eradicate any political uprising that Jesus might lead.

In Graves' story, Jesus was married to Mary of Bethany, the sister of Lazarus. Graves doesn't discuss any children of that union, but if they existed, they would probably have been spirited out of Judea by Joseph of Arimathea the same way that Mary Magdalene's children would have

---

40 *King Jesus*, Robert Graves, Creative Age Press (1946)

been, thereby preserving the bloodline of Jesus, the priest king of the Jews.

Why does this story keep cropping up, generation after generation since the inception of the Christian Church? And why was it so hotly condemned? Is it really because the church didn't want the competition posed by the physical descendants of Jesus? That might have been true in the early centuries, but now, two thousand years later, the church doesn't seem to care. Even after *Holy Blood, Holy Grail* was published, all the Catholic Church did was sneer at the inaccuracies and dismiss it as just another piece of fiction.

Yet the story persists, and there is a reason that goes beyond just another attempt to discredit the Church and defy its authority. Legends of sacred lineages, or people who are descendants of God or other divine beings appear in all cultures. The stories have many of the same features. A male god or divine being comes down to earth and impregnates a mortal woman. Her child or children has special powers that mark their divine lineage. In some cases, the child, usually a male, becomes a semi-divine hero such as Achilles or Cuhulainn. In other cases, the child, usually a female, becomes the mother of a lineage of kings, all who inherit the semi-divine nature of their blood mother.

Such stories abound in Greek, Celtic, and Norse legends. They are also to be found in legends in the Middle East, many of which found their way into both Jewish and Muslim scriptures. Most of these stories were edited out of the canon by the early church, but traces remain.

One such trace is found in Genesis 6:2 "That the sons of God saw the daughters of men that they *were* fair; and they took them wives of all which they chose." Although this story is given only a passing note in Genesis, it is covered at length in an apocryphal *Book of Enoch*. In this book, the 'Sons of God' are angels called Watchers, sent by God to watch over humanity. There are 200 of them led by the angel Azazel. They not only make a pact to descend to earth and marry human wives, they proceed to teach their human charges all manner of arcane knowledge – the secrets of the stars, of charms and enchantments, the nature of plants and roots, metallurgy, and cosmetics. Then, the human wives give birth to giants called the Nephilim: people with special divine powers or knowledge given to them by their angelic sires. The Nephilim eventually run amok and are cursed by God to be drowned in the flood.

Enoch himself, rabbinical tradition has it, is the grandson of Adam and the great grandfather of Noah. He is a just man who has been given the ability to converse with the angels and travel to the heavenly realms in visions. It is he who delivers God's curse upon the Watchers in a language that only he and they understand. It was this self-same Enoch for whom the angelic language developed by Dr. John Dee and Edward Kelly in the 16th century was named: Enochian.

However, there's more. In an Islamic document entitled *The Book of Adam and Eve*, we also find that Adam has been made of the dust of the earth and Eve from his rib, just as they are in Genesis. However, the story of what happened in the Garden of Eden is quite different. In the Islamic text, the Serpent is actually the Archangel Samael, an angel associated with the Sun. It is he who seduces Eve in the garden, not to eat an apple but to mate with him. She becomes pregnant. Subsequently, she seduces and is impregnated by Adam and gives birth to twins, Cain and Abel.

This story resembles that of Castor and Pollux from the Greek tradition in which Leda is impregnated by Zeus in the form of a swan while she is already pregnant by Tyndareus, her human husband. She gives birth to twins, one human and one semi-divine. Castor is the human twin and Pollux the half-divine twin.

In the case of Cain and Abel, Abel is the human twin, the son of Adam. However, Cain is the semi-divine twin, the son of the Archangel Samael, who has semi-divine powers over the physical world, i.e., he can make two blades of grass grow where there was only one before. Eventually, he kills Abel and is condemned to a life of wandering. He sires a bloodline of people with magical powers beginning with a son, Lamech, who begets Tubal Cain, who invents metallurgy, Jubal Cain, who invents music, and a sister, Naamah, who invents divination and prophecy.

Eventually, Adam and Eve have a son called Seth, and it is this son who eventually sires the forebears of the Israelites. Thus, the sons of Cain are cast as enemies and rivals of the sons of Seth – a rivalry which culminates in the Masonic legend of Hiram Abiff and the Temple of Solomon.

Hiram Abiff stained glass window by Charles Snell Allen, 1910,
Tompkins Memorial Chapel, Utica New York.

In this story, Hiram is from Tyre, which makes him a descendant of Cain. Solomon, the son of David, is of the line of Seth. Solomon hires Hiram, a famous master stonemason, to come to Jerusalem and build his wondrous temple. Hiram assembles a large company of masons to undertake the task. However, Hiram wishes to learn to cast the Brazen Sea, a monstrous bronze cauldron used for sacrificial offerings. In a vision, he descends to the underworld where he meets his ancestor, Tubal Cain, who teaches him the secret technique. Hiram reemerges into the upper world, casts the Brazen Sea, and finishes building the temple.

All is well until the beautiful Queen of Sheba arrives in Jerusalem for her arranged marriage to Solomon. She is duly impressed by the wonderful temple and asks to meet the master mason who built it. Solomon, sensing what is about to happen, tries to put her off. But she persists, and finally persuades Solomon to send for Hiram. As she casts her gaze upon Hiram, she instantly falls in love with him. In a fit of jealousy, Solomon bribes three of Hiram's workmen to kill him in three distinctive and horrible ways. To this day, modern masons must reenact this horrible death ritual in order to be reborn as a Master Mason.

In Masonic lore, the sons of Cain, who included Hiram Abiff, were the masters of the elements, people whose divine ancestry gave them a word and a sign by which they could command earth, air, fire, and water. From this mastery came all the ancient the arts and sciences including magic and poetry. Modern science and technology are merely the latest manifestation of this mastery of the secrets of the natural world which this Sacred Bloodline brought to humanity – for good or ill.

The question arises whether this Sacred Bloodline was actually genetic, that is, physical or whether it is only esoteric or spiritual. It is, in fact, both. At one time, there were actual genetic bloodlines in the form of the castes or families that produced the shamans, seers, poets, and priests of a particular tribe or ethnic group. These bloodlines were preserved in the Celtic Druidic and Indian Brahman castes and stories tell us how they took great pains to keep the bloodline pure with arranged and often incestuous marriages.

Over time with millennia of invasions, migrations, intermarriage and mixing of racial and ethnic groups, these shamanic bloodlines have become so diluted and cross pollinated that there is no earthly authority to tell who is or isn't 'of the blood' and able to exhibit the spiritual powers that legend ascribes to them.

However, psychic abilities, often called "the Sight", still crop up in families -- sometimes in individuals whose immediate relatives show no such powers. The blood, apparently, can lie latent or dormant in a particular family, only to be 'quickened' in a particular individual who is mentored, sometimes secretly, by another older family member. This has resulted in many stories in which the magician or witch learned magic from a grandmother, since the women often were the carriers of the magical blood in a particular family.

Also, spiritual bloodlines or groups of souls can be brought back into incarnation again and again. Members of a spiritual family might reincarnate and find each other, often organizing themselves into the surrogate family structures of magical lodges, orders and covens. Many traditional fraternities and sororities that are found in numerous college campuses were originally secret societies where the sons and daughters of particular prominent families could socialize and form secret liaisons that would benefit them and their families later in life.

This is the case of the infamous Skull and Bones fraternity that still exists on the campus of Yale University. As such groups democratized and were forced to take in outsiders, secret subgroups would often form within them where certain select members were bound together by dramatic rituals and dire oaths, forming an inner order within the outer order of the fraternity.

This gives us a quite different perspective on the concept of ley lines. In Paul Devereaux's book, the ley line is the path of the shaman king who is the consort of the goddess of sovereignty, the goddess of the land. This is the meaning of the fact that the horned man guides the seeker to the realm of the goddess. She is the blood mother of the sacred Clan: the ancestress who carries the bloodline of the gods and passes it on to her children.

The Celtic clans viewed their kings and chieftains not as leaders or authorities in the mundane realm, but as people who carry the bloodline or the karmic burden of the clan. This can be seen in the number of names with "reg" in them in ley line lore. Reg (the root of words like "regulate") means to set straight, to lead or guide straight and true. Reg is the movement along a straight line. The major duty of the king or chief was to guide his people along the straight and narrow path by observing all the sacred taboos or decrees of the gods that were placed upon him, even at the expense of his own life.

It is also worth noting that in Celtic society, the chief or king was from the same caste or family as the druid. In the beginning of the celebrated Irish epic, the Tain bo Culaigne or the Cattle Raid of Cooley, we find Queen Nessa out in the meadow with her attendants. The druid Cathbad happens by and stops to speak with her. Knowing that he has knowledge of Astrology, she asks him what that particular hour is good for. It is, Cathbad informs her, a good hour for begetting a king upon a queen. Since Cathbad appears to be the only suitable male in the immediate vicinity, Nessa duly takes him into her pavilion and mates with him. The result is Conchobhar Mac Nessa, who not only figures prominently in the Tain but in the tragic tale of Deirdre of the Sorrows.

Cathbad is able to beget the future king on Queen Nessa because he is of the same caste as she. Nessa is queen by blood right. It is her lineage which confers kingship. Her consort, Fergus Mac Roig, is king only by virtue of being married to her. When she divorces him, he has to step down from the throne. Cathbad the druid, on the other hand, is a shaman who also carries the sacred bloodline of the gods. Therefore, he is the only one who can confer that sacred bloodline on his son, Conchobhar.

We also discover in the Tain that Conchobhar frequently passes on his sacred bloodline to his people by engaging in what would come to be known as the Droit de Seigneur, or the right of a feudal lord to deflower a bride on her wedding night before turning her over to her new husband. If she conceives as a result of that mating, the child will have both a semi-divine father and a human one.

It is also interesting to note that Conchobhar, as distinct from nearly all other Irish kings, is called Mac, or "son of", Nessa, naming himself after his mother rather than his father. Her lineage confers earthly kingship. However, his sacred kingship is conferred by his druid father, whose name he does not bear. Cathbad serves as a remnant of the concept of a divine sire who is unnamed and considered to be not human. So, he traces his human lineage through his mother -- like Merlin would centuries later in the tales of King Arthur. And, like Jesus would in the gospels.

Mary was of the lineage of King David. So was Joseph, or so we are told. But Jesus wasn't considered to be Joseph's son. He was the son of an unnamed, nonhuman, divine father. And Mary is the queen who confers the human lineage of sovereignty while the unnamed divine sire confers the sacred lineage.

So, in a sacred Clan, fealty and lineage is pledged not to a person but to a bloodline – a bloodline of the gods, not of mortals.

Chapter 9

The Lady of the Castle

So, who exactly do we meet when we finally complete the journey and achieve the Castle Perilous, the Grail Castle? For Cochrane, she was fate, the creatress and destroyer. Unhappy mortals understand why she destroys, but the destruction will bring its own sorrow. As the Goddess of Love, she humbles everyone at some time. And that sorrow is perhaps Her greatest gift to the moon-stuck poet.

If Gerald Gardner did one worthwhile thing in the 1960s, he revived the worship of the Goddess. Gardnarian Wicca, as he originally conceived it, was a religion in which the prime deity was a goddess, or rather The Goddess, with many names and many faces and aspects, but considered one deity: God the Mother rather than God the Father.

The Charge of the Goddess, originally compiled by Gardner and later rewritten by Doreen Valiente, is an affirmation which is supposed to be recited by the high priestess at every sabbat. It begins: "Listen to the words of the Great Mother, who of old was called Isis, Artemis, Bast, Melusine, Aphrodite, Cerridwen, Diana, Kuan Yin, Brigid and by many other Names."

The charge then goes on to state, "I am the Gracious Goddess, who gives the gift of joy unto the heart of man. Upon earth, I give the knowledge of the spirit eternal; and beyond death, I give peace and freedom and reunion with those who have gone before. Nor do I demand aught in sacrifice; for behold, I am the Mother of all living, and my love is poured out upon the earth."

All of a sudden, Goddess religion became popular among Neopagan folk of all kinds. Obscure goddesses from a variety of ancient pagan cultures were written about in popular books. Rituals were performed in their names, and their myths acted out, often combining goddess of different (and traditionally warring) cultures, all in the name of "all goddesses are one goddess".

"She is called by many names by many men," Dion Fortune writes in her essay *The Worship of Isis*[41], "but to all she is the Great Goddess, space and earth and water."

But just who was this goddess who emerged from the shadows after nearly two thousand years? According to the feminist writings of the 60s and 70s, she was the personification of Mother Nature, all benevolent and all fertile, who brings forth all living things from her infinite womb. It was she who made the plants grow, the grain and fruit ripen, animals breed and herds increase. And she was the one whom humans, both men and women, propitiated to grant them strong, healthy children. She is the ideal female power, conceived as maiden, mother, and crone, concerned only with women's biological functions of fertility, maternity, nurturing, loving, healing and compassion. And, incidentally, the only female divine power deemed acceptable to a patriarchal religious and secular authority.

In the early Christian era, she was co-opted by the Roman Catholic Church as Mary the Blessed Virgin, the Mother of God. Various church doctrines were proposed to justify her veneration. They even invented a name for what she was -- a hyperdulia, a human woman who, through her selfless service to humankind was turned into a kind of super saint who could be called upon to give aid and comfort to her children. She was called the moon of the church and was sometimes pictured as standing on the crescent moon, surrounded by a halo of stars.

---

41 *Aspects of Occultism*, Dion Fortune, Aquarian Press, 1949.

The Roman Church spent many centuries officially denying that Mary was anything other than a vessel, and that her Son was both God and man rather than half god and half man like so many of the ancient Greco-Roman heroes had been. However, in 1959, unable to erase her from the collective memory of the people, the church was forced to formally enshrine Mary as the Mother of God, a human woman who, because of her obedience and conformity to masculine ideals, was given the privilege of bearing the physical body of the One who would be savior of mankind, the masculine Son of a masculine God who, for all His supposed omnipotence, required a human female to give birth to a human man.

But for all her veneration, Mary was never worshiped as a goddess. That honor was reserved for the Greco-Roman moon Goddess, Diana, the goddess of the witches, who was a different sort of feminine power entirely.

Her worship was widespread in the ancient world and served as a thorn in the side of the early church fathers, a constant reminder of the fact that their conquest of native pagan practices was not complete. Ephesus, in particular, was the site of a large and important temple to Diana. St. Paul's visit to Ephesus and his resulting epistle to the Ephesians apparently did little to persuade the Ephesians as a whole to abandon her worship.

St. John Chrysostom, the Archbishop of Constantinople in the 4th century, writes of Paul's experiences in Ephesus and laments: "But when they knew that he was a Jew, all with one voice about the space of two hours cried out, Great is Diana of the Ephesians. A childish understanding indeed! as if they were afraid, lest their worship should be extinguished, they shouted without intermission. For two years had Paul abode there and see how many heathen there were still!"

Five hundred years later, the author of the Canon Episcopi or Instruction to the Bishops admonishes:

> It is also not to be omitted that some wicked women, perverted by the Devil, seduced by illusions and phantasms of demons, believe and

profess themselves, in the hours of the night, to ride upon certain beasts with Diana, the goddess of pagans, and an innumerable multitude of women, and in the silence of the dead of the night to traverse great spaces of earth, and to obey her commands as of their mistress, and to be summoned to her service on certain nights.

Diana originally was not strictly a moon goddess. She started out as a pre-Roman goddess of the hunt, a woodland patroness of wild animals. Later, she became associated with the Greek moon goddess Artemis who shared many of the same characteristics, and eventually the two became interchangeable.

'Transformation of Actaeon"
Jean Mignon, 16th century

Ovid, in his Metamorphosis, tells the sad tale of Actaeon, the grandson of the king of Thebes. Actaeon was out hunting one day with his hounds. He stumbled upon the sacred grove of Diana and happened to catch sight of her naked, bathing in the pool with her nymphs. The goddess spotted him crouching in the undergrowth. In her wrath, she turned him into a stag, whereon he was beset upon by his own hounds and torn to pieces. A dreadful fate, maybe. However, A.E. Waite would eventually write that to behold Diana unveiled was equivalent in alchemical terminology to attaining the Magnum Opus.

Cochrane wrote that the reason why the Goddess of Love in Britain was depicted as carrying a net was that she ensnares the souls of her lovers with a devotion that very few women are able to command. In her love there is death and she rends her poets/lovers apart before making them all wise.

Diana's sacerdos, or the high priest of her shrine at Lake Nemi near Rome, was called the Rex Nemorensis or King of the Woods. Virgil, in his Aeneid, relates that the Rex Nemorensis was an escaped slave who held his position until somebody else challenged and killed him in a duel, after breaking a branch from a particular oak tree, the so-called Golden Bough. This ever-open succession reveals the character and mission of the goddess as a guarantee of the continuity of the kingly status through successive generations, and serves as the basis for the mystery of the sacred king who must periodically be slain by his rival in J.G. Frazer's *The Golden Bough*[42].

So, we can see the unfortunate Actaeon in a different context, now. He has beheld the White Goddess unveiled and has become the sacred king who bears a stag's antlers. He functions as her consort, her protector, and her shaman or go-between with her human children. He is also her son, who has inherited the sacred bloodline through her and is able to pass it along to humans. He is the king of the sacred bloodline, the Sang Real, the king of the ancestors. As the sacrificial king, he is torn apart by emissaries of Hecate (to whom dogs were sacred) until another successor beholds the beauty of the Goddess and wears the crown of the Horned King.

Diana was also worshiped by women who sought pregnancy or an easy delivery. Eventually, she became associated with Lucina, the goddess of childbirth and the patroness of midwives. Her Greek counterpart, Artemis, was similarly propitiated. Thus, she functions not as a mother goddess *per se*. She herself does not give birth. However, although chaste and virgin, she is the patroness of childbirth and midwifery. This function is similar to the one performed by the Celtic Church's St. Bridgit, a virgin nun who, according to legend, served as midwife to the Virgin Mary.

This reveals her as a goddess not of motherhood in the personal,

---

42 *The Golden Bough*, J.G. Frazier, Published by Macmillan and Co., Limited, London, 1890.

biological sense, but of sovereignty, the mother of a bloodline, tribe or clan. Her purpose is to facilitate the birth of a mortal king, a hero or a priest, become his patroness, and invest him with her power and authority over the powers of the earth. The late Alexei Kondratiev[43] wrote about the Celtic view of goddesses being very similar to that of the Hindus. For Hindus, goddesses are sources of energy. They are often referred to collectively as Shakti and can also be personified as Durga, the supreme virgin goddess who is the source of all energy in the universe.

With the waning of the influence of the Christian church in the late 19th and early 20th centuries, scholars began to take another look at witches. They rediscovered what the early church fathers had known all along and roundly condemned: that witchcraft had its roots in small isolated cults which continued the worship of Diana, the goddess of the moon, of women, of dreams and magic. And that it had continued to be practiced in various forms often in defiance of both the traditional religious and secular authority of Rome – both pagan and Christian.

In 1889, Charles Leland published a book called *Aradia, The Gospel of the Witches*[44], which he claimed had been given to him by a witch in Tuscany by the name of Maddelena. The story is interesting on a number of different levels. Mythologically, it gives a different spin on classical Greco-Roman accounts showing how myths, legends and stories are living organic things that change with the times, and morph into different forms over the centuries.

Aradia is the daughter of Diana, the moon goddess by her brother Lucifer, god of the Sun and the Moon (how it happens that he is named after the rebellious archangel rather than the Roman god Apollo is never explained but is significant). Aradia is sent to earth as a mortal woman by her mother to teach humans the art of witchcraft and how to be free, one presumes, from the influence of the patriarchal Christian church.

---

43 *An Tríbhís Mhór: A Quarterly Journal of Celtic Spirituality* (Imbas Journal) Alexei Kondratiev, 1997.

44 *Aradia: Gospel fo the Witches*, Charles Leland, Published by London: David Nutt, 1899 (1899)

But she makes it clear that it is her mother and not she who is to be adored in the rites and called upon for aid. She is eventually called back to the moon while leaving behind a small group of men and women who carry on the work that she began.

According to Leland, Diana was the goddess of the god-forsaken and ungodly, of thieves, and harlots. Thus, he portrays her religion as a religion of rebellion where the gods that were worshiped were the very gods the Church condemned. If an abusive Church disapproved of these gods, then there must be something good about them, something that can be called upon to aid those who were victimized by said Church. And since the Church embodied everything logical, masculine. and sexually repressive, it would stand to reason that the rebel gods would be emotional, feminine, and sexually permissive.

This transformation was nothing new. It had less to do with Christianity *per se* than it did the patriarchal, materialistic, and aggressively militant authority of the Roman state, which the Catholic Church appropriated after the 6th century. There were, after all, witches in pre-Christian Rome. They also worshiped Diana in her many forms as well as performed magical rituals, particularly of a sexual nature. And the Roman authority persecuted them with as much fervor as the Church would a thousand years later -- and for many of the same reasons.

They were the rebellious ones, the shadow ones, the children of the night, and of the moon. In Rome, Diana was regarded as protector of the lower classes. In fact, the day of Diana's annual festival in Rome and Aricia, celebrated on the Ides of August (around what would later be called Lammastide), was a holiday for slaves. Diana's temple at Ephesus was considered to be a sanctuary for runaway slaves. She is very much the deity of rebellion against the authority of the church, much like her brother and lover, Lucifer, would one day become.

In traditional Witchcraft (as opposed to the neopagan Gardnarian wicca revival) the moon goddess actually has two faces. She is, of course, Diana the huntress. She is the bright moon, the waxing moon, the White Lady. The Orphic Hymn to Diana translated into English by the Renaissance scholar Thomas Taylor the Platonist addresses her thus:

> *Jove's daughter, celebrated queen,*
> *Bacchian and Titan, of a noble mien:*
> *In darts rejoicing and on all to shine,*
> *Torch-bearing Goddess, Dictynna divine;*
> *O'er births presiding, and thyself a maid*
> *To labour-pangs imparting ready aid:*
> *Dissolver of the zone and wrinkled care,*
> *Fierce huntress, glorying in the Sylvan war:*
> *Swift in the course, in dreadful arrows skilled,*
> *Wandering by night, rejoicing in the field:*
> *Of manly form, erect, of bounteous mind,*
> *Illustrious dæmon, nurse of human kind:*
> *Immortal, earthly, bane of monsters fell,*
> *'Tis thine; blest maid, on woody hills to dwell:*
> *Foe of the stag, whom woods and dogs delight,*
> *In endless youth who flourish fair and bright.*
> *O, universal queen, august, divine,*
> *A various form, Cydonian power, is thine:*
> *Dread guardian Goddess, with benignant mind*
> *Auspicious, come to mystic rites inclined*
> *Give earth a store of beauteous fruits to bear,*
> *Send gentle Peace, and Health with lovely hair,*
> *And to the mountains drive Disease and Care.*

In *Witches: Investigating an Ancient Religion*[45] published in 1962, antiquarian and eccentric folklorist T.C. Lethbridge quotes a sixteenth century verse that says much the same thing, only in an earthier fashion:

> *Diana and her darling crew shall pluck your fingers fine,*
> *And lead you forth right pleasantly to sup the honeyed wine.*
> *To sup the honeyed wine my loves, and breathe the heavenly air,*
> *And dance as the young angels dance. Ah God, that I were there.*

But the bright moon goddess had another face. A dark face – that of Hecate, the goddess of the crossroads. She is the dark moon, the goddess

---

[45] *Witches: Investigating an Ancient Religion*, T.C. Lethbridge, Humanities Press (1962)

of the underworld. In popular lore, particularly in more modern feminist treatises, she is the fierce goddess of death, who collects poisons and gives nightmares and madness. She serves as the patron goddess of all who are outcast of patriarchal society – much like her bright sister Diana. Only in her case, she doesn't just provide sanctuary, she provides the means for redress and revenge.

'Hecate'
Artist unknown, British Museum

As the goddess of the underworld who befriended Persephone in Hades, Hecate haunts graveyards and is followed around in her travels by an entourage of ghosts. Eventually she, and not her bright sister, became the patron goddess of witches, identified by cauldrons and cackling hags, bubbling potions, and black cats.

However, Hecate didn't always have such a bad reputation. She originally was a Titaness and had extraordinary powers. She was the daughter of the star goddess Asteria, a bestower of wealth and all blessings of everyday life, and in the human sphere she ruled over the three great mysteries of birth, life, and death.

Hesiod, in his *Theogony*[46], writes that if a man invokes Hecate and sacrifices to her accordingly, he should receive a gift of success. Hecate is accounted for her authority to grant victory and glory in the battlefield as well as to bring the coveted prize to athletes. She not only is revered as a fertility goddess for farming products but also contains the power to assist in fishing and horse riding.

The Orphic Hymn to Hecate invokes her thus:

---

46 *The Theogony, the geneology or birth of the Gods,* an ancient poem written by Hesiod, c. 700 bc,

> *I call Einodian Hecate, lovely dame,*
> *Of earthly, watery, and celestial frame,*
> *Sepulchral, in a saffron veil arrayed,*
> *Pleased with dark ghosts that wander thro' the shade;*
> *Persian, unconquerable huntress hail!*
> *The world's key-bearer never doomed to fail;*
> *On the rough rock to wander thee delights,*
> *Leader and nurse be present to our rites;*
> *Propitious grant our just desires success,*
> *Accept our homage, and the incense bless.*

Fate is like a crossroad. When we stand at the crossroad, we are presented with a choice. We can go this way or that. We can even turn around and go back where we came, if we choose. But we can only change direction when the roads cross and a choice is presented to us. But we must choose, even though both choices have their advantages and disadvantages. The one thing we can't do is stand still.

So, we have two very different goddesses, serving two very different functions within the human psyche. But both are goddesses of the moon, and when it comes right down to it, the moon has only two phases. She is either waxing or waning, either growing or shrinking, either getting stronger or weaker. The New Moon, the Full Moon and the Quarter Moons are all merely stages in the process of transformation from waxing to waning, and back to waxing again. The moon waxes until she is full, but the instant she is full, she begins to wane until she is dark. At that moment, she begins to wax. The New Moon is actually the waxing moon, and the Full Moon, the waning.

So, the moon goddess has two faces, black and white. And when we meet her, we have to deal with both faces. Both aspects of the goddess present their trials, and both bestow their blessing. And just what is that blessing?

In 1948 a seminal book appeared on the subject of the Goddess, presenting a far different concept of female divinity than was currently popular amid the Gardnarian Wica set. It was written by Robert Graves, a British poet and novelist. To him, the White Goddess, or Diana, was the Muse, the patroness of inspiration and the giver of divine madness. The goddess of love and the goddess of death.

> *All saints revile her, and all sober men*
> *Ruled by the God Apollo's golden mean—*
> *In scorn of which I sailed to find her*
> *In distant regions likeliest to hold her*
> *Whom I desired above all things to know,*
>
> *Sister of the mirage and echo.*
> *It was a virtue not to stay,*
> *To go my headstrong and heroic way*
> *Seeking her out at the volcano's head,*
> *Among pack ice, or where the track had faded*
> *Beyond the cavern of the seven sleepers:*
> *Whose broad high brow was white as any leper's,*
> *Whose eyes were blue, with rowan-berry lips,*
> *With hair curled honey-coloured to white hips.*
>
> *Green sap of Spring in the young wood a-stir*
> *Will celebrate the Mountain Mother,*
> *And every song-bird shout awhile for her;*
> *But I am gifted, even in November*
> *Rawest of seasons, with so huge a sense*
> *Of her nakedly worn magnificence*
> *I forget cruelty and past betrayal,*
> *Careless of where the next bright bolt may fall.*

Graves didn't consider the Great Mother, the goddess of fertility and the giver of material abundance, to be the Muse. In his book of essays entitled *Mammon and the Black Goddess*[47], Graves writes:

> There are two distinct, but complementary, orders of women, both of them honoured by poets. First, the ideal woman of patriarchal civilization whom the Greeks deified as the goddess Hestia, the Latins as Vesta; and who is represented in Christianity by the Virgin Mary -- heroine

---

47 *Mammon and the Black Goddess*, Robert Graves, Garden City, Doubleday, 1965

of all old-fashioned songs and stories. Beautiful, tender, true, patient, practical, dependable: the woman whom Solomon described as 'more precious than rubies' -- the guardian of the sacred hearth, the wife-to-be, dreamt of by romantic soldiers in desert bivouacs.

Then the other woman: the multitudinously named White Goddess, a relic of matriarchal civilization or (who knows?) the harbinger of its return. She scorns any claim on her person, or curb on her desires; rejects male tutelage, hates marriage, and demands utter trust and faithfulness from her lovers - treating love not as a matter of contract, but as a sudden, unforeseeable miracle. She punishes the pride of any suitor who dares hope that he will one day make her his wife.

Graves' poem, Ruby and Amethyst[48], describes them as follows:

> *Two women: one as good as bread,*
> *Bound to a sturdy husband.*
> *Two women: one as rare as myrrh*
> *Bound only to herself.*
> *Two women: one as good as bread,*
> *Faithful to every promise.*
> *Two women: one as rare as myrrh,*
> *Who never pledges faith.*

This is significant. It shows that the lady of the mysteries of witchcraft isn't the 3-fold moon goddess of the ancients, the maid, the mother and the crone, the goddess of female biology. Nor is she the earth mother, good as bread, who makes things grow. Cochrane was an admirer (and critic) of Robert Graves, and his goddess is a goddess of magic and the poetry that makes that magic, not fertility – neither of body nor of mind.

"There has been no cause for a fertility religion in Europe" says Cochrane in *The Craft of the Wise,* "since the advent of the coultershare plough in the thirteenth century, the discovery of haymaking, selective breeding of animals, etc."

So, for both Graves and Cochrane, the mysteries were not concerned

---

48 *Collected Poems,* Robert Graves, Garden City, N.Y., Doubleday, 1961

with this world, but the otherworld. The world of the muse, the White Goddess.

And what of Hecate, the Black Goddess? Graves also writes in *Mammon and the Black Goddess*:

> "Nevertheless Ishtar, though the most powerful deity of her day, did not rule alone. At Hierapolis, Jerusalem, and Rome she acknowledged a mysterious sister, the Goddess of Wisdom, whose temple was small and unthronged. Call her the Black Goddess: Provencal and Sicilian 'Black Virgins' are so named because they derive from an ancient tradition of Wisdom as Blackness. This Black Goddess, who represents a miraculous certitude in love, ordained that the poet who seeks her must pass uncomplaining through all the passionate ordeals to which the White Goddess may subject him.
>
> Poetry, it may be said, passes through three distinct stages: first, the poet's introduction, by Vesta, to love in its old-fashioned forms of affection and companionship; next, his experience of death and recreation at the White Goddess's hand; and lastly a certitude in love, given him by the Black Goddess, his more-than-Muse.
>
> The Black Goddess is so far hardly more than a word of hope whispered among the few who have served their apprenticeship to the White Goddess. She promises a new pacific bond between men and women, corresponding to a final reality of love, in which the patriarchal marriage bond will fade away. Unlike Vesta, the Black Goddess has experienced good and evil, love and hate, truth and falsehood in the person of her sister; but chooses what is good: rejecting serpent-love and corpse flesh. Faithful as Vesta, gay and adventurous as the White Goddess, she will lead man back to that sure instinct of love which he long ago forfeited by intellectual pride."

And, we might add, witches as well as poets.

Chapter 10

The Dark Mother, Goddess of Fate

*In the neverending blackness
Of the space between
Yesterday and tomorrow
We will find Her
Mother of both the darkness
And the dawn.
In the silent, breathless hush
Between the exhale and the inhale
Between the systolic and diastolic
Beats of a heart momentarily at rest
She abides.
Change swirls around her
Shifting patterns of light and dark
Earth and Air, Fire and Water
Good and Evil, Female and Male
Yet, she remains
As the still center of the cyclone
The all-seeing eye of the hurricane
Silent
Unmoving*

Timeless
Formless
Nameless
Faceless
Always behind us
Like the dark side of the moon
Like the back of our own heads.
Feet first we enter
Her realm
Until head first we emerge
Bundled into our graves
In a fetal position
Our knees tucked beneath our chins
Awaiting the dawn.
What will we dream in this sleep between
The death rattle and that gasp that heralds
A baby's first wail?
Will the melodrama
Of our life past make us laugh
Or cry?
Will we try to turn away
When we have no head to turn?
Will we try to shut
Our lidless eyes?
Or will we watch the movie
Through its final reel
Alone?
The Hell of the Christians
Holds no such anguish.
And yet
Dawn comes.
We gasp, we wail and rejoin the dance of life
And try not to stumble
Or tread on others' feet.
Set after set
The piper never tires.
We step the figure
Clasping now this hand, and now that

In the traveling measure, the grand hey
First fearful, then graceful
Awaiting the next tune and the next
With tapping toes
And cheerful whistle
Until that day which is not a day
That time which is not a time
In the still of the darkness between nightfall and daybreak
Between the last breath and the first
When finally we are freed from
Images seen only
In the upside-down mirrors
On the rear surfaces of our eyes
We will at last see Her face
And we will find it

Beautiful.

Astrologically, the moon represents instinct, tribal and racial memory, particularly the things we learn at our mother's knee long before we are able to evaluate them logically and critically. All our experiences, our prejudices, our loves and our hates are stored in the Cabbalistic lunar sphere of Yesod.

These are the unconscious things that bedevil us, all of our complexes, secret desires and secret fears -- all those things that are out of the conscious mind that move us to do things that have consequences. And it is these consequences of our actions, moved as they are by unconscious forces sometimes against our conscious will, that manifest as our fate, our destiny. They happen to us as events in the external world only because the cause of them within us is hidden out of our conscious awareness, cloaked in the shroud of denial.

This is why meeting the Goddess of Fate is important. She is a threshold guardian who guards access to the realm of the gods. You don't get past her until you overcome your own fate and become Karma free. As fate, she embodies the external manifestation of our own instinctual imbalances. By making these imbalances conscious, owning them and working to balance them, we overcome fate.

Robert Cochrane wrote that it was not enough to see The Lady. It was better to serve Her and Her will by being involved in humanity and the process of Fate, which was the single name of all the Gods. In fate, and the overcoming of fate, lies the true Graal, for from this process comes inspiration and death is defeated. Therefore, witches are concerned with Fate – for humanity is greater than the Gods, although not as great as the Goddess. When Man triumphs, Fate stops and the Gods are defeated. This is the meaning of magic. Magic and religion are aids to overcome Fate and Fate is the cradle that rocks the infant spirit.

The Gods traditionally consist of the seven guardians of humanity, which are enshrined in the mythology of all ancient cultures. They are personifications of the seven natural forces which correspond to the seven natural instincts of man. They are featured in the days of the week (the names may differ with the culture, but they are the same gods and appear in the same order). They are also the seven planets which appear in traditional astrology. They also rule the lower seven of the ten sephira on the Cabalistic tree of life. They are:

Sun – principle of vitality and ego

Moon – principle of emotion and memory

Mars – principle of desire and will

Mercury – principle of mind and reason

Jupiter – principle of authority and generosity

Venus – principle of love and money

Saturn – principle of limitation and death

The practice of personality centered astrology works extensively with these symbolic principles, charting in a horoscope the various instinctual energies that either appear in harmony or in opposition to each other. For example, if Mars (desire) is in a harmonious aspect (trine) to Jupiter (authority) then you will have a person whose desire for power is met in ruling over others. If Mars is in a challenging aspect (square) to Jupiter, then you will have a person whose desire for authority is thwarted or turns to selfish purposes.

This analysis presents an opportunity to 1) become consciously aware of one's personality issues, 2) take ownership of them (i.e. stop blaming other people or extenuating circumstances), and 3) make a concerted effort to overcome the negative effects of the conflicting forces by disciplining them and balancing them out, either through psychotherapy, meditation, or magical rituals.

Dion Fortune, in her essay *Applied Magic*, wrote:

> "The aim of those who follow this Path is to obtain complete mastery over every aspect of created life. But when we say mastery, we do not mean the mastery of a slave-owner over his slave. Rather do we mean the mastery of the virtuoso over his instrument … The adept who has gained mastery over the Sphere of Luna interprets the message of the Moon to the world and shows forth her powers in equilibrated balance."

If we acknowledge that whatever conflicting forces within our own natures are a result of actions we have performed or attitudes we have held in the past, which determine our present karma or destiny, then it follows that the resolution or balancing of these forces will result in a resolution of the outer manifestations of our karma.

We must, as Dion Fortune further writes,

> "equilibrate the warring forces in our own nature until we can handle our unruly team of instincts and make them draw the chariot of the soul with the power of their untiring speed."

Then, the god forces will no longer be subconscious but conscious and by consciously balancing the forces, then the power of the gods over us will be defeated and karma will be overcome. At that moment, the demons of the underworld take off their scary masks and reveal themselves to be the gods of the starry realm. And we find that we have been in the realm of the gods all along.

The key to this process of overcoming fate is the concept of reincarnation, one of the basic tenets of the Craft as well as most other traditions of the Western Esoteric Tradition. We enter into this world as an infant soul, a spark of divine substance, and through many incarnations full of trials and tribulations we learn the lessons of the earth plane and eventually return to the starry realms from whence we came.

Occultist Manly P. Hall, in his book, *Reincarnation*[49] wrote:

> The purpose of all evolution is to achieve liberation; that is, to produce a personality into which the entity flows so perfectly and completely that there ceases to be any interval between the two. To achieve this end requires the disciplining of the personality. This discipline is made possible only because previous lives have enriched the new personality with sufficient wisdom to desire this discipline. ... Liberation results from the elevation and refinement of personalities through thousands of years of rebirth with the result that at last a personality is emanated which is capable of making the supreme adjustment in which it absolutely negates itself to the entity from which it emanates.

According to the Rosicrucian scholar Max Heindel[50],

> Spirits incarnate only to gain experience; to conquer the world; to overcome the lower self and attain self-mastery. When we realize this, we shall understand that there comes a time when there is no further need for incarnation because the lessons have all been learned. The teaching of the Kathopanishad indicates that instead of remaining tied to the wheel of birth and death, man will at some time go into the motionless state of Nirvana.

---

49 *Reincarnation*, Manly P. Hall, Philosophical Research Society, 1946

50 *The Rosicrusion Cosmo-Conception or Mystic Christianity,* Max Heindel, L.N. Fowler, Imperial Arcade, Ludgate Circus, 1922

Robert Cochrane wrote in a letter to Bill Gray that the pagan land of the dead, Apple Island, Avalon, Caerochren is a place that to the image fixed mind, appears as a wooded countryside, with a bleak seashore. Across deep pasture, lie hills that rise blue heads to the lowering sky. By the sea and across the woods is a small hamlet;

> *There you and I my loves*
> *There you and I will lie,*
> *When the cross of resurrection is broken*
> *And our time has come to die.*
> *For no more is there weeping*
> *For no more is there death.*
> *Only the golden sunset,*
> *Only the golden rest.*

According to the ancient Celtic version of reincarnation, called metempsychosis by the Greeks, we are reborn over and over within the same tribal bloodline. Death, especially in battle, wasn't the tragedy to the Celts that it is to us. It merely meant that the person shed a body that was wracked with pain and went to a place of rest (and feasting, harping, boasting and loving) until it was time to be reborn and take up the tribal work once more. The living would eagerly await the rebirth of the deceased as a baby. They would look for certain signs which would reveal that a particular child was so-and-so reborn and would often help the child take up his or her previous place in society.

This is, in fact, the process by which the Tibetan Buddhists choose their spiritual leaders, particularly the Dalai Lama. When the old Dalai Lama dies, his successor is considered to be the same entity reincarnated in another body. A search is made for the child who can, for example, identify certain objects owned by the deceased, or otherwise indicate that he is the same entity in another body. When the reincarnated Dalai Lama is located, his name is changed, he is taken from his birth parents, and carefully reared so that he can take up his old office again when he matures.

This is common to many tribes. Oblique references to it are even found in the Bible. John the Baptist was considered by the Pharisees to be the reincarnation of Elijah. Jesus himself was asked if he was the reincarnation of Elias or Jeremiah or another of the prophets. In this view, people are not reincarnated as individual souls but as parts of the tribe to which they still belong after death. When deceased members of a tribe are reborn, they return to the tribe because they are parts of it. Through them, the tribe itself is reborn.

In the book *The Fairy-Faith in Celtic Countries*, W.Y. Evans-Wentz[51] wrote:

> ... the Celtic Esoteric Doctrine of Re-birth correctly interpreted does not conceive personal immortality, but it conceives a greater kind of immortality—the immortality of the unknown principle which gives unity to each temporary personality it makes use of, and which we prefer to designate as the individuality, the impersonator. And this individuality is the bearer of all evolutionary gains made in each temporary personality through which it reflects itself: it is the permanent evolving principle.

Later doctrines of reincarnation, mainly taken from Buddhism and Hinduism, were re-introduced into the west by the Theosophical Society in the late 1800s and transmitted by the various esoteric traditions such as the Rosicrucians. This view of reincarnation is less concerned with the rebirth of the tribal bloodline and more concerned with the development of the individual soul. It includes the possibility of lifetimes spent as members of different tribes, ethnic groups, social and economic stations, even different genders in order for the soul to learn all of life's lessons.

We have all known people who seem to be strangers to their genetic families and culture and only find their soul's true home within another totally different ethnic or cultural group. This is often true of people who have parents from two completely different ethnic groups, and they are drawn to either one or the other. Others, however, can find no ancestor no matter how far back that might be from the ethnic or cultural group to which they are drawn, and it can only be concluded that they are born outside their tribe this time around in order to learn a spiritual lesson.

---

51 *The Fairy Faith in Celtic Countries,* W.Y. Evans-Wentz, London and New York; H. Froude, [1911]

One way to reconcile these two views is through the concept of a sacred or shamanic bloodline that somehow transcends ethnic or cultural boundaries. This sacred bloodline is not limited to one tribal or ethnic group, but includes all of them, since all ancient tribes had their priests, seers and shamans. People who are of the sacred bloodline (evidenced by an interest in psychic and magical things and possibly a talent for divination or scrying) always seem to end up finding their way back to magic no matter what their current ethnic makeup.

There is a certain tribe-like feel to this sacred bloodline, but it's not cultural or even genetic: it's spiritual. Joseph Campbell once remarked that Buddhist monks often have more in common with Catholic monks than they have with members of their own families. This is due to the fact that both Buddhist and Catholic mysticism sheds the ritual forms, dogma and doctrines that are common to the laity and are stripped down to their mystic core which reveal more similarities than differences.

Certain spiritual principles, then, are shared among the magicians of all tribes which go beyond the concrete images that appear in different ethnic or tribal mindsets. Magically-inclined people are better able to transcend ethnic and cultural differences and come together in common cause then people who still haven't gotten past the tribal mindset and their identification with the myths and mores of a particular tribe.

And so, the Lady of the Castle finally reveals herself as mother to all who share the sacred bloodline, no matter what their current or past genetic or cultural heritage might be. Bill Gray, in *Evoking the Primal Goddess*[52], writes this invocation to Her:

> *Beloved Bloodmother of my especial breed, welcome me this magic moment with your wondrous womb. Let me learn to live in love with all you are so that my seeking spirit serves the Sangreal.*

Nothing much has changed in 2000 years. Diana/Hecate is still the goddess of rebellion, but it's ultimately a rebellion against spiritual rather

---

[52] *Evoking the Primal Goddess: Discovery of the Eternal Feminine Within*, Llewellyn Publications, 1989.

than worldly authority, against those who would imprison souls rather than bodies, who seek to control thoughts and beliefs rather than just behaviors.

Those of the Sacred Bloodline who seek the Lady of the Castle are the ultimate rebels. By conquering fate, they commit the ultimate heresy of our age or any age. They relinquish all blame, excuses or evasions, evolve beyond their identity as part of this tribe or that and become free to pursue their own personal destiny as individual souls. Now, as Cochrane wrote in 1966, we finally know what 'witches' are.

Chapter 11

The Keys to the Gate

Where do you actually go when you cross the river that separates this world from the Otherworld? Will you actually journey to the realms of the ancestors, see and converse with them in vision and gain a measure of their wisdom and power? Or will you just stay in your own head and experience a personal fantasy that may be entertaining but will ultimately produce nothing? And is there a difference?

Carl Jung called it the Collective Unconscious—that psychological realm similar to our personal unconscious but which contains the images all of the myths, stories, gods, otherworld animals, angels and demons which have haunted all of humanity for thousands upon thousands of years. In his seminal work *Man and His Symbols*[53], Jung postulates the existence of mental forms whose presence cannot be explained by anything in the individual's own life and which seem to be aboriginal, innate, and inherited shapes of the human mind. These images from humanity's more primitive and less civilized past are what Jung dubbed archetypes.

But these archetypes aren't just static images, like bits of broken statuary or faded paintings stored away in some dusty cosmic museum. They live in all of us as dynamic, constantly changing entities. For thousands of years, they have inspired works of art, painting, sculpture, music, and

---

[53] *Man and His Symbols*, Carl Jung, Doubleday & Company Inc., (1964).

fiction. They still do, including those most modern of art forms, movies and videos.

They also invade our dreams, and in some instances our waking minds, often with disastrous and debilitating effects. Voices that give instructions for often destructive acts and hallucinations of beings that are both beautiful and horrifying are so vivid and intense that in some cases they are accepted as more real than the surrounding material world.

In fact, both Jung and mythologist Joseph Campbell considered mental illnesses such as schizophrenia to be a kind of modern shaman's journey in which these archetypes rise up from the depths of the collective unconscious like vengeful spirits and must be confronted and come to terms with in order for mental and spiritual healing to take place.

In a 1979 work by Princeton psychology professor Julian Jaynes entitled *The Origin of Consciousness in the Breakdown of the Bicameral Mind*[54], schizophrenia is postulated to be a modern throwback to a primitive mentality in which the diktats of the tribal culture are told to every member of that tribe by means of voices emanating from the temporal lobe of the right hemisphere of his or her brain. In times of stress, certain chemicals flood the body and trigger neural changes which cause the tribal member to hear voices or sometimes see visions of the tribal god or gods instructing him what to do. In schizophrenia, the modern mind of the patient with its rational consciousness is less resistant to these chemical changes and these neural patterns are triggered in the form of hearing voices either of gods, angels, devils, or other authority figures which tell the patient to do things either in accordance with their childhood upbringing or, in certain cases of demonic possession, things that are directly opposed to it.

Jaynes considered these voices to be authority figures created by the nervous system out of the patient's admonitory experience and his cultural expectations and are more often than not religious. The hallucinations feature religious visions, posturing, ceremony and worship. One patient

---

54 *The Origin of Consciousness in the Breakdown of the Bicameral Mind,* Julian Jaynes, Published August 15th 2000 by Mariner Books (first published 1976).

writes, "I was impelled to address the sun as a personal god, and to evolve from it a ritual sun worship."

One of the most important -- and the most controversial – parts of the theory of archetypes is that they are hereditary. They have a psycho-physiological component to them and some psychological theories postulate that they serve as hard-wired neurological templates upon which experiences and people are organized in order for a developing child to learn to make sense of his or her world.

They certainly contain a cultural component which colors their form and function, but the fact that the most fundamental of them persist from culture to culture, from ancient times to modern, indicates that they form a kind of racial memory that we inherit from our ancestors along with our physical genes.

This realm of the ancestors, spoken of by shamans all over the world, is precisely the realm in which we must journey. Traditional occultists call this realm the astral plane, the plane of existence just above our purely physical one. Theosophist C.W. Leadbetter, in his classic work, *The Astral Plane*[55], wrote:

"It has often been called the realm of illusion – not that it is itself any more illusory than the physical world, but, because of the extreme unreliability of the impressions brought back from it by the untrained seer."

"Why should this be so? We account for it mainly by two remarkable characteristics of the astral world – first, that many of its inhabitants have a marvelous power of changing their forms with Protean rapidity, and also of casting practically unlimited glamour over those with whom they choose to sport; and secondly, that sight on that plane is a faculty very different from and much more extended than physical vision."

Both Jungian Psychology and Classical Occultism agree on several key points about the nature of this realm: It has a biological component.

---

[55] *The Astral Plane*, C.W. Leadbetter, Published by The Theosophical Publishing Society, 1895.

Blavatsky called it kama, the realm of desire. To Jung's teacher, colleague and rival Sigmund Freud, the unconscious was the place where an individual's instinctual biological urges were stored, and the forms taken by these desires appeared in dreams and hallucinations. So, for both the mystic and the psychologist, this is the realm of primitive human urges for sex, breeding, survival, and territory which underlie our deepest emotions and most urgent desires.

It has an objective reality. Not just reality in the sense that everything that we perceive is real to us, but that it is real and alive in and of itself and produces effects in the physical world, both positive and negative. The stuff of the astral plane is energy, not matter. Consequently, the beings that live there are able to appear to human awareness in any form they wish, changing forms and shapes depending upon who is attempting to communicate with them. This is what causes the images that people see in dreams or in psychic vision.

Finally, it has a cultural component. The forms that these beings take will be those that a particular culture or religion teaches its people to recognize. A Catholic mystic will see Jesus and the Virgin Mary. A Tlingit shaman will see raven or bear. A Sioux Medicine man will see White Buffalo Woman or Crow Chief. And a Western European magician will see Raphael and Uriel or Sylphs and Undines. So, Jungian archetypes are the astral forms that these forces and beings take on in order to communicate with us.

Also, from his book *Reincarnation*, Manly Hall wrote,

> The dead Egyptian expected to see Osiris. His expectancy became a thought pattern, and he saw Osiris. In the same way, the Christian will see Christ, the Buddhist will see Buddha, and the Brahman will enter the expected palace of Indra.

Finally, we can navigate this realm by the use of certain selected images or symbols which serve as signposts to get to the place where we need to go, where our own Clan ancestors await us. The Jungian archetypes serve as forms which are embodied by the ancestral powers who, being spirit, have no shape of their own. In modern parlance, the archetypical images serve as access codes to call upon those ancestral powers that we seek. But we don't find them. They find us.

One of the things that distinguishes modern magic from New Age therapy is the fact that these ancestral powers, whether we call them gods, angels or demons, have a will and mind of their own. We can call upon them with all the pomp, ceremony, astrological correspondences and correctly pronounced invocations that we wish. But if they don't want to attend us, they won't. They will heed the call of some people and not others. It is as if they know who are their kin and who are not and will not heed the call of a magician, no matter how sincere, who is not one of their "chosen" people

This is a controversial point, so much so that it formed one of the main lines of fissure between the theories of Carl Jung and Sigmund Freud. For Jung, the "Collective Unconscious" was universal, a repository of all human cultural images and accessible to every human person by virtue of his or her humanity. They exist in a divine realm that transcends cultural forms yet contains them all. The Great Mother, for example, is an archetype which manifests in a variety of cultural forms, but whether she is called Ceres, Demeter, Isis or the Virgin Mary, she is greater than all these identities as an archetype because her existence is a part of the human psyche in general.

For Freud, the Collective Unconscious was tribal. It contained a set of images and patterns that pertain only to the members of a particular tribal bloodline. They manifested as ancestral spirits or totem animals which would appear in dreams and visions and formed the basis of songs, stories and religious rituals. They functioned as templates for tribal behavior, illustrating what to do as laws and what not to do as taboos. Whoever was born into that tribe would inherit this particular set of archetypal images and behavioral patterns along with any distinctive physical characteristics and these would persist even though they might be raised outside of the tribal culture. And this tribal inheritance and identity was nearly always transmitted through the mother.

So, which viewpoint is the correct one? Quite possibly, it is both depending on who is accessing it and why. The two concepts aren't really opposed to each other. They are complimentary. Neither is exclusive. One can be contained in the other. It is a well-known occult axiom that one must travel down into the underworld in order to finally emerge in the realm of the gods. So, it is possible to postulate that one must descend into the tribal psychophysiological underworld of Freud and emerge into the divine archetypal realm of Jung. As above, so below.

Dion Fortune in her essay on the Astral Plane collected in the book *Aspects of Occultism*[56] elaborates on this further:

> The difference between the man who touches astral imagination only and the man who, by astral imagination, touches spiritual actualities, is that the former in his concepts can rise no higher than the astral imagination, and the latter has in his soul spiritual realization and aspiration which he brings through into brain consciousness by means of the astral imagination.

This is where the concept of sacred bloodline comes in. The ancestors know their own. Blood calls to blood and whether we are led to where we need to be depends on a blood tie to the beings in question. Sometimes these blood ties are physical and consist of actual kinship ties to a particular ethnic group. Sometimes they are spiritual, consisting of soul ties, affinities forged in other incarnations that don't necessarily match one's current biological ancestry.

But as every shaman knows, when one enters the Otherworld, one is accepted by one's own ancestors, not someone else's ancestors or some generic, unspecified ancestral force. There are bloodlines on the astral as well as on the physical. And these bloodlines, like astral families, carry with it talents, flaws and karmic debts just like physical families do. And when one summons the ancestral forces, one must summon the entire package, the good as well as the bad. And if those ancestors attend your call, they will bring the entire package with them for you to deal with as best you can.

---

56 *Aspects of Occultism*, Dion Fortune, Published 2000 by Weiser Books (first published 1962)

This is the point where the most difficult part of the Journey comes in. You stand at the edge of the river of time, the river Styx which divides this world from the otherworld, uncertain of what to do next. You have several choices. You can call, summon a guide by virtue of your spiritual bloodline, and go where the guide takes you. Or you can forge ahead on your own, making it up as you go along. You can be conducted over the river by ancient spirits clothed in their culture-specific astral costumes into the collective unconscious, or you can dive into the stagnant pool of your own repressed desires, ego trips, hatreds, angers and frustrations and be devoured by the monster who wears your own face.

One way is the way of shamanism, the other is the way of madness.

Signposts

So, how do you know that you are on the right road? Simple. You look for the signposts.

Roads on the physical plane have signposts to let travelers know that they are on the right road and traveling in the desired direction. Sometimes the signposts show a place name that indicates that the traveler has reached some kind of town or dwelling. Sometimes an arrow will appear at an intersection to indicate what lies at the end of each fork in the road. Occasionally, there will appear an indication of distance, how far one is away from a desired destination.

These signposts are comforting, but not absolutely necessary. They reassure the mind of the traveler that he is, indeed, on the right road and will eventually reach his destination if he remains traveling on that road. However, it's also true that if the traveler remains on the right road and follows it faithfully and steadfastly, he will arrive at his destination anyway without a signpost. The signposts, although useful and reassuring, can also function as a distraction. They can lure a traveler off the road to follow a time-consuming detour – or off a steep cliff to his doom.

Pathways on the astral plane also feature signposts. These appear to the inner vision as particular symbols that let you know that you are on the right path and are being led to the place of the ancestors. They can also indicate to an observer of the journey that the traveler is following the path faithfully and will eventually reach the proper destination.

In many magical traditions, a would-be student or acolyte is sent on a vision quest or solitary inner plane journey before he or she is accepted by a teacher for further instruction. Not only is this done to test the student's resolve, it also serves to determine whether or not that apprentice has been accepted by the ancestral spirits into the tribe as an apprentice shaman.

When the apprentice returns from the journey (provided he survives the ordeal), the elders of the tribe will question him closely and rigorously about his experiences. What images did he see? What obstacles did he encounter? Who, if anybody, came to him to be his guide? From the answers that the apprentice gives, the elders will determine whether he actually was accepted by the ancestral spirits and taken into their realm or whether he just spent his time wandering around the astral plane in the realm of his own wish fulfillment fantasies.

If he encountered the proper ancestral symbols or archetypes of his tribe, the elders would know that he was accepted by the ancestors and led to the sacred tribal areas in the otherworld. If not, it meant that the spirits shunned him and left him to wander about in a personal delusion. If that was the case, he was not initiated into the tradition as an apprentice shaman.

So, what are the key symbols that serve as signposts to the Clan tradition? What signposts do we look for on our journey to let us know that we are traveling in the proper direction? After one leaves the circle of companions and travels alone to the threshold between the physical and the astral realm, the first thing that he or she encounters is a guide from the Other Side. This guide is typically encountered immediately after leaving the circle and guards the gateway to the otherworld which is created on the physical plane by means of ritual and is entered into by means of the trance state.

In some shamanic traditions, this guide is an animal. In the case of the Journey to the Castle, it is human, a particular kind of human. We were told that this human is the blind harper, usually pictured as a cloaked figure with no eyes and carrying a harp. In Western European traditions, this figure is a bard or skald, someone who knows the lore and can impart it by means of poetry or song.

'*The Blind Harper*'
Egyptian Wall Art. Limestone scene from the Tomb Chapel of Paatenemheh, Sakkara. 1333-1307 B.C.E. Museum van Oudheden, Leiden

In bardic traditions, the purpose of the bard is to lead the listener on a journey through the ancestral realms by means of carefully chosen words. The words would be descriptive and would evoke images and emotions from the collective and personal experiences of the listeners. Often, the words were spoken with a particular meter or rhythm resulting from the emphasis placed on particular words or syllables within words. This turned ordinary speech into poetry.

Experimental evidence in neuroscience has suggested that when people hear metered or rhythmic speech (i.e. poetry) the words are processed in a different part of the brain than when they hear ordinary speech. This effect is enhanced when a bard would alternate speaking poetry with singing or chanting the words. If the bard could accompany himself with music from a harp or another kind of stringed instrument, the effect was heightened.

In the days before television, radio or even the written word, the only thing the people in a village or settlement had for entertainment and education was the bard or storyteller. The experience of listening to a bard was not something that happened every day. Bards tended to be nomads. They would travel the countryside from one settlement to another. They would stop at one village, perform for a few days, then travel to another village, perform for a few days and so on.

Consequently, the arrival of a bard was a special occasion. People would literally drop everything and assemble as the bard would tell a tale or chant a poem. Older people might know the tale or the poem and encourage the younger ones to listen carefully. The reason for this was that for hundreds if not thousands of years, the only way that a people could learn about and participate in their shared culture was by hearing and repeating the stories of their gods and ancestors. The bard was a walking repository of what the people were supposed to believe about their ancestry and tribal ways in order to create some measure of cultural cohesion.

But why is the bard blind? Often, shamanic cultures looked upon blindness as an indication that the person has sacrificed physical sight in order to cultivate inner sight instead. He or she can see into the otherworld as opposed merely seeing things in this world. For a bard, being blind is often not an impediment but an advantage. Even for sighted people, stories, poems, and musical instruments can be learned by ear rather than by means of written scripts or musical scores. Furthermore, learning a poem or a song by ear can bypass the tyranny of the written word (or musical note) and encourage more variations and improvisation of the material rather than adhering slavishly to what the written form is supposed to be. So, our guide turns out to be a poet/musician who is not only familiar with the ancestral lore but is skilled in imparting it in a way that excites the spiritual senses and sees into the Otherworld besides.

However, this mysterious figure can also assume the form of the dark man, the hooded man, or the horned man. Whatever form he takes, he is the sacred king that serves as a guide and psycho-pomp to the underworld and the realm of the Goddess. In Celtic and Greek tradition, he would have also been a bard since the bards were priests, aspects of the sacred king who, like Orpheus, conducted the worshipers by his music and poetry to the realm of the gods, and suffered himself to be sacrificed by being torn to pieces by them.

These two forms can also be combined in the figure of the horned piper. The figure of a man bearing the antlers of a totem animal is as ancient as the paintings on the walls of the caves at Lascaux in France. But as we have seen, an effective shaman is also skilled in music, poetry and dance

– skills that help him or her lead the people away from this realm and into the realms of their ancestors to learn the lessons, laws and taboos of their culture.

In some traditions, the guardian is mounted on a horse. In Appalachian conjure tradition, the guardian of the gateway to the Otherworld is the "Dark Rider" that the conjurer summons at the crossroads to serve as a messenger from this world to the realm of Old Fate, a form of the Goddess that corresponds exactly to that of the Lady of the Castle. In some cases, he not only conveys messages, he conveys the magician himself across the boundaries into the Otherworld where he can take his petition to Old Fate personally. The purpose of the Blind Harper, whatever form he takes, is to carry the seeker across the boundary between our world and the underworld so that the denizens of that realm can be accessed.

The second key is the river that separates the living from the dead, this world from the otherworld. In the mythology of many cultures, a soul after death must cross a river, an ocean or some body of water to get to the afterlife. In some traditions, this river can only be crossed by a mysterious figure in a boat who will, for a price, row the newly departed soul to the other side. It is for this reason that bodies are still buried with pennies over the eyes or a coin in the mouth in order to pay the ferryman and ensure that the soul of the departed will reach the other side without mishap.

In many ancient cultures, the afterlife itself was by definition the realm of the ancestors. In traditions as diverse as Greek and Jewish, the newly dead person is not alone but joins a lot of other people in some kind of Elysian field or Summerland. Those other people are the ancestors, both ancient ancestors and more recent relatives who have gone before you. The idea that you might encounter people other than ancestors or relatives is a modern one. In ancient tribal cultures, there *were* no other people in the Otherworld other than ancestors or relatives.

Another important key is the oak tree which serves as the door or the portal to the Otherworld. As one of the Celtic Chieftain trees of the Celtic Druids, the oak was known as *Duir*, the wood from which castle doors were fashioned because of its hardness and strength. From its boughs come the lintel and door posts and from its trunk come the timbers of heroes' coffins. People gathered beneath its spreading branches to settle disputes and hear the words of teachers, seers, lawgivers, and in later centuries preachers preaching the Christian gospel.

The rose is another key which has a rich tradition in Western European magical lore. The rose in folklore is a symbol of secrecy. Discussions of important matters are conducted *sub rosa*, literally "under the rose" and are considered to be secret or not revealed to outsiders upon pain of death or banishment. Such secret discussions often involved life or death matters, and revelation of which might often result in dire consequences for a family or a people. In Scottish legal proceedings, a rose was literally suspended from the ceiling to remind everyone in attendance that whatever was revealed was to be kept secret.

The rose is also a totem plant and in the later middle ages was featured as a heraldic device which identified whoever wore it on a shield as a member of a particular family. The infamous War of the Roses was fought for years between the House of York, whose device bore the white rose and the House of Lancaster whose device bore the red rose as to who would inherit the throne of England. The Tudor King Henry VIII used as his device a white rose surrounded by the petals of a red rose to indicate his legitimacy as the successor of both York and Lancaster and painted it on the ceiling of his private chamber where secret state decisions were made.

The rose is also used as a token to access the realms of fairy. In the Scottish ballad of Tam Lin, a princess goes to a haunted forest and plucks a double rose from a rose bush. Tam Lin, a human knight who has been imprisoned by the Queen of the Fairies appears and gets her with child. He tells her that she can only win his freedom by waiting by the side of the road on Halloween night when he rides with the fairy folk and pulling him down from his horse as he passes her. He warns her that the fairies will turn him into a variety of horrid shapes. But if she continues to hold onto him, eventually the Queen of the Fairies will be defeated, and he will be free.

Roses also grow from graves to symbolize that the spirits of the dead survive after death. In the ballad of Barbara Allen, a young man dies for love of a beautiful young woman named Barbara Allen, who has spurned him. After his death, Barbara regrets her actions and decides to die herself for love of him. From his grave, there grows a rose; from hers, a briar. They both grow unimpeded until eventually, they entwine in a true lover's knot to symbolize the triumph of love over death.

Botanically, the rose (family *rosaceae*) is a relative of the apple (genus, *malus*). The swelling that appears on the base of the rose after the petals have dropped off is called a rose apple. The apple is another plant with a wide variety of mythic and symbolic associations, not the least of which was its identification as the fruit from the tree of good and evil that Eve tasted and its association with the Isle of Avalon or Apple Island where King Arthur was ferried after his mortal wound by Morgan le Fay.

The castle is the realm of the Queen of the Otherworld, the Black Goddess or Old Fate. Her castle spins without motion between the elements. It serves as the final destination of the actual and metaphorical journey. Once there, we have arrived in the realm of the gods, the time outside of time, the world between the worlds where gods and mortals meet, and the Valhalla where heroes and the chosen ones of the gods go after death to await rebirth.

Carmarthen Castle
Carmarthen, Wales
Photo by Ann Finnin

The word "castle" itself comes from the Latin word "castellum," which means "fortified place." A castle was originally little more than a mound surrounded by rock or wooden walls, accessible only by gates made of a hard wood like oak and a moat in which water could be channeled. The people of the tribe lived in a village on the mound, and when a rival tribe invaded them, they could take up the bridge across the moat and close the gates to prevent entry as well as fight off the invaders from positions on top of the walls.

In the high middle ages, castles became more sophisticated. A tall structure with tiny, inaccessible windows was made of stone located on the top of a steep hill or rocky crag and was often surrounded by a deep moat, high walls with battlements and turrets accessible only by gates that were made of iron. This structure served as a home for the ruler, his family and his retainers, and was supported by a surrounding village of peasant farmers and artisans.

During times of peace, the castle gates were opened, the bridge across the moat was let down, and people could come and go into and out of the castle environs. Often, fairs were held in the castle grounds where farmers, artisans, performers, and others offering both goods and services could congregate to sell their wares. The ruler might send servants to buy goods and engage entertainers like bards and musicians.

But during times of war or invasion, the bridge over the moat would be raised, the gates closed and the towers and battlements fortified with soldiers who would rain arrows, boiling water, molten lead or anything else down upon whatever invaders were able to climb up the mountain, cross the moat, and assemble at the foot of the stone towers. Often, the peasants and artisans in the surrounding village would be permitted to enter the castle grounds for protection from the invaders.

Eventually, a castle became the symbol of the fortified dwelling place of a royal bloodline and the tribe which it served. When it was under siege, it was inaccessible by any rational means. The only way in was to be invited in and then it was only entered by some kind of secret entryway known only to the chosen few.

Using the Keys

One of the purposes of ritual is to recreate in the physical realm the images on the astral that guide us where we should go. Consequently, the physical ritual space is constructed to reflect the astral signposts so that when we travel in vision, we go where we are supposed to go. To this end, the circle is set up as described by Evan John Jones and Doreen Valiente in *Witchcraft: A Tradition Renewed*.

If the ritual is to be held outdoors (preferable but not necessary), a circle is cut in the turf with a knife. Traditionally, this would be done by taking one's cord, fixing one end in the center and tying the other end to the knife to make sure that the circle was actually a circle with the right dimensions, that is, large enough to contain a coven of thirteen.

Next, the cardinal directions (north, south, east and west) are marked with stones or candles. The elemental associates for these cardinal points correspond not to those described in the Golden Dawn, which provided much of the source material for the Gardnarian version of Wicca, but instead correspond to the four Scottish Airts, directions or points of the compass.

Each Airt is the home of a spirit or spirits with a particular color association as described in the following rhyme.

East is red for break of day.

South is white for noontide hour.

West is twilight gray,

Black is North for midnight power.

It is interesting to note that the word airt, when used as a verb, means to point out the way, direct or guide. This relates to the use of airts in the Sacred Path described in Chapter 12.

Roy described the cardinal directions as castles, each with an elemental designation and a ruler. They are:

> 1. A castle surrounded by fire that lies upon the East, ruled over by Lucet.
>
> 2. A castle under the depths of the Sea, laying towards the West ruled over by Node.
>
> 3. A castle in the clouds laying towards the North, ruled over by Tettens.
>
> 4. A castle builded upon the earth and surrounded by trees, laying towards the south, ruled over by Cernunos."

Note that the elements are arranged around the circle as polar opposites:

East: fire vs. West: water.

North: air vs South: earth.

Now, we have created the boundary between this world and the Otherworld. The circle becomes the Castle, Caer Ochren, in Roy's words, *"turning four times to the elements."* The cut in the turf becomes the river between the worlds which must be crossed to leave the mortal realm behind and enter the abode of the dead. In some rituals, it is actually filled with water from the cauldron.

Then, a fire is placed in the center of the circle to symbolize the Rose from the Grave. The Stang placed at the north end of the circle becomes the Horned Piper, the sacred king as messenger of the Goddess who is the only one who can conduct us into Her presence.

The doorway is symbolized by the besom or broom which is laid across the opening to the circle. The group is led one by one across the bridge and through the door of the castle where they are greeted by the Lady and purified.

So, we have made the symbolic journey in ritual. All that remains is that we make the journey in vision. As described in Chapter 4, we turn the mill, fall into a trance and allow the Horned Piper to lead us into the Spiral Castle where we meet the Lady face to face.

One final use for the keys involves the most secret of esoteric traditions. These images can serve as building blocks in the astral edifice that houses the Otherworld where Clan members go when they die. In one of his letters to Bill Gray, Roy wrote that when he was dead, he would go to another place that he and his ancestors created. Without that work it would not exist, since for many eons of time the human spirit had no abode. Then, by desire to survive, it created the pathway into other worlds. Nothing is gotten by doing nothing, and whatever humans do now creates the world in which humans exist tomorrow. The same applies to death; what humans have created in thought, they create in that other reality. Desire was the very first all created things.

Many mystical traditions claim that when we shed our physical bodies, we go to a place on the astral plane with which we are familiar. In the 18th century, philosopher Emanual Swedenbourg wrote that when a person's soul separates itself, it is received by good spirits, who likewise do it all kind offices whilst it is in consort with them. If, however, the person's life in the world was such that he cannot remain associated with the good, he will seek to be disunited from them also, and this separation is repeated again and again, until he associates himself with those whose state entirely agrees with that of his former life in the world, among whom he finds his own life. Then, together they live a life of similar quality to that which had constituted their ruling delight when in the body.

However, the reason why it is so familiar to us is because we ourselves have had a hand in creating it by our dedication to the symbols which make it up. Just as we dream in certain symbols that have meaning to us, after we have shed our objective awareness along with our sensory organs at death, we retreat into an astral world which is made up of the symbols which the past members of our faith or our culture, our ancestors in the spiritual rather than the biological sense, used in their rituals and meditations.

Astral imagination, whether expressed in vision or ritual or both, is a process of construction. In our minds, and in our dreams, we build images as vehicles and signposts for accessing the inner realms. To the extent that the keys that we construct in our imaginations are not just our wish fulfillment fantasies but are accurate according to the ancient patterns is the extent to which we will be able to unlock the doors to the inner realms and enter the world of the ancestors -- the collective unconscious rather than our own personal unconscious. In the former case, we can actually change the collective reality. In the latter case, we stroke our own egos and change nothing.

So, we create our own reality with our thoughts, both in this world and in the otherworld. These archetypal and ancestral images are the building blocks with which we do this. Bards and storytellers, by their art, can teach us how to do this on an individual basis by describing the images in song, story, and poetry. However, by the use of ritual, done properly and effectively, we can do this together and create a shared reality that will provide us with a home on the astral plane. Then, when the silver cord is severed, and we leave our physical bodies behind and we will travel across the river to return not again.

Chapter 12

The Sacred Path

The ultimate sacred journey is the pilgrimage. A pilgrim sets out upon a journey to visit some sacred place where the spiritual realm touches the earthly realm and merges with it. By visiting the sacred place on the earth plane, the devout pilgrim is also visiting it on the spiritual plane. This sacred place could be a shrine or a church, a temple or some special place where miracles have been performed or witnessed. It could also be the home of a deity or the birthplace of the founder of a religious tradition, or the place where a religious figure or saint is buried.

Nearly all religious traditions include the pilgrimage in their devotions. Devout Muslims are directed to make a Hajj or a pilgrimage to Mecca once in their lifetime. Medieval Catholics made pilgrimages to Compostela, Rome or Jerusalem. Modern Catholics travel to Fatima or Lourdes hoping to be healed of wounds or illnesses. Hindus also make pilgrimages to holy cities which are said to be the birthplaces of gods or ancestors. And the Japanese, both Buddhist and Shinto, will make a Junrai or pilgrimage to places of spiritual power such as mountains or shrines.

The form that these pilgrimages take varies with the religious tradition. Some pilgrimages are journeys to a single destination. Others constitute 'sacred tours' of a number of different sites. Still others are very structured and consist of a particular number of sites in a certain order with prayers, meditations and other spiritual exercises that are to be performed before embarking on the journey, while on the journey, at each site, and after returning home.

The reasons for making the pilgrimage are as varied as the pilgrims. Some go as part of their religious practice or as a sign of their devotion. Others go, as medieval Catholics did, to gain grace and forgiveness of sins. Some pilgrims have more personal reasons for making the journey. They will visit a sacred place to have questions answered by the guardian saint or deity. They may travel to a place where miracles were said to occur in order to witness their own miracle or manifestation of the divine.

But in all cases, the common features are that the destination is considered sacred or spiritual, and the pilgrim must make the journey personally, himself or herself, either alone or with others. The act of making the journey itself is as important as the shrine or sacred place which is to be visited and must be undertaken with devotion and reverence with a spiritual purpose uppermost in the mind. One is not just a tourist.

At its heart, this concept of pilgrimage constitutes a journey into the kind of sacred landscape that Paul Devereaux describes. The purpose is not just to visit the shrine or sacred place. The greater purpose is the journey itself, made slowly and deliberately, paying attention to the road, the signposts and lesser shrines along the way and interacting with the other pilgrims traveling upon the same road heading for the same destination. And once the destination is reached, the pilgrim enters into sacred space. The shrine, temple, church, or mountain is a place where the earth-bound traveler can touch the sacred, the numinous or the miraculous and come away healed, blessed, forgiven, or otherwise spiritually changed forever.

The Clan is no different. It has its own pilgrimage, its own sacred landscape where the spiritual and the earthly realms meet. In an interview with John in 1991, he told us the source of Roy's inspiration. "A lot of it came from Norfolk," he said. "But whether it was Roy's original material or old George who had been involved with Norfolk people before and sent it back through Roy, I can't be quite sure."

If that was indeed the case, then Roy could have trod the Peddar's Way. The Peddars' Way is a walking track in Norfolk. There are two branches, one along the seacoast, and one which runs inland in a southerly direction. A section of this latter branch consists of a remnant of a Roman road which was established after the defeat of Boudicca, Queen of the Icini in AD 61. It winds around for several miles, running through woodlands, between farms and fields, up and down hills, and between ancient sites and more modern structures.

Peddar's Way Signpost
Photo by Ann Finnin

Some parts of the Peddar's Way consist of paved roads which can be easily traveled by car. However, some parts are hiking trails and walking paths that lead over hedgerows and through pastures, skirt streams and wind down hillsides. Ideally, one should tread the path on foot like early pilgrims did using the act of walking like a sacred dance, swaying to the rhythm of the footsteps and eventually entering a trance-like state in which the wind rustling in the leaves overhead, the water trickling in a stream, the cows lowing and the birds singing become voices that speak to the soul and prepare the pilgrim for the moment of arrival at the shrine.

The Five Mysteries

Like the *Old Straight Track* which connects stone circles and ancient monuments in Watkyn's book, the Peddars Way connects a number of ancient shrines that are said to guard mysteries that the pilgrim confronts in the journey along the sacred path. These mysteries involve mystical gateways to the Otherworld, and the symbol used to represent this gateway determines the nature of the mystery. By visiting each site and performing a ritual or meditation, the pilgrim prays that the gateway to the Otherworld will be opened and the mystery revealed.

The Mysteries (from the Latin *mysterium* and Greek *mysterion*) were secret rites or doctrines taught by the various mystery schools that proliferated in the Greco-Roman world. These existed in addition to the exoteric religions of the time, in which the general public could attend without really understanding the doctrines. A woman might go to the temple of Hera to leave an offering to the goddess to insure the faithfulness of her husband. A man might sacrifice to Mercury to insure the beneficial outcome of a business deal. And for most of the Greco-Roman world, that was all that religion was.

In the mystery schools, however, only a small, select group of people participated in the rites. These people were carefully schooled in the esoteric doctrines taught by the schools, which went far beyond the outward expression of religious devotion and became initiates in those schools. Once they had achieved the status of initiate, they were sworn to secrecy regarding the rites and doctrines and vowed never to reveal them to outsiders. Thus, the mysteries, which tended to be experiential rather than doctrinal, were preserved from profanation by people who had neither the instruction nor the inclination to understand them.

It's ironic that Christianity started out as a mystery school in which dedicants would study the scriptures for a time until they were ready to be initiated by the rite of baptism. At that point, they were entitled to participate in the ritual of the Mass which, with its mystery of transubstantiation, required instruction to properly understand and appreciate its significance.

However, Christianity harbored a heresy that rendered it incompatible with Roman state religion. It insisted on exclusivity. Most of the other mystery schools of the time were not rivals of the state religion. They did not seek to replace it, only to augment it with less superficial and more deeply spiritual doctrines. Christianity not only harbored certain 'non-roman' beliefs and concepts, it insisted that it was the only true religion and that the Imperial cult was evil. This attitude led to their persecution in a way that other mystery cults of the time did not suffer.

When the Roman Catholic Church eventually became the dominant exoteric religion of Western Europe, the mystery schools re-emerged. Many of them practiced the same pagan rites they had preserved for hundreds of years, only now they were considered evil and heretical and were persecuted with the same fervor that the Roman state had persecuted the early Christians. They also taught certain doctrines, such as reincarnation and goddess worship, that the Church condemned.

So, they retreated underground, and their rites and doctrines were largely transmitted via oral tradition. And their sacred shrines were ordinary places – often old and abandoned relics and ruins that most people disdained – and only had a mystical significance to those who were initiates and understood the mysteries that the places symbolized.

Roy maintained that in the days when the Clan actually consisted of blood families, each Clan guarded one of the sacred sites along with the Mystery that it embodied and the power for which it served as an access point. If it is not possible to actually visit the shrine or place of power, one can employ the symbols represented by the shrine in a ritual to access the same power.

The rituals, as Roy originally described them, consisted of little more than an outline of certain symbolic actions. A few meaningful words can be added if desired. But a full ritual script is not necessary and can be counterproductive if one is worrying about saying the 'right' words at the 'right' time and not meditating on the powerful visual symbols that the ritual employs. Again, the purpose of these rituals is to use certain symbolic props to recreate the shrine within the ritual space and then to meditate upon the symbolic representations of the power in order to 'unlock' the mystery.

There is a great deal of controversy in Craft circles regarding 'real' vs. 'fake' ritual props. One school of thought on this topic maintains that the substance that the ritual implement is made of has power in and of itself regardless of the form it may take. A ritual, after all, isn't a stage performance. It's an attempt to create on the physical plane those powers that exist on the inner planes. The best thing to use to symbolize a sharp knife is a sharp knife.

Consequently, if the ritual calls for a sword, even a modest one, provided it is forged of real iron, will work better than the most elaborate pot-metal stage prop. For years, the Roebuck had a policy of requiring swords and athames to be made of real iron, since we were part of the Clan of Tubal Cain and thus were the kin of the Blacksmith God. We had one member who didn't want to work with a traditional blade, but instead worked with a pair of hand-forged iron shears. It worked, because in her case, the shears constituted a tool of her trade and served the same function as an athame, that is, an extension of her will and power.

However, this can cause other problems. If the ritual calls for a cup of wine, then grape juice won't do. Wine is wine, not just red liquid and the spirit of the alcohol is a large part of why it is used in ritual. People who have issues with alcohol can honor the cup even if they choose not to drink the contents. It is not necessary to actually eat or drink things that one must avoid for health reasons. But 'watering down the ritual' by using fake substitutes can sacrifice a lot of the power that the ritual is attempting to access.

Finally, there is a problem with obtaining actual ritual implements that used to be common but are now obsolete and difficult to find, especially in a city. Sometimes, one has to spend years haunting antique shops and swap meets for things like pitchforks, knives, sickles, cauldrons, animal skulls, deer antlers, and ram's horns. Once found, they are often expensive and require extensive cleaning and repairs – provided you can find them at all.

Another problem can arise with regard to the sacred plants and woods that are specified in the ritual. Again, the plant has power beyond its symbolic meaning. But there are places where they are almost impossible to find, particularly in areas that do not have a climate suitable for growing them. An effective alternative would be to research a plant from the same genus or family that does grow in the area or to grow it yourself under controlled conditions with seeds or cuttings.

At the end of the day, all you can do is your best. However, it is interesting that the more a group performs these rites, even with props that are less genuine and more symbolic, the opportunity to procure the real object will present itself. It is as though the guardians on the inner planes see the sincere effort and reward it with the means by which to access the power more completely by arranging it so that the required object or plant becomes available.

'Grimes Graves'
Thetford, Norfolk, England
Photo by Ann Finnin

The Cave and the Cauldron

A cave is a natural underground space large enough for a human to enter. Caves form naturally by the weathering of rock, either by wind or water, and often extend deep underground. Early humans used them for shelter, warmth and protection. However, they were also considered to be gateways to the underworld, guarded by fearsome beasts which had to be either subdued or placated in order to gain access to the innermost depths by means of trance-induced visions.

The famous caves at Lascaux in France are a case in point. The paintings depict scenes of hunting – herds of animals and hunters armed with spears. But it also depicts the now iconic image of the shaman, a man dressed in a deer hide and stag antlers.

Imagine yourself a young man of twelve or so taking your initiation as a hunter. You have spent several days in that cave without food or human contact. You don't know if it's day or night. The only light is a small fire that throws flickering shadows on the walls. After the third day or so might not the painted animals begin to move, and the shaman speak to you? Will his message to you be interpreted by the tribal elders as indicating that you have passed your test and are now a full-fledged hunter?

There is also another kind of cave. This was the man-made cave or mine which was dug deep into the earth to claim a treasure guarded by the denizens of the underworld. This treasure could be gold or silver, gemstones, or iron ore. But even before the age of iron or bronze, there was another treasure sought by humans from the underworld.

Norfolk is dotted with prehistoric flint mines. One of these, Grimes Graves, is one of the most well-known. Since the site is owned by the National Trust, it can be visited, and descending into its depths is an amazing experience. Flint was used before metal to make tools and weapons, but one has to go deep underground to get it and it was considered a gift of the gods of the underworld.

Photo by Dave Finnin

The mystery of the Cave and the Cauldron illustrates the necessity of descending into the underworld in order to find the cauldron of inspiration and transformation. In this cave dwell the three goddesses that John described as the three Norns but can also be seen as the Moirai or fates, the daughters of night.

There are three Fates: Clotho, the spinner, who spins the thread of life; Lachesis, the measurer, who chooses the lot in life one will have and measures off how long it is to be; and Atropos, she who cannot be turned, who at death with her shears cuts the thread of life.

Celtic lore often depicts goddesses as having three faces or three forms. Examples are the three Bridgets, which were later Christianized as the three Marys who keened at the foot of the cross and the three weird sisters in Shakespeare's Macbeth. Most notably, Hecate, the goddess of the Dark Moon, the underworld, witchcraft and sorcery, is depicted as having three faces. So, the three fates are actually three faces of one goddess, the Dark Lady of Fate herself.

In the Cave and the Cauldron ritual, three women gather around a cauldron. The Magister approaches them and asks who they are. They reply that they are three who keep the cauldron; one to stir, one to serve and one to see as the fates decree. The first woman takes up the sword and stirs the water. She then sprinkles the quarters with water, working widdershins.

The second takes a ladle and fills a cup with water from the cauldron. She offers it to the goddess, then serves everyone in the circle, with the Summoner being first to be served.

The third kneels before the cauldron and acts as seer while everyone else treads a slow, silent, widdershins mill. When the seer is finished, she stands up and the mill stops.

It is noted that this rite is divinatory in nature and not performed in a cast circle. The Summoner stands guard during the rite and therefore is the first to be offered the cup.

St. Bruno's Church, Berriew, Wales
Photo by Ann Finnin

Chapel of St.Mark, Appleton, Norfolk
Photo by Ann Finnin

The Rose Beyond the Grave

The Norfolk area is also replete with old ruined chapels which had been in use several hundred years ago and fell into disuse when the population of the countryside migrated to the city. Some are quite large, well preserved, and are still in use as parish churches.

Some, however, are so tiny that they couldn't have been parish churches and are located far from the nearest village. The roofs are gone, but the arches and towers remain. Many have graves in the floor. Some have ancient rose bushes that crawl along the stone walls and arches.

The mystery of the Rose Beyond the Grave symbolizes death and rebirth. Death is the ultimate mystery, and what happens after death is the ultimate test of faith. In his article *The Rose Beyond the Grave*,[57] John wrote that it doesn't matter how much we delve into our innermost being to dredge up past-life experiences. In the end all that we have left is our personal belief in the existence of a soul and of a life beyond the grave. It is only when we cross from life to death that we are able to find the true answer to the secret that we call the Rose beyond the Grave.

In this ritual, an open grave is recreated on an east-west axis with the headstone in the east. If this ritual is done indoors, the grave can be marked by a rectangle of stones or bricks measuring roughly four feet across and six feet long with a headstone aligned to the eastern wall.

The Magister hallows the circle by sprinkling drops of water at the four quarters. Then, he sprinkles a few drops into the grave and drops a single red rose into it with the flower pointing to the headstone. The other members jump or step across the open grave to enter the circle. By doing so, they have placed themselves 'under the rose' and are sworn to secrecy about their experiences in the circle. The quarters of East, South and West are hallowed, but not North since the North is hallowed along with the grave.

The mill is trod until all have received their visions. Bread with salt sprinkled on it and wine are shared with the Maid pouring a libation to the Lady of the castle. Then all exit over the grave and back to the world of the living once more.

---

57 John Johns, Evan. (2012). *The Rose Beyond the Grave*. Pomegranate: The International Journal of Pagan Studies. 13. 48-52. 10.1558/pome.v13i5.48.

The Stone Stile

Out in the Norfolk countryside, fields and pastures are separated by hedgerows which in themselves are a deception. They aren't just bushes. They often consist of thick vines, some with sharp thorns, which hide rock walls, some at least six feet high. They are impossible to climb over. But instead of gates, which could be left open allowing cattle to escape, stone stiles or steps are built into the walls which allow walkers to climb over the wall and cross over from one field to the next. But they are often well hidden. One must know where they are.

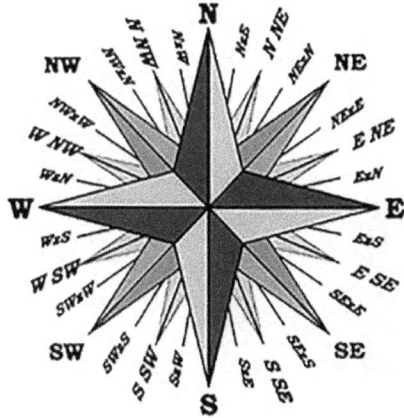

The Stone Stile is the mystery of how to navigate across the sacred landscape. This is one ritual which is best done outdoors. The Magister first casts the circle by marking the four quarters with wine to symbolize the god and marking the eight cross quarters with water to symbolize the goddess for a total of 12 points. If he uses a compass, he can use magnetic north as a starting point. These directions can be marked by small stones or other markers if desired.

By doing this, he has created a compass or wind rose showing the 12 classical points from where the twelve traditional winds arose. The compass rose was used by navigators that crossed the ocean in sailing vessels with only the stars as their guide. This 12-wind compass rose dates from the time of the ancient Greeks. It was adopted and refined by the Romans and used throughout medieval Europe.

The twelve points are:

North	North by Northeast	South by Southeast
South	Northeast	Southeast
East	North by Northwest	South by Southwest
West	Northwest	Southwest

Once again, we find the symbolism of the airts who not only mark the actual compass points, but also serve to predict the nature of the winds that might arise from the twelve directions that either aid or hinder the sailor in his journey. By treading the mill within the compass rose, you can navigate between the worlds by finding the location of the Stone Stiles by which you can cross the boundary between the worlds.

'Castle Acre'
Norfolk, England
Photo by Ann Finnin

The Castle of the Four Winds

Ruined castles like Castle Acre also dot the countryside in Norfolk. The ruins are like the chapels. They have walls and windows but no roofs, and are open to the sky, letting the winds from all four directions whistle through them. There, we perform the mystery called the Castle of the Four Winds.

The Castle Perilous, or the Castle of the Four Winds, is the home of the ancestral goddess. This marks the apex of the journey along the sacred path. We have communed with the ancestors, experienced rebirth, found our bearings, and learned our fate. We have now arrived at the castle turning without motion between the elements. And we are also back where we began, in the sacred circle.

This ritual should be performed by a solo practitioner or small group. It is significant that a traditional circle isn't cast and that the besom bridge is not crossed. This can only mean that we are not outside the castle when we perform this ritual, but within it.

This ritual involves building three concentric circles within the sacred space, each with a particular meaning, using the stang in the center as a pivot point. You are, in essence, not casting a circle representing the castle but casting the castle itself as a vehicle for death and rebirth.

The first circle represents life, labor, and physical manifestation. It is produced by sprinkling salt around the circle. We go from the duties of physical life to the exploration of the spiritual realms.

The second circle represents the process of sacrifice that the aspirant must perform in order to cross the river. It is produced by sprinkling the ashes of willow and birch. Both willow and birch are Chieftain trees and symbolize mourning and rebirth respectively.

The third circle represents the 'river of time', the boundary between our world and the otherworld, the moat of the castle that only admits those who are 'of the blood.' It's produced by asperging the circle, starting in the north and proceeding first to the east, then the south, then the west, with a mixture of water, wine, vinegar, and salt.

Candles are now lit in the four directions beginning in the east, moving west, then south, and finally north. Note that we are not going around the circle, either widdershins or deosil. We are pacing the compass rose and summoning the airts or the four winds.

At each point of the compass, we kneel on one knee, make a fist, thump the ground three times, and summon the elemental spirit of the airt to blow through the castle. We summon the spirit of Fire in the East, the spirit of Water in the West, the spirit of Earth in the South, and the spirit of Air in the North, just as described in the circle casting ritual.

In the center of the circle we place a knife at the foot of the stang to represent the male principle. We take our power, intellect, and will and lay it at the foot of the sacrificial king. We place a cord, tied with eight knots with a noose at one end on the tine of the stang to the practitioner's left. We become Odin, hanging on the world tree by the will of the three-fold goddess so that we might acquire the Sight.

The Stang and Cord
Photo by Dave Finnin

We slowly pace the mill around the stang with our hoods up, 3x3 or nine times. Finally, we extinguish the candles in the order East, West, South, and North, spiraling deosil beginning in the south and going around three times until all the candles are out. Then, we leave the circle.

The Mound and the Skull

As you drive along the Peddar's Way, Neolithic burial mounds dot the countryside. You will be driving along a field or pasture, and suddenly you will see a mound rising up from the surrounding field like a woman's breast. In some cases, you can actually park by the side of the road, enter the field, and climb the mound.

A long barrow along Peddar's Way in Norfolk
Photo by Ann Finnin

Neolithic mounds, such as the famous one on Salisbury plain called Silbury hill, are similar to the ones found all over the British Isles. They marked a burial place -- not of an ordinary mortal – but a chieftain or king who had often been elevated in song and story to the status of a god. After the burial, the mound could be used as a worship site for the tribe (much in the same way that important people in the parish were buried in the parish church) who would feel that as they communed with the gods, their departed ancestral leaders who were buried there would be joined with them.

Photo by Dave Finnin

The mystery of the Mound and the Skull is how to connect with the ancestors.

In this ritual, one obtains a human skull. The skull should be real if at all possible. In most places, skulls are not illegal to have provided they are actually purchased from authorized dealer of medical specimens and not dug up out of a graveyard somewhere. A real skull carries with it powerful energies that are worked with in the ritual. However, an anatomically correct replica of the kind used in science classes will do until the opportunity arises to get a real one. And, if the ritual is performed with sincere intent, a suitable ancestor will no doubt appear.

The ritual was described by Cochrane in an article entitled *The Witches' Esbat*[58] which appeared in *New Dimensions*, November of 1964. He describes it as, "a combination of fiction and fact since the full ritual cannot be described." Of course, the reason that it couldn't be described is that it didn't actually happen. Apparently, it was supposed to occur, but for various reasons, it did not. This ritual is what should have happened.

It takes place inside a cave, as did many of Cochrane's rituals. But we suspect that this cave was used as a way of accessing the inside of a burial

---

58 *The Witches' Esbat,* Robert Chocrane, New Dimensions, Vol. 2, No. 10, November 1964.

mound. This isn't stated *per se*, but the rest of the ritual suggests that this was the intent.

The circle is arranged so that the skull is placed in the center and elevated above the floor, impaled by the blade of a sword and tied securely to the hilt. The blade is stuck into the earth.

The ritual begins by treading a maze pattern, then pacing around the fire. The cauldron is emptied into a moat around the periphery of the circle and all enter the circle with the Maid tossing a piece of cake onto the ground after her.

The Magister stands in front of the skull and, lifts up five fingers and chants "UEIOA." The rest of the company tread the mill in silence, hoods up, concentrating on the work. Green lights flash around the skull. The group calls "Master, master." A figure appears, exuding strength and wisdom. He is greeted, then the ritual is over.

When we performed this ritual, we used dark beer instead of wine. Since we were in the temple, we didn't pour the wine. We sprinkled the dark beer around the perimeter of the circle. We performed the maze pattern before entering the temple, tossed the cake over the threshold, and treaded the mill. Dave invoked with five fingers and the chant of "UEIOA." However, we called "Tubal, Tubal" instead of "Master, Master."

And yes, it worked.

Chapter 13

The Question of Authority

One of the main issues that has bedeviled the modern Witchcraft movement from its inception has been one of authenticity – who was a 'real' witch and who wasn't. The debate still rages on between the eclectics and the traditionalists as to just whose tradition is genuine and whose is made up.

Consequently, even if a witch has spent many years building up a workable tradition from personal inspiration, work, and research, she can claim no authority over anyone else. Nobody is compelled to listen to her, read what she writes or do as she says. She has no right to determine what Wicca is since she is just one independent practitioner among many.

But if she has an initiation in a genuine tradition, even though she personally has done nothing much of note, then she has borrowed robes to wear. Everyone else must take her seriously because she is an initiate of (insert famous name here) tradition. And even though she has done no work, run no group, written no rituals, and taught no students, she is an important person and has the right to tell everyone what they must do to be considered a real witch.

This particularly true in America where the quest for authenticity is more desperate than it is in Europe or Britain. There has never been an officially established, uncontested, religious or spiritual authority in this country -- no Church of America that everyone must join and acknowledge as the real religion. Immigrants came to this country from all races, religions and cultures, and effectively left their secular and spiritual authorities behind. They clustered together in a tapestry of diverse traditions, each with their separate beliefs and practices.

There were certainly skirmishes and turf wars between different traditions, and between rival groups within the same tradition for local supremacy. However, after two or three hundred years, particularly in big cities, the result was a marketplace of religious and spiritual ideas where each religion and sect, whether new or old, had to set up their booths and attempt to sell their religion to a spiritual seeker on the basis of merit alone. And the seeker could choose the one that appealed to him the most, regardless of his ethnic or religious background. This was true in the cunning traditions as well.

Many Americans come from immigrant families who had originally practiced folk magic traditions in their native countries for hundreds of years. Originally, these families settled in rural areas sequestered away in hidden valleys in Appalachia or among the German speaking families of the Pennsylvania Dutch, where outsiders rarely ventured until recent times.

In later years, those traditions found their way out of their rural valleys and into the wider venues of cities and towns, often cheek-to-jowl alongside similar traditions from other cultures. In the cities, immigrants of various cultures freely intermarried with each side of the family, bringing their own traditions to the table, and the children and grandchildren would learn both.

However, as families were separated in the early twentieth century by war, economic upheavals, or natural disasters, younger generations never got to learn the family traditions from their grandparents the way previous generations did. So, they turned to imported traditions that were similar to the forgotten family traditions but did not require them to be taught by relatives and were able to join without presenting any *bona fides* that they belonged there by blood or family affiliation.

Many times, seekers possessed a half-forgotten family talent, perhaps a latent psychic ability, but had no idea what to do with it. So, they would join a group with lots of ritual and lore and interesting (and often obscure) practices that was run by someone who had some kind of initiation in a particular European or British tradition. They would then adopt the authenticity of that tradition instead of their own family tradition.

The standard story they heard was that the person running the group had been initiated into, or had advanced standing in, a supposed genuine craft tradition from somewhere in Europe, and possessed some kind of official mandate to bring this genuine tradition to America. If a seeker was found to be suitable, whatever that process might entail, he or she would be taught the tradition, brought into the group and initiated. Then, he or she would be considered to be a genuine magician or witch rather than an eclectic and would have the right to pass judgment on the rest of the wannabes that he or she might encounter at various gatherings and meet-ups.

This process becomes important because with the claim to authenticity comes authority – and credibility. Those who have an initiation in an authentic tradition feel that they have some measure of authority in the community rather than the "wanna-blessed-bes" who just made it all up. And authority means the perceived right to be the arbiter of what is genuine craft and what is not.

An initiation into an alleged-authentic tradition might mean a greater chance of having a book published by a well-known publishing house, and having it read by newcomers who want to know what real witchcraft is all about. A book with a jacket that informs the reader that the author is a high-ranking initiate in the XYZ tradition that has its origins in the 'mists of time' will sell better than a similar book whose author spent thirty years taking bits and pieces from various magical traditions and concocted a method of magic practice that happens to work.

The author with the supposed authentic credentials might also be considered as a *de facto* expert on what the Craft really is and may be asked to speak at various academic and institutional symposiums. Someone who pieced their tradition together does not have the credibility -- or marketability -- as one who has the authentic *bona fides*, however spurious they may be.

True eclectics have rebelled against this notion for a very good reason. They often sense that the so-called genuine groups are no more genuine than they are. The credentialed author in question could be the inheritor of a tradition which itself was founded by a person who made it up. In some cases, the ostensibly authentic tradition was fabricated out of whole cloth by a previous generation across the ocean, where it was easier to cover up their tracks.

Indeed, the last thirty or so years of digging up the antecedents of Gerald Gardner's work has suggested that Gardner himself had no more connection with any kind of ancient traditional craft than many of the modern day eclectics. He had a vision and a source of inspiration. He did research, wrote rituals, ran a group, and essentially fashioned a reconstruction that happened to work. However, people in his own day called him a wannabe, a showman, and an eclectic. And even in England at the present time, Gardnerians are given no more authority in the wider Craft community than any other reconstructed tradition.

But by the time Gardnarian craft came to America, it was peddled as an ancient tradition that had been dug up complete and fully preserved out of a peat bog, and if you were lucky enough to get an initiation into one of its covens, you were a real witch. If you weren't, you were only a wannabe. In fact, some branches of American Gardnerians treated their third-degree initiations like a kind of apostolic succession, considering that they and only they are entitled to pass self-proclaimed genuine Wicca to whomever they deemed worthy. This was the trap that we fell into back in 1975.

As I mentioned in *Forge of Tubal Cain*, we had been denied admission into the 'official' Long Island Gardnarian line by someone who had received no more training and done no more work than we had, but who had received a weekend third degree from the New York coven and was now authorized to return to California and determine who should be a real witch, and who was destined to remain beyond the pale.

So, when in 1986 when we were formally initiated by John into The Clan of Tubal Cain, we couldn't help feeling as though we had finally been accepted into a tradition that we believed to be even more genuine, not the warmed-over ceremonial magic and questionable sexual practices of the American Gardnerians.

However, we were wrong. One of the reasons why should have been obvious to us when, in 1994, John abandoned Roy's tradition completely and produced *Sacred Mask, Sacred Dance*. Despite what he had written to us about what he claimed to be Roy's secret tradition, in the book he actually went so far as to question Roy's legitimacy, and suggested that whatever else Roy might have had, he may not have had the traditional background that he claimed:

> Was Cochrane a real magician of the old tradition, or was he just another magical trickster, a "tregetour" or mountebank who jumped on the occult bandwagon, as some people who never even met the man now claim that he did? Perhaps what is written here will go some way to help people to make up their own minds about him and not prejudge or blindly accept everything claimed for both him and his works. After all, even during his lifetime his harshest critics often were those who had worked with him! But even then we still had the feeling that what he did was very different from the usual run of occult workings. So what was so special about the way he worked all those years ago?

During the process of writing his first book with Doreen Valiente in 1991, John must have discovered what Doreen had already known, that Roy was no more of a hereditary witch than he was, and that Roy's background in traditional craft was either grossly exaggerated or made up out of whole cloth. That meant that there was nothing sacrosanct about Roy's tradition. It could be modified and abandoned altogether, which he eventually did in the *Sacred Masks, Sacred Dance* book.

We were shocked at the time, but we shouldn't have been. There were a number of attempted reconstructions of the so-called witch cult in Britain around the time of the repeal of the Witchcraft Act in 1951, of which Gardner's was only one of the most well-known. Most of the reconstructions were based upon a small number of pseudo-scholarly works which gave as their sources the folklore surrounding witches as well as the alleged confessions that were wrung from accused witches who likely faced a horrible death if convicted. The information in these works was often unsubstantiated and deliberately lurid in order to shock their pious Christian readers into worrying that the Devil was lurking under their beds, just waiting to carry them off to hell for the slightest infraction.

In her book, *Witch Cult in Western Europe*[59], anthropologist Margaret Murray took a different tack. The medieval witch cult, far from being anti-clerical and Satanic, was actually a survival of a pre-Christian pagan religion which worshiped the Goddess and the Horned God as the givers of fertility. This appealed to Gardner, who designed his coven to be run by a High Priestess who was the representative of the Goddess, with the High Priest as the representative of the Horned God playing a secondary role.

However, this interpretation didn't match the evidence from other sources. There were many involved in the Witchcraft movement in the 1960s who considered Gardner nothing more than a showman and a fake. Several anonymous contributors to the various Craft newsletters such as *Pentagram*, edited by Gerald Noel, disputed the claims that the various Gardnarian luminaries were making to having the one true right and only Craft tradition. One of them, who called himself "Taliesin", claimed to be a hereditary witch from a clan similar to Roy's. He pointed out that Dr. Murray had glossed over the fact that the Horned God of the medieval cult showed unmistakable Middle-Eastern characteristics and that the Goddess was never so much as mentioned either by witches undergoing trial or by those who were trying them. The allegiance of the covens was given unswervingly to their god, not to a goddess.

Evidence also pointed to the fact that the coven leader was not a woman but a man, not a High Priestess but a Magister. According to John, often the Magister was a member of the aristocracy and owned the land on which the coven held their rituals. He presided over the meetings, often providing food for the feast afterward. He also provided protection for

---

59 *Witch Cults in Western Europe: A Study in Anthropology*, Margaret Murray, Published by Clarendon Press, Oxford (1921).

the meetings since he was often the only one in the group who actually owned a sword. He was known to the coveners only as "the Devil", no doubt to protect his identity in case they were questioned by inquisitors. Roy at one point referred to himself as "the Devil, in fact" when describing himself as the magister of his Clan.

If this structure sounds familiar, that's because it matches the accounts of the North Berwick witches who bedeviled the English King James VI in the early 1600s -- a time when every political dispute was also a religious dispute, and the Protestant fear of devils, demons and Roman Catholic magical practices ran rampant. In the case of the North Berwick witches, "the Devil" was none other than Francis Stuart, the 5th Earl of Bothwell and James' cousin who had a claim to the Scottish throne, and this fact might have contributed to James' legendary terror of witchcraft.

And the king had every reason to be afraid, it seems, of both witchcraft and treason. The coven, consisting of well-to-do townsfolk, seems to have directed its magical activities to ensure the destruction of James VI and his reign. They were accused primarily of sending storms to sink the ship that carried James and his new bride, Anne of Denmark, back to England.

James, a devout Calvinist, presided over the trial personally. One of coveners apparently convinced the king of her magical abilities – and sealed her fate -- by whispering into his ear the very words that he had said to his bride on their wedding night. James needed no further proof. She, along with all the members of the coven, were tortured and executed with only Francis Stuart surviving. This touched off a wave of horrific witchcraft persecutions which extended even across the Atlantic into Colonial America.

Murray's work has since been discredited as inaccurate, fanciful, and extremely biased. The existence of a monolithic witch cult that survived unchanged for fifteen centuries in Europe is extremely unlikely, or it would have suffered persecution long before the fifteenth century just like the Cathars did. And that meant that there was certainly no unbroken line of succession from any Murrayite witch cult to the followers of

Gerald Gardner, contrary to what has been claimed on both sides of the Atlantic.

Similarly, Leland's work, particularly his conversations with Italian witches recorded in Aradia, has also come under intense scrutiny. When other Italian speakers translate the invocations given in the book, they turn out to mean something entirely different than what Leland said they did. There is also no scholarly evidence that there was any kind of organized witchcraft movement in Italy during the time in question -- at least, one that practiced the kind of rituals that Leland claimed -- any more than there had been in England. So, it is entirely possible that Leland assembled the Aradia material from bits and pieces of his earlier works on Gypsy and Etruscan folklore for either political or money-making purposes. And that would include the entire 'Lucifer, brother of Diana' connection.

Still, wrote Taliesin, the Murray material gave Gardner a starting point. From there, his own far-from-small intelligence and great imagination, allied to a seasoning of Crowley and a strong injection of Leland's books of gypsy sorcery and the esoteric Etruscan and Florentine witch cults, produced the greater proportion of what today makes up the rites, rituals, witty sayings, wise saws and general fun and games of modern witchcraft.

Bill Gray was also extremely critical of what was being passed off as witchcraft during the Gardner era. In his book *Magical Ritual Methods*, he decries the "self-acclaimed 'witches' inventing ritualistic covers for sex-naughtiness." He goes on to say that, "the so-called 'Witch' rites linked with primitive paganism depend on ritualized sex practices and symbolic slaughter dramatized in the forms of sadism and masochism known as 'bonding and beating'." He concludes with, "The completely phony 'Witch-rites' purchasable from various sources are mainly modern inventions."

These accusations left only the cunning craft that actually had been practiced, more or less continually, since the early 1600s. Unlike Murray's witch cult, the cunning folk had no Grand Master or centralized authority. They plied their trade as independent individuals, and passed on their craft in a rather haphazard fashion to their descendants. So, it is possible that there were people in the witchcraft movement in the 1960s who actually had family ties to the practitioners of this craft.

However, there was no evidence that Roy himself did. Roy had claimed at one point that he and his wife had been Thames "bargees": people who piloted the cargo barges down the Thames river. The bargees belonged, apparently, to a small group of families who, like gypsies, practiced a traditional form of cunning craft which including trance work, spells and invocations, and maintained a tight-lipped secrecy about their activities in front of outsiders. There is no evidence that either Roy or his wife were members of such a family. Still, it made for a compelling narrative. Consequently, there arose a craft movement which proposed to replace Gardner with someone who had less of a ceremonial magic background and more of a hereditary and shamanic background. Roy either considered himself, or was considered by others, as this likely successor.

And he certainly could have been. He was a much younger man and a more poetic writer than Gardner, as well as a creative and visionary ritualist. And he had the august if shadowy presence of William G. Gray in his corner. With a couple of published books under his belt written with the same inspirational force as his letters, Roy could very well have toppled Gardner from his pedestal, and what came to be known as Traditional British Witchcraft would have been very different.

But that didn't happen. As the years went by, Roy's compelling story about his hereditary past began to wear thin. People who in the beginning had believed his story, began to question his credentials. One by one, they declared him a phony and his story fake, referring to him as a "weirdie" and a "hysteric."

And the dominoes continued to fall. Doreen Valiente herself, who had worked with Roy and his group, came to the conclusion that he was not a hereditary witch after all. Roy's brother, apparently, had no knowledge of the Craft, or anything to do with it. Even Roy's widow eventually confessed to the fact that everything Roy had claimed about his craft was "all lies." He had only come into the Craft about eight years previously through a man named Charles "Chalky" White after answering an advertisement in a local newspaper. His story continued to unravel until finally, just two years after Gardner's death, Roy fell victim to the '*Curse of Tubal Cain*' and took his own life.

Fifty years later, it is interesting to speculate on what kind of craft Roy Bowers could have promulgated, given his talents. But there is one thing that these fifty years have revealed: modern witchcraft, no matter what its luminaries and prophets claim, was not passed down unaltered from sometime in the shadowy past. It was reassembled using modern materials, on the barest shred of an ancient template that had been abandoned for hundreds of years.

Dion Fortune wrote in *Applied Magic,*

> Whatever it may be in the East, the lines of contact on the physical plane in the West have been so utterly broken and destroyed with historical time that they have to be pieced together like ancient pottery. Experience proves, however, that when a certain amount of piecing has been done and the pattern appears, it is possible for the psychic to pick up the inner plane contacts and reforge the link. This is what is actually done in the modem Mysteries.

Fortune goes on to say:

> "A great body of tradition exists, though scattered and concealed, and the student in whom the inner eye is open can penetrate its significance when he studies it. If he aims at being an initiator and training students, it is necessary that he should codify this knowledge and reduce it to an intelligible system; the value of an occult school depends in large measure on the manner in which this purely mundane work has been done. The Ancient Wisdom must be correlated with modem thought if its significance is to be made available for the student."

In short, the modern Craft, in all its iterations, is a reconstruction. And nobody has any more right to try their hand at such a reconstruction than anybody else, on either side of the Atlantic.

That being said, however, lineage in an established tradition is still vitally important for a number of obvious and not-so-obvious reasons. A tradition, if it's been around for a few decades, represents a body of knowledge and procedures that somebody had to do a lot of work to put together. Craft traditions are not dug intact out of peat bogs. They are put together over years of dedicated and often difficult work. Book and primary source research, creative writing of rituals, chants and spells, trying the rituals out on a small group of people who may or may not appreciate being magical guinea pigs, writing the results down, revising them, scrapping them if necessary, and so on all contribute to the corpus of a working magical tradition.

The dominant Craft tradition of modern times, the Gardnarian tradition, was put together in this fashion. Even before he retired to London to start his coven, Gardner spent decades in dedicated study and exploration of every source of magical practice that he could get his hands on. And the result was far from finished when he died. Those who came after him, in particular Doreen Valiente, refined it further, making the pieces fit together and made it work for a group of modern people. It has taken us in the Roebuck four decades to do the same and, as such, I have nothing but admiration for the efforts of the Gardnerians, even if I don't particularly agree with some of the results.

When a student takes initiation into such a tradition, after having studied it intensely for a year or two, there remains a permanent stamp on the student's magical practice. The first magical tradition you learn stays with you, no matter how many subsequent traditions you study afterwards. Attitudes towards the gods, who those gods are, methods of working, what you do in circle, what you say, and how you invoke are things that you learn in your first circle, and they color almost everything else that you do going forward.

Indeed, it's almost impossible to scour that training from your aura no matter how hard you try. Since these things are most often learned by rote without questioning them, they are embedded deeply into the unconscious and will emerge whenever you do ritual. Your lineage is truly engraved upon your brow, as the ancients say. This is why phony Gardnerians in particular are so obvious. They may claim they have a Gardnarian initiation, but if they don't act like Gardnerians in a circle, then they haven't had any Gardnerian training, even though they might have gone through a ceremony or two over the course of a weekend.

There is another subtler issue that Dion Fortune talks about, and that is the question of the psychic contacts. Every tradition that is more than a fantasy role playing game reaches up into the astral plane and attracts spiritual beings into its group soul. These can be angels, demons, gods, ancestors, fairies, genii or whatever, but if the group is genuinely practicing a modern version of an old tradition, it will attract the spirits that attended that old tradition. This doesn't happen automatically, nor by fiat. For example, just because somebody claims to be practicing a fairy faith doesn't mean the fairies are actually in attendance, especially in cases when fairies are actually aiding the work rather than coming in to mess it up.

Just because one is practicing an Egyptian or a Celtic tradition and invoking Egyptian or Celtic gods, doesn't mean that those gods are in attendance. On the other hand, they may be in attendance well enough, but they aren't the whitewashed Victorian versions of those gods that one reads about in books. And this is where traditions often go on the rocks. The gods they invoke are Victorian fantasies. If the actual gods deign to show up, they usually end up causing trouble rather than bestowing power and enlightenment.

Consequently, those modern reconstructions of ancient traditions that plug into genuine astral patterns and cosmic contacts will thrive, while those that function as nothing more than the personal wish fulfillment fantasies of the people that attempt them will not. And like seeds sown in fallow ground, some will grow and thrive, and others will wither and die.

However, the personal backgrounds of those who sow them are of no importance in the grand scheme of things. The ancestral guardians choose the ones who are more likely to succeed in their reconstruction efforts, not those who have some kind of bloodline. And at the end of the day, the traditions themselves will determine who speaks for them, and who does not.

Authentic magical traditions still exist. Their astral influence is real, and initiations into those traditions are genuine and powerful. But the proof that the initiation has actually taken place and that the initiate is carrying on a genuine tradition rather than a personal magical fantasy game is going to be evident only after years of work, not after several ceremonies conducted over a three-day weekend. The initiation, whatever it consists of, is only the beginning of the process anyway. Those who use their initiation - even if it is into a genuine tradition - as *'Letters of Marque'* to justify their own power trip are going to fall by the wayside when the going gets tough.

What we probably should have done back in 1986 is take our hands-on adoption from John, go home and integrate the Clan material into the growing Roebuck, rather than attempt to run the Clan of Tubal Cain as a separate group. There was nothing wrong with the Roebuck. Ten years after its founding, the Roebuck was a functioning coven, and we had worked long and hard to make it that way. It had a useful and integrated training system, and a structure that encouraged individual magical growth while providing a means of keeping anybody, from the high priest and priestess on down, from imposing their personal will on the rest of the group. Our Clan adoption served to hook us up with the wellhead of ancestral power. But we had to provide the conduit for that power.

Now that thirty years have passed, there are elements to the story of our quest for Roy's tradition that we either didn't know or hadn't realized the significance of at the time. The first thing was the importance of our meeting with Bill Gray. In our zeal to discover the roots of Roy's tradition, we made the mistake of not paying more attention to Bill's work on the Sangreal. After all, we had left ceremonial magic behind – or so we thought.

It wasn't until much later that we came to realize the significance of his influence on Roy's work. The Rollright Ritual had just been the beginning. For the next thirty years, everything we learned about Roy's tradition seemed to have Bill's signature all over it. From the basics of turning the mill, to the vowel chant, to the five mysteries, we found ourselves following in Bill's footsteps as much as we did John's.

And then, there is the mystery of Roy's cord. We know that Bill performed a ritual after Roy's death to untie the knots in order to set Roy's spirit free. We also know that he wasn't alone when he performed that ritual. He had a couple of his own students with him. We have since spoken to one of those students and have verified that the cord in our possession is indeed Roy's cord. Why did Bill not give the cord to John after Roy's death? Why did he hold onto it himself for fifteen years just to give it to us after having known us for only a few short hours? What did he know that we didn't? And what influence did he have on John's declaration in 1987 that the Roebuck was the only true inheritors of Roy's tradition, even though John was later to rescind that declaration after Bill had died?

John had originally told us back in 1982 that any member of Roy's Clan could adopt someone else into the Clan. One didn't need to be the leader of the group in order to do so. And, in fact, at the time we were adopted into the Clan, John actively denied being the leader. Hence, the letter informing us that we were the leaders, and that he and whoever he was working with at the time owed their position to us.

However, somewhere during the course of the next ten years, that obviously changed. It has been apparent to us that John, for all of his talent and knowledge, was not immune to the lure of the inherited mantle of authority. Even after repudiating Roy in print, he continued to use his connection with Roy as a means to establish himself as an authority within the greater craft community as the one and only heir to Roy's tradition. Eventually, after years of being underground, he decided to accept students and start his own version of the Clan.

Fair enough. No one here was disputing his right to start a group of his own and explore Roy's teachings according to his research and inclination. We certainly had no issue with him doing so, despite what he had written to us in 1987. We, in fact, welcomed a sister Clan in England with whom we could share information and research so that both Clans could carry on the work that Roy begun.

In his last letter to us, he wrote to us that at May Eve when he passed on the stag's head wand over to someone else, he would float a candle over the falls to signify the oath of leadership has been dissolved and that he was no longer leading his Clan. We couldn't help noting that he specifically said his Clan not THE Clan. It was his group that he was turning over to someone else, not ours, nor the Clan in general.

Again, something changed somewhere along the line. After John's death, someone claiming to be his successor informed us that as active magister of the Clan of Tubal Cain, John appointed her as THE Maid of Tubal Cain in 1999. She went on to state in no uncertain terms that Tubal Cain was a British born and British led group. The American branch was a kindred group only. The mantle was passed from Roy to Jane to John to her and to her appointed magister in true traditional succession. There are no others.

So, rather than being a *Sister Clan*, we were at best only a cadet branch. A bastard line. We shared the same bloodline through John, but they were the legitimate branch, and we were not. However, we were subsequently assured that, if we wished, we could take an oath of fealty to John's legitimate successors and be officially brought into the main line. Our years of work and service to the Clan were commendable and duly noted. However, we could only be legitimate by submitting to the authority of John's appointed successors. We would not be, nor could we ever be, their equals.

I don't think that was how Roy had intended the Clan to be passed on. There was never supposed to be only one line of succession, legitimate or not. The Craft is not the Roman Catholic Church. That was always our strength across the many centuries of persecution. The more groups there are practicing a tradition independently of each other, the greater the probability that the tradition will survive.

But that also means that no one person or group, on either side of the pond, has the right to claim possession of the tradition. We don't deserve to be kicked to the curb after thirty years just because our existence proved to be inconvenient to those who would claim exclusive right to it. It belongs to all of us, or it belongs to none.

In a strange way, discovering that Roy wasn't a genuine hereditary witch actually frees us from any allegiance to, or domination from, those who claim to be the legitimate heirs to Roy's tradition. They are only doing what we have done – taken Roy's information and inspirations and wove them into their own personal ritual framework. If we aren't genuine, then neither are they.

It appears to be a hallmark of those who inherit established traditions that they feel they must jealously guard it against those who would seek to claim their own legitimacy and refuse to acknowledge the authority of the new leaders of the parent group. However, this ploy will continue to work so long as the authority of those who inherit the tradition is accepted by others.

If not, then a rival group can turn around, give the so-called legitimate inheritors of the tradition the old middle-finger salute, and merrily go ahead with running their own reconstructed group. There is no power that can stop them. And, indeed, if they have been truly connected to the wellhead of ancestral power and authority, the rival group will not only thrive, but possibly outlast the supposed 'more legitimate' heirs. If they have not, then they will fall apart once they have severed ties with the parent group.

In her essay "The Occult Field Today" (included in the volume entitled *Applied Magic*).

> The wind bloweth where it listeth not where it is chartered by established authority.

This is particularly true in the case of Americans who take initiations into British Witchcraft groups. Americans have always had a fascination for magical traditions from the British Isles – traditions which often have the same roots as the traditions that came to the New World with their ancestors nearly three hundred years earlier. They learn these traditions easily, and often become quite proficient in the practices and rituals.

Some of them are inspired to make it their life's work and found groups of their own. However, in true American fashion, they reject the authority of the British heirs of those traditions and establish their own versions, often with identical rituals and practices, but without the blessing or authorization of the British hierarchy who consider their American counterparts to be upstarts.

In his book *Occult America*[60], Mitch Horowitz tells the story of Paul Foster Case, an occultist who had been part of the American branch of the Order of the Golden Dawn. The Order, after the death of S.L. McGregor Mathers, was being administered by Mather's widow, Moina who ran the order – and the lives of her initiates – with an iron fist.

Case, who had achieved a high degree within the Order wanted to marry another member of the lodge. Moina Mathers, who advocated celibacy for high level initiates, objected. After heated letters back and forth, Moina Mathers expelled Case from the lodge. Undaunted, he founded the Builders of the Adytum (BOTA), which is still in existence today and provides occult information to anyone who has a genuine interest, regardless of race, creed, or previous experience – in defiance of the original secrecy and obedience demanded by the British Golden Dawn lodge.

This is the source of the common accusation that Americans steal traditions that they aren't entitled to have in order to set themselves up as authorities on those traditions and receive money and credibility therefrom. A great deal of heated rhetoric flies back and forth across the Atlantic regarding who are the rightful heirs to a particular tradition, and attempts are made to discredit the American rivals to the claim by various means.

One method of doing this is to deny the legitimacy of the rival's initiation or adoption into the tradition. Years, sometimes decades, after the initiation occurred (and after the founder of the group is conveniently dead) the self-proclaimed legitimate heirs of the tradition will deny that the leaders of a rival group were ever given a valid initiation. The excuses for this vary. Sometimes, it is claimed that the initiation was performed just for show, to make a visitor with a relationship to the founder feel at home and accepted. Sometimes, it was because there were irregularities in the ritual that was performed – deliberately or not – making it

---

60 *Occult America*, Mitch Horowitz, Bantam 2009.

somehow invalid. If it was deliberate, then the initiate was never told otherwise, and was intentionally fooled into thinking that he or she was an accepted member of a tradition when, in fact, he or she was not.

However, in all cases, the validity of the initiation was denied. And since the initiation/adoption wasn't authentic, then the initiate's membership in the tradition wasn't either. Furthermore, and perhaps most significantly, anybody who the initiate subsequently brings into the tradition also lacks legitimacy.

If the rival group disputes this, a custody battle can be fought on the founder's grave over who will be the legitimate inheritors of the tradition. Often, this battle is only resolved when the group splits apart and some members go with one claimant, and the rest go with the other claimant. The two sister groups then become ferocious adversaries, each excommunicating, defaming, and vilifying the other while claiming that they are the only real group, and that the members of the other group are heretics and schismatics.

Again, from *The Occult Field Today*[61]:

> Mystical organizations are not long-lived things; they seldom survive the generation that had personal contact with the founder. As soon as the original impulse loses its momentum, senility sets in, and they have to be reborn amid throes unspeakable. Old bottles will seldom hold new wine, and reform usually takes place by schism rather than by expansion and restatement.

When one scratches the surface of such disputes, one finds that the real underlying reason for a particular group's insistence on an exclusive right to a tradition is the fear of competition for the promotion of, and profit from, a body of work that they had no hand in developing. If this were not the case, then it wouldn't matter that there were groups in other parts of the world who claim the same lineage, and who practice their own version of the tradition. It's only when there is money and prestige at stake that self-proclaimed legitimate heirs want an exclusive right to

---

[61] Essay from Dion Fortune's book *Applied Magic*, Aquarian Press, 1962.

a spiritual tradition. This isn't a hallmark of spirituality and religion. It's more of a feature of trade union protectionism where economic competition is squelched, perhaps due to the fear that the competing group might be more effective or truer to the original intent of the actual founder.

There are a number of ways that people can legitimately inherit religious and spiritual traditions. Ideally, they would study for many years with the founder until the founder dies, then take up the fallen mantle, and carry on the founder's work. However, in the real world, this rarely happens. For one thing, there is always someone waiting in the wings for the founder to die or retire to claim ownership of the tradition and snatch it away from those who worked with the founder to develop it.

Another thing that often happens is that an opportunistic newcomer will take advantage of the founder when he or she is either old, ill, or otherwise incapacitated, and convince him or her to officially make the newcomer the heir apparent, while denigrating those members who had been the most active in the development of the group.

Sometimes the newcomer will offer the founder money, flattery, personal service or sexual favors, and thereby secure some kind of official designation such as a written letter or signed charter and will promptly turn around and excommunicate the older more experienced members of the group – some of whom may have official charters of their own – as heretics and usurpers.

The larger and more public the group, the more there is to be gained by claiming the right to copyrighted materials, possible revenue from the exclusive publication of those materials, use of a trademarked name, or other advantages. In this case, the only thing that the other members can do is either go along with the arrangement for the advantages or break away and form an illegitimate rival group which is continually excoriated in official publications and communications.

To the victors belong the spoils, and the people who claim that they have the official inheritance are seldom the people who actually know about and worked the tradition. Often, the original teachings of the founder are conveniently pushed aside, and more self-serving teachings and practices substituted in their place. Any writings left by the founder will be edited and expurgated to the point where it will be nearly impossible to determine what the founder's original teachings actually were. Consequently, over time, the teachings of the group will show less and less resemblance to the teachings of the original founder, even though his or her name will still remain attached to them.

What authority will such a group retain on a spiritual and moral level, even though it may possibly retain legal authority? And why must anybody continue to follow them, unless they, as in the case of the Roman Catholic Church, ally themselves with secular authority and impose an outward obedience by means of physical force and threats of bodily or financial harm?

In most western countries, such spiritual authority backed by physical force is less official, but subtler. If a group breaks away from the parent group and forms a rival heretical or schismatic group, then about all that happens is one gets insults, unfounded accusations and anonymous exposes of wrong doing, which rarely if ever include any proof or even any details of said wrong doing.

In some extreme cases, there can be sabotage and secret acts of vandalism or anonymous threats of harm to anyone who aids and abets the heretics. Sometimes, such threats can sink to the depths of harm against innocent family members, children, or pets. Even though such threats of bodily harm are not coming from official sources, that doesn't make them any less horrifying, and the lack of a known perpetrator makes any kind of legal redress impossible.

And it isn't even those groups with tangible assets such as money, publications, a trademarked name or media presence which are targeted. Any group which has dared to defy those who claim any kind of spiritual or religious authority is subject to acts of retaliation. If a rival group – especially one with its own claims to authenticity – succeeds in defying the authority, then the whole edifice of that authority threatens to come crashing down. Heretics tend to beget other heretics, and a resistance movement grows.

Spiritual authority is highly addictive, and anyone who threatens to cut off the supply earns the wrath of those so addicted. It goes beyond simple physical obedience. There is a deep-seated need in many people to have one's own views of the cosmos accepted as true and right, and to somehow destroy anyone who dares to question it. This is pretty much the definition of fundamentalism and religious fanaticism in any faith. To have a divine power say, in effect, you have the only true and legitimate view of how the universe works is a strong intoxicant.

This becomes toxic when the divine being says not only is your view true and legitimate, but you have the right to impose that view on others to your personal advantage as a reward for having the correct view. There is a tremendous temptation to turn personal problems into religious doctrine, and instead of taking personal responsibility for those problems, justify them by some kind of divine revelation, and force others to accept those problems as right and just.

The final ingredient in this toxic brew is the view that any activity is justified, even those activities that directly contradict the teachings of the founder (i.e., lying, cheating, defamation, threatened or actual violence) if it forces other people to accept your view, acknowledge your authority, and most importantly submit to allowing you to taking the advantage of them, all the while proclaiming that you aren't doing it for you own glory, but for the sake of some divine power.

This is the darker side of lineage that nobody likes to talk about. When you accept initiation into any tradition, you not only adopt the practices and beliefs of that tradition, you also accept your share of the group's karma. This can be good, in the case of a tradition which has been positive and helped people, or it can be not so good in the case of a tradition which has spent years hurting people out of pride and love of power.

Most traditions have a mixture of good and bad, and the student who aligns himself with a tradition will genuinely wish to discard the bad and enlarge on the good. But attitudes about magic and the purpose of magical power and knowledge are learned along with how to cast a circle and invoke the gods. The student will end up accepting all of it as a package deal. This, too, is engraved on the brow.

If you sign on to a tradition that has actively done evil in the past, then you must participate in the clean-up operation, or find yourself drawn into the same evil attitudes and practices that the group has perpetuated. In magic, the traditions that conjure demons or dark gods in order to have the power to prey on their fellow humans will tend to attract students who have that unconscious desire, even though they might not admit to it or even be aware of it. They may even formulate a desire to use the negative power for good, but will fall into evil anyway and justify their actions in the ways that the group has justified them in the past. This is particularly true if the would-be initiate has been a member of the tradition in a previous incarnation of both the tradition and the initiate. If it all feels familiar, that's because it is.

All traditional groups have their positive and negative sides, just as a sword has two edges. But a group that has genuine power resulting from contacts with psychic entities will attract people on their wavelength for both good and ill. And the more powerful the group mind, the more work and dedication it will take for an initiate to turn the tide from negative to positive expressions of that power. Some people never do this and eventually end up adopting the negative aspects as the *raison d'etre* of the tradition and scorning the positive as heresy. And thus, we enter the realm of the '*Shadow Clan.*'

Chapter 14

The Shadow Clan

Finally, we knew the nature of the shadow that had been dogging our heels ever since we first heard of Cochrane's work. I discussed it at length in my book *The Forge of Tubal Cain*. It was a force, readily identifiable and omnipresent, that took over student after student. The names of the people were different, but the scenario was the same.

First, there was a desire to avoid hard and thankless work and study. Second, there was a desire for attention and admiration that was not earned by any merit. Third, there was anger that the attention and admiration wasn't immediately forthcoming. Finally, there was a willingness to follow the lead of someone who enabled them to blame others for their failure – someone who wanted authority but was also unwilling to do the work to achieve it.

This pattern was so pervasive and so predictable that one member insisted that the entire 1734 tradition was cursed and that anyone who tried to work it would come to some bad end. We couldn't disagree. We had sensed it as well. And we have since discovered that we weren't the only ones who had sensed the presence of this shadow.

At first, we were under the impression that the curse had begun with Roy's suicide. However, the more we learned about his death and the circumstances that led up to it, the more we became convinced that Roy had been only a victim. The curse itself seemed to be a great deal older. Roy wasn't the first to have fallen into its clutches and he wouldn't be the last.

There is a grim story that Doreen Valiente relates in her diary regarding a blood sacrifice that Roy was supposed to have performed towards the end of his life at the bequest of his mistress. The lady had apparently provided a live cockerel which Roy was supposed to have killed as part of a curse upon the lady's estranged husband to bring about his death.

What evil actually befell the gentleman in question is not recorded. But if Roy had actually performed a ritual like that – something so contrary to what he had been writing about for nearly ten years -- it would explain the sad and cryptic message in his last letter to Joe Wilson written barely a month before his death.

He admonishes Joe never to be like he had been for a short while, arrogant in the knowledge of power, for Fate soon tripped him up, and brought him home across his black horse. Now, he lay like the knights of old, wounded and without hope.

Lord Acton (1834–1902) famously said that power tends to corrupt, and absolute power corrupts absolutely. It's a rare human being who can command power without personally being corrupted by it. Yet, there are always those who will desire power anyway. They will tell themselves, and everybody else, that they intend to use the power for good rather than evil. They insist that they will use the power to help people rather than harm them. After all, power in and of itself is neither good nor evil. It is a natural force, like electricity, which exists everywhere in the universe and can be harnessed for good or evil depending on the mind and heart of the magician who wields it.

As a member of the Clan of Tubal Cain, there is a power that comes to us as a birthright from our semi-divine ancestry. But something seems to happen to people to attempt to harness that power, even for so-called noble purposes, without paying the coin.

We wondered what it was. We knew its modus operandi, the way it worked, and the kind of person that it worked on. But it wasn't until we were confronted with the Luciferian streak in the Clan that we were able to finally identify it and put a name to it.

It was hubris – the curse of the Shadow Clan.

The most important discussion of hubris in antiquity is in Aristotle's *Rhetoric*[62]:

> Hubris consists in doing and saying things that cause shame to the victim…simply for the pleasure of it. Young men and the rich are hubristic because they think they are better than other people.

Some poets, especially Hesiod and Aeschylus, used the term hubris to describe wrongful action against the divine order marked by excessive pride toward, or defiance of, the gods, particularly by a semi-divine hero. Such a hero would become so full of himself that he would think that not only was he better than mere mortals, he was so special that the laws of the gods didn't apply to him and he could break them with impunity.

'Nemesis'"
Alfred Rethel 1837

In the *Iliad*[63], the immortal hero Achilles is sent by the gods to fight for the Greeks against the Trojans. However, Achilles is angry with the

---

62 *Aristotle's Rhetoric*, Aristotle, Treatise on the art of persuasion, 4th century B.C.E

63 *The Iliad*, Homer, Ancient Greek epic poem set during the time of the Trojan War, 762 B.C.E.

Greek king for stealing a slave girl that he fancied. So, in a fit of pique, Achilles hides among the women in order to avoid taking his place at the king's side in battle as was his duty. He even gives his armor to his mortal human friend to wear in his stead to fool the Trojans into thinking he had joined the battle – a deception that led to his friend's death. This act of hubris leads to his downfall. Eventually, the only place where he was vulnerable, his heel, is pierced by an arrow shot by the son of the Trojan king – and guided by the hand of the goddess Nemesis.

A related concept from the Celtic culture is that of the *geis*. The geis was a ritual obligation laid upon a hero that would either forbid or command an action to avoid shame or the wrath of the gods. The more powerful the hero, the greater the number of geisa that were laid upon him, and the more dire the consequences if he breaks them.

Take the case of Cuhullan, the hero of the Irish epic tale the *Tain bo Culaigne* (The Cattle Raid of Cooley). Cuhullan, like Achilles, is a semi-divine warrior hero, the son of the god Lugh. As the story unfolds, we discover that he has been placed under two geisa: he must never eat the flesh of a dog, and he must never refuse to eat food offered to him by a woman.

The *Tain* records many instances where Cuhullan displays his supernatural prowess in battle. However, in his pride, he refuses to mate with the Morrighan, the Irish goddess of sovereignty. It is an act that is required of him to become a Sacred King. But he spurns the goddess and refuses to assume the sacrificial role. His refusal is not only an insult to the goddess, it's an act of hubris – a rejection of the sacred duty that accompanies the superhuman power he wields.

In retaliation, the Morrighan disguises herself as an old woman, approaches him at a banquet, and offers him the flesh of a dog to eat. He finds himself in an impossible position of having to break one geis to avoid breaking another. Knowing that he has been defeated by the goddess, he eats the dog meat and seals his fate.

Being a child of the gods carries with it a great responsibility as well as a great power. Like the semi-divine heroes of old, we are put here on the earth to serve a purpose. But that purpose is to do the will the gods, not pursue our own pleasure or ego gratification. When we abandon our purpose to pursue our own pride and vanity, Nemesis comes for us. How do we decide if our purpose serves the gods or only serves ourselves? It's actually quite difficult to know – at least at first. When we feel enthusiastic about doing something important, it feels very good – so good, in fact, that we want to do nothing else.

The word enthusiasm comes from the Greek word *entheos*: filled with the power of a god. While we are filled with entheos, we are plugged into the cosmic power source. We have, at least for a short while, transcended our mundane human existence and have become a part of something far greater than our present-day human personalities. We have a cosmic mission to perform. But what happens when that good feeling stops coming from enthusiastic service to a greater purpose and starts coming from stroking our own egos? Things start to go very wrong.

In an odd little book entitled *The Goblin Universe*[64], author Ted Holiday relates a story about Joan of Arc. At the beginning of her career, Joan heard the voices of beings she called angels guiding her to put the young Dauphin Charles VII on the throne of France. Miraculous events followed her until she accomplished that purpose. Then, the voices fell silent. One can only assume that the angels' purpose had been accomplished. Joan was now expected to give up the battle, return to her home, and get on with her life.

However, she stubbornly continued battling the English invaders. Her goal was now to trounce the English, quite possibly out of political or ethnic hatred rather than because of any divine mandate. Apparently, the angels weren't concerned with defeating the English and withdrew their support, leaving Joan on her own. Without the voices to guide her, she found herself at a loss to know what to do. So, she turned for counsel instead to a warrior with a sinister past – a man by the name of Giles de Rais.

The strategy didn't work. The battle with the English went from one

---

64 *The Goblin Universe*, Ted Holiday, Llewellyn Publications (1986)

defeat to another. The carnage on both sides was horrifying. Joan at one point realized this. She is said to have sat on the bank of the Loire and wept at all the bodies floating downstream in the bloodstained water. However, Giles de Rais, a French nobleman who presumably had a personal stake in an English defeat, seemed not to care about the death toll, and calmly sharpened his sword while the bodies drifted by.

Finally, Nemesis stepped in. The English eventually proved victorious. Joan was burned at the stake for witchcraft, and Giles de Rais went on to commit acts of cruelty and degradation that made his name synonymous with evil and depravity for the next six hundred years.

It's very exciting to be devoted to a purpose greater than oneself, to be filled with entheos for a divine cause. But once the purpose of the gods has been fulfilled, people often find that their part in that divine cause abruptly vanishes. For a while, they have left their human problems behind, and played a role in a kind of mythic drama. But the drama eventually ends. Once their part in the greater whole has been accomplished, they are expected to go back to their mundane, ordinary lives, and solve their own personal karmic problems.

This is, of course, not as gratifying and exciting as acting in a mythic drama, so people are understandably reluctant to give it up. And it's not fair, really. Often people devote many years to some kind of transcendent cause, only to find that their part in that cause abruptly ceases to exist. They are replaced by someone else, the cause changes direction in ways that they don't like, the people around them no longer depend on their advice and help, and suddenly they are extraneous, obsolete, and unnecessary.

So, they try to continue playing their accustomed role even though their participation is no longer required. From that point on, nothing works right. The energy and charisma they once had is no longer there. People no longer listen to them. It suddenly becomes impossible to maintain their former position on the basis of their effort alone. They become angry and take it out on the people who still have a role to play. They lie and manipulate, threaten and intimidate, to get their former associates to take them seriously again. But all it does is generate trouble and ill-feeling, and seriously compromises whatever the divinely ordained purpose they had been so enthusiastic about in the first place.

This is the difference between entheos and hubris. When we have to depend on other people to shore up our position, support us with time, effort, money, and attention, then we have ceased to do the work of the gods and are only serving our vanity. When we have to tear down others in order to rise, when we have to lie, deceive, and manipulate in order to maintain our position, then we know that we have offended the gods, and Nemesis is close at our heels.

All esoteric teachings stress the necessity of living in both worlds, of not only doing magical work, but also having an ordinary life with mundane work, hobbies, families, and personal relationships. A balance must be maintained between the magical work and mundane work, or else enthusiasm turns into obsession. After all, according to Cochrane, the will of the gods is that we overcome our own karmic issues in order to be of greater use to them the next time around. Eventually, we must take our bows, exit stage left, and return to our mundane life with all the humbling and annoying duties that go with it.

If it's only our ego which is getting fed, rather than our desire to do the will of the gods, then we won't retire gracefully once our magical work is done. Even though we are no longer plugged into the cosmic wall socket, we will continue to try to shine with our own light rather that with the light of the gods. And when our light dims, which it eventually does, we will seek to steal power from others in order to maintain the illusion. We turn into a vampire.

The vampire as described by Nigel Jackson in his book *The Compleat Vanpyre*[65] is a useful metaphor in understanding the Shadow Clan. When the power of the gods is withdrawn from us, we die in the magical realm and must return for a time to the mundane realm to live and work. If we don't want to do this, then we must feed upon the life force of others to maintain our place in the magical realm. We do this not by means of sucking their physical blood but sucking their psychic blood.

---

65 *The Compleat Vampyre*, Capall Bann Publishing, 1995.

We feed on their entheos. We seduce them with promises of love, wealth, or power in order to gain their attention and sympathy. Then, we insist that they serve us in some way.

This service can be sexual or financial. It can be in the form of physical labor or emotional support. It can simply be functioning as a sycophant who greets every idea or request with praise and approval whether it has merit or not. In extreme cases, the service will consist of lying, cheating, or stealing. Sometimes, the service will consist of being an attack dog to tear down a rival or a defector. And always, things are done in the shadows, behind the scenes, behind everyone's back since the machinations cannot stand up to the cold, clear light of day.

To the victim, this is exciting for a while. There is something strangely alluring about serving someone who promises a share of the spoils or a means to get back at someone that the victim doesn't like. The problem is that the vampire has no intention of making good on the promises. When the victim is no longer of use, he or she is abandoned without a backwards glance.

Who becomes a victim of the vampire? The same kind of people who want something for nothing, who want the adulation without the effort, who want authority without earning it. It is someone who, in medieval parlance, is willing to sell their soul to the devil in exchange for power over others. Someone who is guilty of hubris.

'Teuflspakt Faust Mephisto'
Julius Nisle, 1840

The classic case of this devil's bargain is, of course, that of the story of Johannes Faust. In the German legend, Faust is a would-be magician, someone who is studying magic for the sake of personal enlightenment – or so he thinks. Someone else knows better. One day, Faust receives a visit from a debonair demon called Mephistopheles (possibly derived from the Hebrew word mephitz, meaning "'distributor", and tophel, meaning "liar") who offers him seven years of unlimited power over others in exchange for his soul.

Faust agrees, and the pact is sealed. With Mephistopheles's assistance, the first thing Faust does is become young again in order to seduce the beautiful Gretchen. Although innocent and naive, Gretchen has a weak spot in her character – a love of jewelry and fine clothes – which allows her to fall under Faust's spell. For seven years, Mephistopheles assists Faust in one act of debauchery and cruelty after another, destroying not only his rivals, but Gretchen herself until the seven years are up. Then, the demon gathers up the protesting Faust and carts him off to Hell.

How does one escape the vampyre? One refuses to fall prey to it in the first place. In our experience of the Shadow Clan, every time members fell victim to the Clan shadow, it was because they wished to take a short cut to power, to reap where they had not sown, to parade about in borrowed robes, and feign authority that they had not earned through hard work and dedication, and insist that everyone buy into the sham. Along comes the vampyre who promises these things if the victims will surrender their will – and their higher values of loyalty and honesty – and do what they're told.

The people who put themselves in a position to be a victim of the vampyre either think they are immune, or actually want to surrender to the predator. They are willing to give in to the personal gratification and ego trip that the vampyre offers in exchange for the loss of psychic energy. That is why there is such an erotic component to the vampire legends. Sensual pleasure, a feeling of personal vanity and pride, and the sense of being special is the price that is accepted in exchange for the soul.

The problem is that the pleasure is phony. Like fairy gold that gives the illusion of great wealth, it vanishes with the dawn, leaving only emptiness. The pleasure comes from the illusion of being special, of being beloved, of being powerful, without having to do that which earns those things in the real world. And when the illusion fades, there remains only disillusionment and anger. Then, they turn with unbridled fury on someone who has the real thing. If they can't have it, then nobody should. Especially someone whom they deem unworthy, that is, someone who isn't taking their advice or being led by them.

You see this all the time with people in the mundane world. Someone else gets a professional promotion that was denied them, and the person becomes a target of unreasonable hate and vindictive attacks. It isn't really very different on a spiritual level, except for the ability to convince themselves that they are doing it for the gods, or some other selfless purpose.

People who choose this fate go around and around the karmic wheel, lifetime after lifetime, desiring that which the gods in their wisdom deny them, yet not being able to swallow their hubris and do the work and personal sacrifice necessary to earn it. Usually, they are harmless, pathetic souls, except that they can make a lot of noise, and cause a lot of distraction, especially if they attract those like themselves who want the easy, cut rate path to enlightenment and magical power. But this power usually turns out like a fake Gucci bag. It only impresses people who either don't know what a real one looks like, or don't see that the fake one falls apart and looks ratty after a short while.

In order to wield true spiritual authority, one must be willing to do the work to achieve mastery and credibility on one's own merits rather than on the efforts of others. Only then can one conduct one's magical affairs with genuine knowledge and experience rather than as a deceptive, self-deluding fantasy game.

Sometimes, it means that one must set aside the ritual implements, the books and the robes, and go back to the mundane duties for a while – often for years. These duties include working the bread-and-butter job, paying the bills, taking care of children and animals, attending to a spouse or partner, fulfilling obligations to a parent or an employer or a school – in short, all the responsibilities to others that are all too often abandoned when one plays the cosmic role of Great Magus or Witch Queen for too long. These are divine duties, too. They also serve the will of the gods by forcing us to grow up, to learn to deal with the limitations of the physical world, and take responsibility for ourselves, to work out our karma, and prevent new karma from being built up – in short, to use the hammer and the square of a child of Cain to make ourselves into more useful tools so that when our divine work presents itself again, we are able to perform it more successfully.

This is the alternative to becoming a vampyre and joining the Shadow Clan. One can actually get busy and do the work of magic. One can study the tradition, do the meditations and visualization exercises regularly even if nobody is watching in admiration, perform the rituals faithfully whether they work or not, and whether or not they produce nifty visions in which the gods tell you how wonderful you are.

Instead of spending your time criticizing the work of others, you can do your own work and allow it to stand or fall on its own merits. It always seems to be the case that when you are actively engaged in meaningful occult work, all the while trying to maintain yourself in the material world, there is increasingly less time and energy to spend denouncing others.

Finally, you must take the uncomfortable but required journey into the underworld in which you face your own personal demons, take responsibility for your own actions, and realize that ultimately you are nothing more than a part of a larger purpose. Your personal wants and needs are not the main priority of the universe, and the goal of your efforts is to further the greater good, not your own self-aggrandizement. This means you must do what Achilles and Cuchulain failed to do – that is, put aside your hubris, lay your own personal ego on the altar of sacrifice, do your duty to your gods and to your people, and earn your right to become a priest or priestess of the Great Goddess.

JOURNEY TO THE CASTLE

Chapter 15

Lord of Light, Lord of Darkness

Just who is Lucifer anyway? It depends on who you ask. According to Milton's *Paradise Lost*[66], Lucifer (whose name means 'morning star') was the most beautiful angel in heaven. When Jehovah made Man, He set his new creation, made in the creator's own image and likeness, above the angels. He required that Lucifer and the other angels bow down and worship Man. Lucifer refused and fomented a rebellion against Jehovah, who banished him and his followers from heaven.

'Lucifer'
Mihaly Zichy, 1887

He and his small troop of rebellious angels fell to earth where they attempt to corrupt Jehovah's most prized creation by persuading one of them, the woman Eve, to eat a fruit that Jehovah has forbidden them to

---

66 *Paradise Lost*, John Milton, Published by London: [Samuel Simmons for] Peter Parker, Robert Boulter & Mathias Walker (1667).

touch, telling them that they would surely die. This is a lie, however, and Lucifer knows it.

He informs Eve that she has been duped. The fruit contains knowledge that will make humans as gods, thereby usurping Jehovah's power over them. Eve eats the fruit, persuades Adam to eat as well and, sure enough, their eyes are opened. They finally see themselves as they really are and all Jehovah can do is toss them out of their garden paradise and force them to "earn bread by the sweat of their brow."[67]

So, is Lucifer the bad guy or the good guy? The Catholic Church, as expected, roundly condemned Lucifer for tempting Eve. It branded Adam and Eve's disobedience to Jehovah's dictate as original sin which every human is guilty of at birth and which required Jehovah to send His Son to expiate. Later, the Protestant churches would echo this attitude. Eventually, all Christian churches, who didn't agree on much, agreed that disobeying Jehovah (and, by extension, His church) was the most horrible crime that a human could commit, and that eternal suffering in the fires of hell was just punishment.

However, not everyone agreed. In the *Hypostasis of the Archons*[68], a Coptic document, the traditional story of man's disobedience toward God is reinterpreted as a universal conflict between knowledge (*gnosis*) and the dark powers (*exousia*) of the world, which bind the human soul in ignorance. The ancient mystery religion promised to make man aware of his divine origins and make him as the gods, knowing good and evil.

In Gnostic philosophy, the god Jehovah was the Demiurge who created man for his own selfish interest, trapping spiritual beings in the prison of matter. Lucifer was regarded as the hero, savior, and friend of man, who revealed the sacred mysteries which the Demiurge jealously withheld. Lucifer is also associated with Prometheus, who stole fire from heaven to give to humanity, thereby giving humans the power of gods. When

---

67 (Genesis 3:19)

68 *Hypostasis of the Archons (The Reality of the Rulers)*, from the Nag Hammadi Library

Jehovah forbade Adam and Eve the fruit of the Tree of Knowledge, Lucifer persuaded them to defy Jehovah's edicts and eat the forbidden fruit anyway, thereby giving them "gnosis" or enlightenment – the knowledge of good and evil.

"Lucifer, the Light-Bearer!" writes 33rd Degree Mason Albert Pike in his *Morals and Dogma of the Ancient and Accepted Scottish Rite of Freemasonry*[69], "Strange and mysterious name to give to the Spirit of Darkness! Lucifer, the Son of the Morning! Is it he who bears the light, and with its splendors intolerable blinds feeble, sensual or selfish Souls? Doubt it not![i]

Consequently, Lucifer is seen as the embodiment of reason, of intelligence, and of critical thought. He stands against dogma – not only the dogma of God but all other dogmas. He stands for the exploration of new ideas and new perspectives in the pursuit of truth. He is the model of human freedom to know good and evil and to choose between them.

However, this freedom brings with it a price. Humans who have eaten the forbidden fruit can no longer remain in blissful ignorance and childlike dependency, relying on Jehovah's minions to save them. They have to make their own way in the world. As Rosicrucian scholar Max Heindel points out in his treatise *Freemasonry and Catholicism*[70], "having repudiated the authority of Jehovah, they must work out their own salvation in their own manner." This is the basis of Freemasonry, and the craft of Tubal Cain.

I have specifically not identified the Luciferian Craft as the Shadow Clan. It is not. In its pure form, it has much to teach. The name Lucifer comes from the Latin words lux or luc (light) and the suffix -fer (bearing); Thus, Lucifer literally means "light bearing". His strong light can illuminate the denizens of the underworld so they can be seen clearly without

---

69 *Morals and Dogmas of the Ancient and Accepted Scottish Rite of Freemasonry,* Albert Pike, published by the Supreme Council of the Scottish Rite, Southern Jurisdiction of the United States, 1871

70 *Freemasonry and Catholicism,* Max Heindel, The Rosicrucian Fellowship, 1921

distortion, and his power can be used to bring those denizens under the control of the magician's conscious will.

However, the power of Lucifer can go seriously septic. Like any source of great power, it can be a lure to the unwary and an intoxicating drink to the bored and the lazy. The power, and the rush that such power brings in its wake, can become an end in itself rather than a means to a higher end. One can become addicted to it. It is the psychic equivalent of crack cocaine.

For Manly Hall, writing in *Magic: a Treatise on Esoteric Ethics*[71], Lucifer is:

> ..the spirit of excess, the flaming son of rashness and the ruler of sense gratification, over which he wields dominion with the scepter of serpents. Those who fall victims to his power do deeds of violence, not because he wills it so, but because they have this spirit of energy and pervert him themselves. Lucifer is the light-bringer; he is transmuted by man into the fiery demon of war and hate.

"Lucifer is the power that stirs up in man all fanatical," wrote Rudolf Steiner in his lecture *The Ahrimanic Deception*[72]. "All falsely mystical forces, all that physiologically tends to bring the blood into disorder and so lift man above and outside himself."

John Milton in *Paradise Lost* describes Lucifer as arrogant and proud. Unwilling to subjugate himself to God (and to God's creation, man) he foments rebellion against God, arguing that God ruled as a tyrant. His rebellion fails, and he is cast down to hell. However, he declares, "To reign is worth ambition, though in Hell: Better to reign in Hell than serve in Heaven."

---

71 *Magic: a Treatise on Esoteric Ethics,* Manly P Hall, Los Angeles, Calif. : Philosophical Research Society, 1978.

72 *The Ahrimanic Deception,* Rudolf Steiner, presented in Zurich on October 27, 1919.

However, as historians Will and Ariel Durant once wrote, today's rebel is tomorrow's tyrant. History has borne this out time and again. Whenever a group of people is oppressed, the spirit of Lucifer arises to overthrow the oppressors and free the people from their chains. However, that same Luciferian fire, rebelliousness -- and self-righteousness -- that inspires people into rebelling against repressive authority will make them supremely intolerant of anybody rebelling against them when it is their turn to rule.

In 1971, psychology professor Philip Zimbardo[73] conducted an experiment in which 24 male students were randomly assigned roles as prisoners or guards in a mock prison set up in the basement of the Stanford University Psychology building. Participants were given instructions based on the role to which they were assigned, either a prisoner or a guard. The experiment was to last six weeks.

The participants adapted to their roles well beyond Zimbardo's expectations. The guards enforced authoritarian measures, and ultimately subjected some of the prisoners to psychological torture. Zimbardo claimed that participants were given no instructions about how to behave. However, critics have argued that his briefing of the guards gave them a clear sense that they should oppress the prisoners. Only later did Zimbardo admit that this was the case.

Many of the prisoners passively accepted psychological abuse and, at the request of the guards, readily turned on any other prisoners who attempted to prevent it. After one of Zimbardo's graduate students questioned the morality of the study, the entire experiment was halted after only six days.

The results clearly indicated that ordinary moral people, when put in positions of power over others, will often turn abusive and evil. This is done primarily by reducing the status of others to something less than oneself, so that one is seen as superior to those over which one has authority. This justifies any abuse that is necessary to maintain that authority. The study was an exploration of the effects of tyrannical

---

73 The Stanford Prison Experiment, Aug 14, 1971 – Aug 20, 1971

leadership in the mundane world. But the results have implications for magical work as well.

"Lucifer's sin is what thinkers in the Middle Ages called "cupiditas," wrote Zimbardo in his book *The Lucifer Effect*[74]. "For those suffering the mortal malady called cupiditas, whatever exists outside of one's self has worth only as it can be exploited by, or taken into one's self." To a person suffering from cupiditas or cupidity, other people are little more than herd animals which exist only to serve the purpose of their masters. They have no rights of their own and deserve no consideration or respect as individuals or, least of all, as equals. This is the essence of hubris.

'Lucifer'
Franz von Stark, 1890

Zimbardo's work doesn't emphasize this, but the Lucifer effect seems to be the most obvious when people are somehow given power and moral authority that they have not earned through their own efforts and carries with it no responsibility or consequences. In the Stanford Prison experiment, the role of guards and prisoners were randomly assigned to avoid any self-selection bias, since that is the way most psychological experiments are conducted. Therefore, the people who were assigned the role of guards were given power and authority over the prisoners without having to do anything to earn it. They didn't go through any kind of training or evaluation. Most were college students with little or no experience with positions of authority and had expended no effort on their own or had even shown any talents in that direction before being assigned to the role.

The kind of arrogance shown by the Shadow Clan seems to be the most apparent among people who inherit a religious tradition from the person who actually did the work to put it together, usually by means of being

---

74 *The Lucifer Effect*, Philip Zimbardo, [Random House], [Rider, 2007.

a favorite or a sycophant rather than an active co-worker in the process. And to those who, through pride, laziness, or lack of self-discipline will not do the hard, selfless work to earn their place at the ancestral table, it can be the source of the hubris that justifies the perverse psychic vampirism of the Shadow Clan. They feel entitled, due to their superiority, to use their fellow man for fodder for their own egos. And once given some measure of authority, will turn into tyrants themselves – ironically just as bad if not worse than the tyrants against which they rebelled.

Still, the Shadow Clan serves an important purpose. The purpose of a predator is to weed out the unfit – in the predator species itself as well as in the prey. This is the survival of the fittest -- a notion that Charles Darwin didn't invent, but only chronicled. Take wolves and deer, for example, in an established ecosystem. The deer breed more than the wolves. In a favorable environment, more deer are born than die of old age, disease or injury. If left to themselves, they would soon produce more individuals than the environment could support. They would outstrip their food source. The green leaves and shoots that they feed on would never grow to maturity. The vegetation, unable to produce new leaves, would die back or produce toxins. Eventually, the vegetation would disappear entirely, and the entire herd would starve to death.

So, the herd must be culled. The number of individuals must be decreased. To put it bluntly, a certain percentage of the deer have to die before they have a chance to breed. But the process can't be random. The culling must be selective. Some individuals must die and some need to live long enough to reproduce. If too few deer die, the food supply will continue to diminish. The vegetation will continue to be stunted and will suffer permanent damage. But if too many deer die, the genetic diversity within the herd will decrease and the herd itself will die out completely. A balance must be struck.

Enter the wolf, a predator exquisitely adapted to the hunting of deer. A pack of half a dozen wolves can effectively control the population of a herd of deer numbering hundreds. Wolves like most healthy predators only hunt to feed themselves. One kill will last them for days and once they have made their kill, they leave the rest of the herd alone. But wolves are also sensible creatures. When they select an individual deer as their prey, they will choose the immature, the old, the sick or the crippled. The last deer they target will be the strong, alert, adult buck or doe – the individuals, in short, that are the most physically fit and whose offspring will increase the overall strength of the herd.

As much as this might be a problem for the individual deer that is targeted by the pack, it actually helps the herd as a whole. The less fit individuals are taken out of the herd leaving the available food for the individuals who are stronger and more fit. These individuals are the ones who eventually live long enough to breed, thereby strengthening the gene pool of the herd. Then, when a particularly harsh winter comes along, or a period of drought, the herd will survive rather than dying out entirely.

So, what does this do for the wolf pack? The same thing, actually. As a predatory species, a wolf's ability to bring down a deer several times its size and weight depends not only on the strength and agility of the individual wolf, but how well each wolf functions within the pack. The wolf that is strong, healthy and socially adapted will live long enough to breed the next generation of the pack.

A wolf pack is subject to the same laws of population genetics as the deer herd. Too many genetically deformed individuals, whether physically or socially, and the pack will not be able to bring down enough deer to survive. As long as the deer in the herd are strong and healthy, the wolf must also be strong, healthy, and socially well adjusted. Consequently, in a stable ecosystem, both the predator and prey are subject to the same natural selection in order to ensure that the individuals who breed are the strongest and most fit of their particular species.

This sounds harsh, perhaps, to big city pagans. But this is the law of that same Mother Nature that big city pagans claim to worship. Without the sacred dance of predator and prey, both species would become weak and deformed and eventually become extinct.

Magic, when done properly, is difficult work. There is the sacrifice of a great deal of time, energy, and money with very little personal gratification to show for it - or even indications that one's efforts have been successful. It is easy to succumb to the process of entropy and slow down, lose focus, and let slide on minimal effort. The predations of the Shadow Clan can keep magicians on their toes and give them a reason to keep on keeping on.

Several vampire legends actually illustrate this well. The usual story goes roughly as follows. A vampire has been ravaging a bunch of innocent, helpless people. Some are devoured like prey. Others are seduced by the erotic overtones of the entire feeding process, submit to the vampire, and become vampires themselves.

However, along comes a person with the knowledge of dark powers, the self-control to resist the erotic (and illusory) seductions, and the courage to use his or her knowledge to do what is necessary to destroy the vampire. He or she destroys the vampire, and all is well in the village. This forms the basic plot of Bram Stoker's classic 1897 novel, *Dracula*[75].

The way of dealing with werewolves (or other werebeasts) was similar. Someone with a knowledge of magic or ancient wisdom would summon the courage and fortitude to face the werebeast and wound it with a magical implement. When the werebeast returned to human form, its body would retain the wound and it would die.

Both vampyres and werewolves also share the same way of perpetuating their kind. If one falls under the spell and allows oneself to be seduced by the erotic lure of the creature, one will be bitten by it. In the case of the vampire, you will appear to have died. But when night falls, you will rise from your grave as a vampire yourself, and you will go and seek the blood of a victim. If you are bitten by a werewolf, you don't die. But at the next full moon, you will change into a werewolf yourself and go seek a victim to bite.

In both cases, the victim refuses to believe that he could possibly be a victim. He might scoff at the very existence of the creature and disregards all warnings to protect himself. This invariably leads to the person falling victim to the creature and becoming one himself. It is significant that the only way to protect oneself from a vampire or a werewolf is to

---

[75] *Dracula*, Bram Stoker, Constable & Robinson Limited, England, 1897,

not only believe that the creature exists but understand its nature and not be afraid of it. Ultimately, then, knowledge of the nature of the evil and the courage to face it without either fear or desire is the way to defeat it.

So, the Shadow Clan reveals a harsh but ultimately useful function. They motivate struggling magicians to keep fighting the good fight and not allow complacency to make them weak and ineffective. They are the grist for the mill.

But more importantly, they serve as a grim reminder that any one of us, at any time, is capable of letting pride, vanity, laziness, and desire for self-gratification at the expense of others lure us into the clutches of the Shadow Clan. There, but for the grace of the gods, go we. There is nothing inherent in anyone practicing magic that renders them immune to the lure of the Luciferian hubris that lies at the heart of the Shadow Clan. We are all susceptible. That knowledge alone should keep us humble if nothing else will. Humility in the face of divine power is the only antidote to the poison of hubris.

The 'Journey to the Castle' is not an easy one. It's like a mountain trail -- narrow, uphill, rocks and ruts to stumble upon and trip over. There is a sheer, rocky cliff on one side of you, and the yawning cavern of the bottomless abyss on the other side. A sensible, materialistic instinct for self-preservation is whispering in your ear, "Don't bother. Stay somewhere where it is safe, pleasant and comfortable. Don't risk it, or you will surely perish."

Then there are the spiritual authorities of all stripes that run churches and religious organizations who look at the hardships as punishment for the desire to go on the journey in the first place. They are the ones who will say that the safest place is with the herd with the good shepherd telling you where to go and what to believe. To be a heretic is to be an outcast.

And they are right. If you go on the journey, you go on your own. You don't get to take the seal of approval from some established authority with you. Such approval means nothing in the underworld. Your own personal merits and demerits constitute the only passport you will ever have. And that must be something you earn, not something bestowed upon you by another mortal. And if you fail, you have only yourself to blame.

It is tempting to look upon that failure to complete the journey as a result of weakness or stupidity. Certainly, unwise choices affect the journey. But often people must quit the journey temporarily to take care of the consequences or obligations incurred by an emotional decision to get married, have a child, take care of an ailing relative or accept a job which pays a great deal of money, but leaves them little or no free time and energy to pursue a spiritual path.

These are not bad or unwise choices in and of themselves, but they are not choices that make the journey easier or more pleasant. Often, these choices bring pleasures of their own which make the journey seem not worth the effort. We'd rather sit in a comfortable place, doing pleasant things with people we love rather than face the trials of the journey.

Unlike many things in life, nobody has to make the 'Journey to the Castle.' Far more people abandon the path for the sake of life's little pleasures than as a result of any opposition by demonic forces. In fact, the demonic forces can sometimes make the path easier by demonstrating the importance and desirability of the path and what lies at the end. It is a lot more difficult to give up if someone or something is slavering after you. If there is nothing nipping at your heels, then why keep on running?

Ultimately, the journey is like most other spiritual paths. There is nobody, nothing, no force in either this world or the Otherworld which can tear you from the path if it truly your will to travel upon it. If you leave the path, it is because you do so yourself. Physical disasters and serious illness can retard your progress for a time, but can't cause you to abandon the path forever. If nothing else, you can find the path again in a subsequent incarnation. And there are those who will claim that it takes many such incarnations treading the path in order to reach the end.

We are, of course, talking about the 'Journey to the Castle' as a metaphor for the spiritual journey that leads down into the underworld of ancestral spirits, and finally emerges into the starry realms of the gods. Only then do we discover the ultimate truth that the ancestors and the gods are one in the same.

They are us.

Chapter 16

The Journey to the Future

Cupidity is a bad thing – isn't it? One would think so. Surely, it can't be right and just to live off the life force of others, no matter who they are. It's not only bad for them, ultimately, it's bad for us. It cuts us off from the source of divine power and reduces us to vampires, werewolves and con artists who have no other source of sustenance than to plunder and prey on our own kind. And they *are* our own kind, whether we like it or not.

One of the hallmarks of both hubris and cupiditas is a marked contempt for those humans who are not "of the blood": ordinary people concerned with ordinary things, like the muggles of the Harry Potter stories. They are to be ignored, used if they prove useful, but then cast aside when used up. Their welfare is no more to be considered than that of animals – often less. Any feelings of compassion or pity towards them, any empathy, sense of affinity or desire to help and succor them are viewed as a weakness and a waste of time. And any laws which mandate treating them with respect and consideration don't apply.

This doesn't seem to be a desirable way of exercising our divine power, does it? And yet, the occult field during the last century or so has been rife with attempts to justify cupiditas and celebrate hubris. In spite of the cautionary tales told by the bards and poets for thousands of years, those who are "of the blood" are convinced that they are exempt from karmic law and can violate it with impunity, to the detriment of ordinary humans.

Aleister Crowley wrote in his *Confessions*[76], "Ordinary morality is only for ordinary people." This statement can be interpreted to mean that powerful semi-divine heroes, like Achilles or Cuhullain, are exempt from any kind of moral code that specifies karmic consequences for deliberately disregarding the rights of others. That is, until Nemesis, in whatever cultural guise she happens to appear in any particular story, ruthlessly shows the hero that cosmic laws do indeed apply to him and proceeds to administer it to his detriment. What goes around, comes around. Even if you're Lucifer himself.

Does it have to be this way? Christian bashing is a fashionable pastime among both secular humanists and Neo-pagans these days. Many enlightened people sneer at Christianity, calling it a ruse used by the church to distract people from their physical misery and keep them from revolting against their oppressive masters. Christianity has also been cast as the mortal enemy of science and humanism, determined to abolish reason and intellectual inquiry, and consign people forever to superstition and ignorance.

It is certainly true that medieval Catholicism, in the form of the Holy Office (otherwise known as the Inquisition) declared open season on magical practitioners of all stripes and persecuted them as witches or sorcerers. And of course, Protestant regimes burned or hung as many witches as Catholic regimes did. In fact, it seems as though one of the few things that Catholics and Protestants agreed on was the verse in Exodus, 'thou shalt not suffer a witch to live.'[77]

However, dismissing Christianity as a whole on the basis of this might be tossing out the baby with two thousand years of dirty bathwater. After all, one of the central tenants of Christianity, according to its founder

---

[76] *The Confessions of Aleister Crowley : an autohagiography*, Aleister Crowley, (Originally titled *The spirit of solitude : an autohagiography*) Mandrake Press, 1929

[77] Exodus 22:18

anyway, is to "love your neighbor as yourself. There is none other commandment greater than these." What's so wrong with that?

One of the ideas that the enlightenment seemed to have inherited from both the Catholic and Protestant (particularly Calvinist) doctrine is the idea that humans *en masse* are ignorant and selfish children who must be guided and protected by an enlightened elite, and can be exploited with impunity, so long as it's justified as being done for their own good.

As tempting as it is to point accusing fingers at Christianity for this idea, it actually came from the ancient Greeks. In *The Republic*[78], Plato states that the common people cannot be trusted to rule themselves, but rather should be ruled by a "philosopher king" aided by an elite caste of "guardians" who weren't above telling the people "a noble lie" in order to keep them from pursing their own selfish interests, and make them "more inclined to care for the state and one another."

The only thing different in our present time is who these philosopher kings are. The classical Luciferians of the eighteenth century (the majority of whom were members of the aristocracy) did not desire to free the ordinary people from their superstitions. They just wanted to wrest them away from the authority of the Church. The peasants are still to be controlled and manipulated, only to serve a different master and benefit a different group of elites.

In many of the legends surrounding the Shadow Clan in the form of shapeshifters and vampires, the prey were seldom members of the aristocracy. They were more likely to be ordinary people whose only crime was abandoning the pagan beliefs of their ancestors, converting to Christianity, and moving to the towns to make a better material life for themselves and their children.

The vampires and shapeshifters are always portrayed as outcasts, throwbacks to a bygone era who practice a dimly remembered ancestral shamanism. Unwilling or unable to adapt to city life, and envious of the

---

78 *The Republic* is a Socratic dialogue about justice and order written by Plato c. 380 B.C.E

wealth and prosperity offered by bourgeois mercantilism, they wreaked their vengeance on the prosperous townsfolk and dared an ineffective and clueless Christian clergy to stop them. This often is viewed as a metaphor of how city life and material prosperity severs people from their attachment to the land. The darker, predatory forces of nature rise up in vengeance and wreak havoc upon people who once feared them, but now scoff at them. This might be true enough on a personal, psychological level, but if one scrapes the surface of this argument, one often finds something else: a bad case of sour grapes.

Over the last few centuries, well-to-do townspeople found that it was more pleasant to go to a handsome church building and nice, friendly priests dressed in white and gold vestments for their spiritual needs rather than an old bad-tempered cunning man or woman who lived out of town in a dirty, smelly cottage. Naturally, the cunning folk resented it. And resentment turned into desire for revenge.

In one version of the Faust tale, Faust summons Mephistopheles with the best of intentions. The city where he lives is being ravaged with plague and try as he might he can find nothing in his magical texts that will stop it. In desperation, he summons Mephistopheles, and offers his soul for a spell which would stop the plague.

Mephistopheles duly grants his wish. The plague is halted. But instead of being grateful, the pious townspeople shun Faust as a sorcerer and a heretic. In a fit of pique, he decides that the townspeople weren't worth the effort, and that he has wasted his time trying to help them. He summons Mephistopheles again, only this time he wants to indulge his sensual appetites at the expense of those same townspeople. Mephistopheles complies, and Faust's downhill slide begins.

A lot of so-called neo-shamanic books published in the last thirty-or-so years are little more than angry screeds against modern society and its Christianity, capitalism, and industrial technology. How dare these materialistic Christians have food and comfort while we, who still worship the old gods of nature, live in hunger and poverty? The people have sold their souls for money. They're all sitting comfortably in church, and not supporting the shamans anymore. Well, we'll show them. We'll turn into werewolves and torment them.

Nigel Jackson, predictably, blames the Catholic Church. In the *Compleat Vampyre*, he writes:

> The Catholic church, then as now, a monstrous machine of oppression and an enemy of human diversity and freedom, rooted out these followers of an ancient shamanic creed and crushed them without remorse or compassion as indeed they have continued to do over the centuries throughout the world.

And while this is true in many instances, the church authorities (not only Catholic but Orthodox and later Protestant) tended to not act in these matters unless somebody in the village ratted out a neighbor as being a sorcerer and accused them of some kind of magical wrong-doing directed at livestock or children. Often this was a tribal conflict.

In *Vampyres*, Jackson goes on to say,

> An interesting insight into the dynamics of ethnic prejudice in Eastern Europe is given by the fact that the Voudokiaki [i.e., vampyres] are often thought to be the aggressive witches of neighbouring peoples, thus they are sometimes regarded as Turkish, Venetian or Italian or of some nationality bearing enmity against the Slovenians and their land."

In the case of sorcery, the Church was actually quite selective in just whom they condemned. Often the local church would side with the dominant or conquering ethnic group (who had the money and the power) to the detriment of the conquered. It was often the members of the subjugated tribe who were subjected to the tender mercies of the local church authorities if they were perceived as getting a little too uppity and had taken to hexing the children and horses or poisoning the local wells.

However, the persecutions by the Catholic Church didn't end with the Protestant Reformation (who also burned witches and sorcerers) or even with the so-called Enlightenment. Even when nobody was being burned at the stake anymore, the problems continued and, one might argue, just got worse. Instead of society persecuting the sorcerers and shamans as heretics, they persecuted them as either mentally ill or predatory con-artists. Again, from *Vampyres*:

> In this respect, our ancestors who knew that werewolves roamed the forests at midwinter and who honoured the wild Horned God of the Beasts enjoyed a far greater degree of psychic vitality and health than the demoralized, neurotic and enslaved dwellers in modern urban centres whose stress and anxiety levels far outstrip the material comforts of a tunnel-vision consumerism with its attendant work-ethic.

Maybe. But then again, this doesn't explain why these ancestors abandoned the forests at midwinter and escaped to the modern urban centers in the first place. After all, one doesn't see too many present-day neopagans abandoning their material comforts and going back to the forests for much longer than a fortnight holiday. It isn't long before they are anxious to abandon the forests and return to their material comforts, as anyone who has organized a pagan-themed weekend camp out will attest to.

Ultimately, the persecution of shamans and shapeshifters by clerical authority in whatever form it took was not really a religious or spiritual conflict. It was more of a social and economic one. This is the envy and anger of one authority that has been supplanted by another, with the tributes going to the new rulers rather than the older ones. It also has nothing to do with Christianity either *per se*. There were vampires and shape-changing witches and sorcerers in pre-Christian Rome and they preyed upon the well-to-do Romans just like they would prey on well-to-do Christians centuries later. To call it a pagan vs. Christian struggle misses the point.

To the Romans, anybody who lived outside the cities in the countryside were Pagani or Pagans, no matter what gods they worshipped. If the pagani wanted to increase their material prosperity, they abandoned their subsistence farms and their tribal practices, and moved into the city. Once they did, they ceased to be pagani and became Romans. The pagani who were left behind got poorer and poorer – and angrier and angrier. And those who still had their ancestral shamanic skills decided to have their revenge on those who abandoned their ancestral ways for a more comfortable material existence in the city.

With the rise of Christianity, nothing much changed. Christianity was always an urban faith. It began in the towns and cities of the Roman empire, and its early adherents were the prosperous middle class – merchants, artisans, government functionaries -- and the laborers who were their slaves. It never was a religion of the Pagani who lived and farmed the countryside. It was a religion of the city, and it depended upon city life for its structure and tenants.

Once the pagani moved to the city, they adopted the religion and culture of the city, which might include Christianity. But even if it didn't, the Pagani were Pagani no longer. After a couple of generations, they discarded their ancestral gods – and the shamans and sorcerers who purported to speak for those gods – as being irrelevant to their new way of life.

Cochrane wrote that some witches claim that there is a greater need in the world for fertility of mind than body. But that is understating the general facts. Morally and socially, Western Europe has advanced more without the 'Old Craft' and its attendant superstitions than it ever did with them.

Occultists in general and the cunning craft in particular have spent the last 1500 years locking horns with the Christian church in all of its various forms and denominations. However, the doctrinal differences between the Western esoteric tradition and early Christianity (especially Gnosticism) are actually quite small. Both have their roots in the writings that originated in the 1st and 2nd centuries after Christ. Some of these, such as the *Corpus Hermeticum*[79] and Ptolemy's *Tetrabiblos*[80], ended up in the literature of the Western Esoteric tradition. Others, such

---

79 *Corpus Hermeticum;* the core documents of the Hermetic Tradition dating back to the early Christian period.

80 *Tetrabiblos,* written in the 2nd century A.D. (C.E.) by Claudius Ptolemy is one of the oldest surviving texts on the philosophy and practice of Astrology.

as the Gospels, the letters of Paul of Tarsus, and the visions of John of Patmos, ended up in the Catholic canon. Which writings were adopted by the Church and which were not depended more often than not on whether they supported the authority of the growing church rather than their philosophical content.

However, once the church consolidated its doctrine and spread westward to Europe, it often adopted and co-opted both the practices and general outlook of the indigenous paganism it encountered, as we have seen. Priests and bishops were drawn from the local population and carried with them their native tribal ways. The only thing that changed was that they acknowledged the church as their spiritual authority rather than the ancient gods and their shamanic priesthood. So, the dispute between tribal shamanism and the Church eventually turned into little more than a power struggle between rival spiritual hierarchies to determine which would prevail over the mass of the population, who were increasingly being seen as only resources to be fought over and exploited rather than fellow humans to be nurtured and served.

When the Church allied itself with the military might of the Roman empire, it looked like the Church would emerge as the winner. And the history of Western Europe reflects the fact that if a tribal warlord converted to Christianity, the church would ally itself with him and make him into a king. In exchange, the new king would bring the newly conquered people under the Church's authority and allow the church to exact its own tribute. And the native shamans were pushed farther and farther into the shadows to be vilified and burnt at the stake if they caused any trouble. The children of Cain became the children of the Devil.

The tide turned in this battle around the end of the 16th century when the Church fragmented into Catholic and Protestant factions, and both became more concerned with warring against each other rather than with sorcerers and magicians. The children of Cain took this opportunity to organize into the fraternities and secret societies, such as Freemasonry and Rosicrucianism, that eventually spawned the Enlightenment. Eventually, the Enlightenment prevailed, and the Church, both Catholic and Protestant, was pushed into the fever swamps of superstition.

But, as historians Will and Ariel Durant have noted in their monumental work, *The Story of Civilization*[81], once the Enlightenment gained supremacy, it ended up being as ruthless, self-righteous, and cruel as the Churches that it replaced. Oppressed during the Middle Ages, it turned into the oppressor of the Enlightenment and as many people suffered and died at the hand of science as did at the hand of religion.

It is sad that the things that gave Christianity the spiritual power it once had – love, charity, faith, compassion, devotion, self-discipline, and dedication to a cause greater than one's own personal gratification are the very things that the Church threw out in her quest for worldly power. This was the reason that Jesus told Lucifer to go pound sand when Lucifer offered him worldly power.

The Gospel of Matthew states, "Again, the devil took him to a very high mountain and showed him all the kingdoms of the world and their splendor. 'All this I will give you,' he said, 'if you will bow down and worship me.'" Jesus replies archly that "Thou shalt not tempt the Lord thy God." Later he tells his disciples in the gospel of John that "my kingdom is not of this world." Thus, by rejecting the temptations of hubris, Jesus eventually died the sacrificial death of a Sacred King.

The Church, scarcely 300 years after Jesus' death, cheerfully took Lucifer's bargain and become a ruthless and cruel institution rather than the source of hope and compassion that its founder intended it to be.

Centuries later, the children of Cain would come along and offer enlightenment and liberation in place of superstition and ignorance. It is a shame that they chose to throw the same spiritual baby out with the dirty bathwater as the Church did when it was their turn at the helm of the spiritual ship and seek power and exploitation rather than service to their fellow man.

In *One: The Grimoire of the Golden Toad,* Chumbley writes that at the culmination of a particular ritual, the "Lord" would come amid the Glories of the World, instructing the aspirant to kneel before him. Then,

---

81 *The Story of Civilization* (11 volume set) 1935-1975, Simon & Schuster

all that the aspirant sees shall be his. All the aspirant need do is meet the Lord's gaze and kneel. Then, he can proclaim himself as the Devil's master and have the Devil deliver to him all the promised glories. Basically, what is happening here is that the practitioner of this rite is taking the place of Jesus in the Biblical temptation in the wilderness -- only instead of telling the Devil to begone, he takes the Devil's bargain and kneels at the Devil's feet, insisting that he is the Devil's master. Might Faust have thought that too, before Mephistopheles eventually hauled him to hell? Cupiditas.

Do other humans exist only to be used and have worth only to the extent that they are useful, both for economic and sexual gratification, or do they exist not as a separate species, but our younger brothers and sisters who need help and guidance to advance along the evolutionary path? Are they fellow humans or are they prey?

Imagine a scene in Hell at the annual dinner of the Tempters' Training College for Young Devils. The Guest of Honor gets up to speak:

> "Your dreaded Principal has included in a speech full of points something like an apology for the banquet which he has set before us. Well, gentledevils, no one blames him. But it would be in vain to deny that the human souls on whose anguish we have been feasting tonight were of pretty poor quality. Not all the most skillful cookery of our tormentors could make them better than insipid. Oh, to get one's teeth again into a Farinata, a Henry VIII, or even a Hitler! There was real crackling there; something to crunch; a rage, an egotism, a cruelty only just less robust than our own. It put up a delicious resistance to being devoured. It warmed your innards when you'd got it down."

The speaker in this passage is the redoubtable Screwtape in the 1959 essay *Screwtape Proposes a Toast*[82] by C.S. Lewis. Screwtape makes it quite clear that the devil, "Our Father Below," has no use for humans save as food. In fact, the whole of the Screwtape letters centers on the idea that humans cannot be fed upon until after death. They must be snatched

---

82 *Screwtape Proposes A Toast*, C.S. Lewis, was first published in The Saturday Evening Post on December 19th, 1959.

away from The Enemy (i.e. God) at the point of death much in the way that a wolf will snatch a straying sheep that lags behind when the herd is locked up for the night behind sturdy gates. And the annoyance of the devils at the salvation of one of the sheep consists of nothing more than being deprived of a meal. It is the fury of the vampire who is driven back by a cross at the moment when he or she is about to sink hungry fangs into the throat of a victim.

It is also worth noting that the devils themselves are by no means safe from such predation. Their job is to bring human food to the other devils or become food themselves. In his last letter to Wormwood, in which the young devil bewails the fact that his "patient" has died and gone to heaven, Screwtape gleefully informs him that as a consequence of his failure, his spiritual essence will be consumed by the other demons, especially by Screwtape himself. That this is a common practice is revealed when Screwtape warns the assembled graduates that, "Your career is before you. Hell expects and demands that it should be - as mine was - one of unbroken success. If it is not, you know what awaits you." There might be honor among thieves, but there doesn't seem to be much among the children of Lucifer.

This question presents itself to all of us at one time or another. Given that we are of the blood, is our purpose on this earth plane to guide and aid those ordinary mortals that Crowley sneers at or are we entitled to feed off of them and use them for our own ends no matter what harm it might cause them? Are we justified in using lies, deception, and trickery to frighten them into doing what we want them to? And if we are, does that make us any better than the Church who once burned us at the stake?

It's easy to use past persecution as an excuse for present tyranny. Psychologists know that this attitude is how abuse is perpetuated in families, where the abused child grows up to become the abusive parent. Yesterday's victims become today's oppressors with great regularity, as present geopolitical patterns show. And today's oppressors will in turn become tomorrow's victims and the cycle perpetuates *ad infinitum.*

It doesn't have to be this way. There appears to be an unspoken taboo against saying, as I am saying here, that for much of the last two thousand years, people adopted Christianity precisely because their tribal paganism and the shamans that presided over it, had failed them. Paganism had become at best irrelevant, and at worst dangerous to the ordinary person. Whether we want to admit it or not, Christianity was in large part adopted by the population of a country because their tribal shamans had, as religious authorities tend to do, become corrupt.

When the Roman Empire disintegrated in the 5th century and largely withdrew from Western Europe, there was perhaps an opportunity for the European tribes to return to their former, peaceful, nature-worshiping ways. They didn't. Instead, they warred brutally against each other for several centuries with each tribal warlord inflicting bloody massacres on helpless members of an opposing tribe. There was a reason why this period in history was called the Dark Ages.

Where were the tribal shamans during all of this carnage? What could they do while their people were being hacked apart by invading warlords? Dress up in animal skins and dance? Chant poetry? Determine auguries from the flights of birds? Brew hallucinogenic potions? What they did do was enter the fray on the side of their own tribe and contribute to the carnage, invoking their tribal gods for aid in slaying the rival tribe. They do it still, in some parts of the world.

Bash the Catholic Church if you will, but from the 5th century through to the 20th, Christianity with its comforting and unifying theology was discovered to be preferable to the ordinary person than trickster shamans and their cunning craft. One of the compelling messages of Christianity was that it transcended tribalism. People of all tribes were brothers and sisters in Christ and could lay their tribal affiliations aside, if they wished, and unite for a common purpose in the spirit of *agape*.

To an ordinary person who was not of the blood, moving to the town, taking up a trade, and converting to Christianity was preferable to staying out in the countryside like their tribal ancestors had. For all the hardships (from our modern perspective) of living in towns, the people enjoyed material comforts that they didn't have in the country, and if that material comfort meant being nominally Christian, then so be it.

The tribal shamans had nothing to compete with it and turning into werewolves and hag-riding horses didn't help the situation any.

There is a reason why ordinary village folk abandoned their tribal paganism for the religion of Christ. It wasn't just that they got a better deal from urban Christianity, or like Cochrane once remarked in a letter to Bill Gray, converted to Methodism in order to participate in Sunday afternoon socials. Another thing that is lost in this tussle is why Christianity was as successful as it was with the ordinary people even as it was scorned by the shamans.

It's easy to blame it on a desire for money and material comforts. And indeed, countries that became Christian tended to also become prosperous. But both Catholicism and Protestantism has also flourished in times and places marked by desperate poverty. Even in such environments, the people continue to cling to the comfort of the church and its ministers when logic would perhaps suggest that they return to their old pagan ways, since Christianity had so obviously failed them.

Some do, perhaps. But the majority do not. For every person who shuns the Church and frequents the local witch doctor or curandero[83], a dozen others will cluster at the feet of the statue of the Virgin in the local church, light candles, and tell their beads.

When one peels away the dogma, doctrine, ritual, and hierarchy that has encrusted it like lichens for nearly two thousand years, what emerges from Christianity is the idea of caritas, or charity. A higher power, with loving intentions, has sent enlightened souls to this earth to help and aid their fellow humans on their journey to enlightenment, even at the expense of their own comfort, human desires, and their very lives. And this is not only a Christian concept, but is mirrored in mystical Buddhism, Hinduism, and Islam as well.

Consider the Mahayana Buddhist bodhisattva, Avalokitesvara (the Chinese pictured this bodhisattva as female and called her Quan Yin). Avalokitesvara was a human being who after many lifetimes of

---

83 (Spanish) A traditional or folk healer/shaman

concentrated self-discipline had perfected his soul to the point where he was about to enter Nirvana. As he was leaving the earth plane forever, he heard the anguished cries of humanity, who were grief stricken that he was leaving them behind.

Overcome by compassion, he vowed that he would not enter the bliss of Nirvana until every single human soul was able to precede him. Until then, he would spend as many lifetimes as it would take in service to his fellow humans to enable them to do so. He is here still, it is claimed, inhabiting the earthly body of the Dalai Lama.

This is the one mythic image that is missing from the whole Luciferian mythos - the one which formed so much a part of Roy's and Bill Gray's work - the concept of the Sacrificial King of royal or holy blood (the Sang Real) who willingly and joyfully allows himself to be killed in order to benefit the tribe.

It's interesting to note in his first book of his Sangreal Sodality series entitled *Western Inner Workings,* first published in 1988, Bill Gray describes in a chapter called Paganistic Principles a group of modern pagans practicing a kind of precursor to the Grail mysteries. Although this group of pagans remained unnamed in his book, Bill told us that that chapter was based on his correspondence with Roy, and the letters he allowed us to copy bore this out.

"The master would take on the disease," Gray says of these unnamed pagans. "If he couldn't get rid of it, he might die of it. His solemn duty was to take on the ills of others. If need be, he might have to die on behalf of his people like the old sacred kings."

Magical power doesn't come cheap. It has to be paid for by someone. And the Magister, if he is working along the ancient lines, will willingly pay it for his people, if not with his life, with his willingness to become the lame king and undergo rebirth on behalf of the entire Clan.

As Roy wrote to Bill, the ancients knew that if man draws out power from the Cosmic Well, he must sooner or later replace it with something better if the social continuity is to survive. The keynote of this survival is sacrifice, and the ancients sacrificed their very best in order to replace the energy loss. Thus, the basic law behind the techniques of magic and fate is that nature abhors a vacuum. With this in mind, mystics and magicians alike attempt to lift the world fate by replacing that which is empty or negative with that which is positive.

This is precisely what is meant by paying the coin. And it also explained why the role of the Magister had been deliberately watered down by Doreen and John in *Witchcraft: A Tradition Renewed.* John had claimed that each seven years a sacrifice had to be made by the Magister in order to keep his sacred role in the Clan. He was right.

Since 1984, every seven years brought a crisis the shook the foundations of our claim as Magister and Maid of the Clan of Tubal Cain. The first crisis came in 1991 when we thought we had better do John's ritual in order to stave off the anger of the gods, and to dodge the ultimate payment that Roy had paid.

And, it worked - for a while. But in seven years' time, we would face another crisis which occurred in 1998, when John rescinded whatever authority he had given us and essentially called us liars and frauds. We managed to prove him wrong, but it meant that we had to redefine our role in the Clan. We stopped performing Clan adoptions and essentially, if not officially, merged the Clan with the Roebuck.

And, sure enough, seven years after that, in 2006, we faced another crisis. After the attacks on the World Trade Center in 2001, Dave had gone to work for Homeland Security. But after only a few years on the job, he developed arthritis in his knees. He went on disability long enough to undergo a knee replacement, which we hoped would fix the problem.

It didn't. The pain resulting from damage to the nerves was so excruciating that he had to take a mind-numbing array of pain medications. So, for several years, he was unable to perform his duties as Magister and other male members of the group had to take on the role.

This was precisely the time that John's successor in England wrote to us demanding that we renounce our claim as Magister and Maid on our website. In addition, there were several calls from our own group for Dave to resign as Magister. Whatever legitimacy we had once had, it appeared that we had it no longer. It seemed as though, after all these years, the gods were calling in their markers.

But Dave decided not to give up. He went cold turkey off the pain medicines and eventually recovered his health. But it was a long and painful process and it necessitated another reorganization of the group and a restatement of purpose. We lost several people during those years, particularly those who desired more in the way of exciting rituals and opportunities for increasing personal power and position.

We persevered with the assistance, support and patience of those members who remained with us. It took a lot of time and effort, especially since many of us had to juggle the demands of work and family. But now, forty years after we first discovered the writings of Robert Cochrane, the Roebuck still meets, still teaches, and still strives to serve the community by performing open rituals and participating in charitable projects. We have an active daughter group and a number of related groups with whom we can share information and techniques.

Gray says in *Western Inner Workings*,

> You should have realized by now, what is at the bottom of our Western Inner Tradition: self-sacrifice." To serve. What a concept. As Gray says, "The Sacred Kings sought to serve their people through their sacrificial deaths. Kings voluntarily reduced themselves to slaves so that slaves might eventually become Kings in their own right. ... Our Grail [that is, our Sang Real] is a spiritual service which seeks to enliven those who should awaken to inner realities while yet on earth.

In other words, *caritas*. What does this service accomplish? "... to achieve individual independence for souls seeking such relationship with spiritual solidities rather than accept without question whatever they are told by establishments opposed to spiritual, and possibly, temporal liberty," Bill Gray explains. It is the 'Idealism of Individuation.'

"Ye shall be as gods," the Sacred Serpent told Eve in the book of Genesis, "knowing good and evil." However, knowing good and evil is one thing. Choosing one over the other is another thing altogether. As children of Cain, we have inherited the ability to choose one or the other. Heaven help those ordinary people if we choose wrongly.

Now, at the tail end of the Piscean age, we who are of the blood need to ask ourselves, just who are we? Just why do we have these psychic gifts that ordinary humans don't have? And, more importantly, how can we use our gifts constructively rather than using them to get back at Christianity for real or imagined slights? Can we not acknowledge and harness the darker side of our natural being without using it as an excuse to wreak vengeance on people whose distant ancestors once oppressed us?

If we of the Clan of Tubal Cain are going to reclaim our divine birthright as light bringers, we are going to have to grow up, do the work we need to do, learn humility and compassion, and assume responsibility for our past mistakes. Then – and only then - can we finally take our place in the world not as ruling elites, con artists, or predatory vampyres, but as priests and healers, bards, shamans, and visionary artists in order to help all of our fellow humans to further advance up the ladder of spiritual evolution, even if we gain little by way of attention and material rewards for our efforts.

For all his faults and failings, Roy Bowers showed us one way of attaining this goal. But it entails work, sacrifice, humility and the need to do battle with the Shadow Clan dwelling within our own psyches in order to master our own fate. Otherwise, we will fall prey to hubris and succumb to the temptation to abuse our knowledge to reap where we have not sown at the expense of our fellow mortals; instead of healing and enlightening, we will resort to chicanery and deceiving.

But for every decision to deceive there can be a decision to enlighten. For every vampyre or werewolf who feeds on the life force of another, there is a healer and a shaman who can call down the power of spirit into the mortal realm and alleviate suffering with a word or the touch of a hand. The choice is ours to make.

Which shall we choose?

INDEX

A
Abel (Biblical), 130
Abiff, Hiram, 58, 131
Achilles, 129, 217-218, 225, 240
Actaeon, 138
Adam (Biblical), 130, 228-229
Adam and Eve, The Book of, 130
Adams, Frederick, 34
Adom Kadom, 123
airt(s), 173, 188, 189
All Hallows, 22
Allen, Charles Snell, 131
altar 15, 34, 35, 53, 117-118, 225
Amlodhi 114-115
angel(s), 16-18, 21, 85, 129-130, 142, 159, 160, 163, 204, 219, 227
 -Archangel 32, 123, 130, 140
 -Fallen 85
Anglo-Saxon 36, 72
An Tribhis Mhor, 140
Annwn, Predui 72
Aphrodite 135
Appalachian 169, 194
apple 130, 171
Apple Island 155, 171
Aquarius 120
Aradia 140, 200
Aradia, Gospel of the Witches, Charles Leland 140
Archbishop of Constantinople 137
Artemis 135, 138
Arthur, King xi, 28, 134, 171
Asteria, 143
astral 52, 109-110, 161-166, 175, 204
 -objective 52
 -plane 109, 161, 164-166, 175, 204
Autohagiography 240
Avalokiteshvara 115, 251
Avalon xiii, 155, 171
Avebury 34, 42
Azazel 129
Azoetia, The, Andrew Chumbley 82-83
Aztec 26

B
Backwards Prayer 82
Barclodi-ad-y-Gawres 42
bard 71, 86, 108, 167-168, 172, 239, 255
 -Shaman 108
 -Poetry (bardic) 108
Bast, 135
bear, 162
belladonna, xi
Beltane, 22
Bible, 17-18, 21, 155
Bodmin Moor, 42
Boudicca, 179
Bowers, Roy, x, xii-xiii, 33, 47, 49-57, 60, 62-65, 71-82, 85-88, 95, 174-175, 178-179, 181, 197-199, 201-202, 207-207, 213, 216-216, 223, 235, 252-253, 255
 See also Robert Chochrane
Bracelin, Jack, 56
Brahman, 132, 162
Branwen, 68
Breton, 22
Bridget, 184
Bridget, Saint, 139
Brigid, 135
Bryn-Celli-Dhu, 42
Buckland, 56
Buddha, 162
Buddhism, 156
Buddhist, Buddhists, 155, 157, 162, 177, 251
 -Mahayan Bodhisattavi, 251

C
Cabala, 32
Caerochren, 155
Cain, 82-84, 130-131, 224-225, 246-247, 255
 -Child or Children of, 225, 246-247, 255
 -Jubal, 130
cairn(s), 35, 41-42, 83
Callanish, 40
Campbell, Joseph, 157, 160
Canberra, Wicca Conference 56
candle(s), 15, 51, 58, 72, 173, 189-190, 206, 251
Canon Episcopi, 137,
capitalism, 242
caste(s), 19, 21, 132, 133, 241
castle, 30, 40, 51-52, 54, 72, 171, 172, 188-189
 -Acre, 188
 -Caer Ochren, 174
 -Harlech, 68

-Of the Four Winds, 88, 188
-Perilous, 135, 188
-Carmethan, 171
-Grail, 135
-In the clouds, 174
-Journey to, 40, 51-52, 54, 67, 88, 111, 167, 188, 236-237
-Lady of, 135, 157-158, 169, 171, 186
-Spiral, xiii, 174-175
-The Cave and the, 78
-Under the sea, 174
-Upon the earth, 174
cat(s), 102, 105, 107
Cathars, 199
Cathbad, 133-134
Catholic, 17, 22, 122, 177-178, 240-241, 243
-apologist, 122
-bishop, 63
-Cannon, 246
-monk, 157
-mystic, 162
-medieval, 177
-Roman, 136, 181, 199, 207, 212
Catholicism, 229, 240, 251
cattle, 34, 177, 133, 187, 218
Cattle Raid of Cooley, The, 133, 218
cauldron, 108, 131, 143, 174, 184-185, 192
Cauldron, The, 79
Cauldron, The Cave and the, 88, 183-185, 192
Celtic, 19-26-27, 68, 71-72, 129, 132-133, 140, 155-156, 168-169, 184, 204, 218
Ceres, 163
Cerridwen, 108, 135
Chaco Canyon, 40
chakra, 123-124
chalice, xi, 15, 128
Chapel of St. Mark, Appleton, Norfolk, 85
Charge of the Goddess, 135
Cheltenham, 47
Chichen Itza, 40
Christian(s), 17-18, 20, 22-23, 27-28, 90, 136, 140, 162, 170, 181, 198, 240, 242, 244-245, 251
-Clergy, 22, 242
-Mystic, 154
Christianity, 17, 35, 90, 141, 180, 184, 240, 242, 244, 245-247, 250-251
Chumbley, Andrew, 82-85, 87, 89, 247

Church, The
-Celtic Catholic, 139
-Christian, 20, 123, 129, 140, 228
-Catholic, viii, 20, 90, 128-129, 136, 141, 181, 207, 211, 228, 243, 246, 250, 246
circumambulation, 78-79, 81, 197
Clifton, Chas, 78-79
   Sacred Mask, Sacred Dance, 78-79, 81, 197
cloak, 54
Chochrane, Robert, x-xi, 29, 34, 48, 63-64, 78-79, 100, 117, 121-122, 135, 138, 145, 153, 155, 158, 191, 197, 215, 221, 245, 254, 254 *See also Roy Bowers*
Compass Rose, 187-189
Compostela, 177
Conchobhar Mac Neesa, 133-134
cord, 29, 49, 53, 173, 190, 206
Cornwall, 41
Corpus Hermeticum, 245
Cosmic Miller, 117
Cromlech, 33, 43
Crowley, Aleister, 82, 111, 200
   -*The Confessions of Aleister Crowley*, 240
Cuhulainn, 218
Cultus Sabbati, 82-85
cunning craft, 83, 89, 200-201, 245, 250
cupiditas, 232, 239, 248

D

dagger, 15-16, 53
Dalai Lama, 155, 252
Dark Mother, 149
David, King (Biblical), 131, 134
Dee, John, 17, 130
deer, 98-99, 105, 110, 117, 233-234
   -antlers, 182-183
   -hide, 110, 183
Demeter, 163
demon(s), 16-18, 21, 27, 137, 159, 163, 199, 204, 214, 222-223, 225, 230, 249
demonic
   -forces, 237
   -possession, 160
deosil, 118-119, 189-190
Deschend, Hertha von, 114

-*Hamlet's Mill: An Essay on Myth and the Frame of Time,* 114
Devereaux, Paul, 34-37-38, 133, 178
   -*Shamanism and the Mystery Lines,* 38
devil, 20-21, 84, 106-107, 137, 160, 198-199, 222, 246, 248-249
Devil's Eye, 42
Diana, 135, 137-143, 144, 157, 200
djinn, 18
dog(s), 102-103, 105, 139, 142, 218, 222
dowser(s), 37
Dragon Project, The, 37
druids, 19, 21, 132-134, 169
Durant, Will and Ariel, 247
   -*The Story of Civilization,* 247
Dyfed, 42

E
eagles, 97, 105
Eden, The Garden of, 130
Eisteddford, 22
element(s) 16, 69, 91, 123-124, 131, 171, 174, 189
elemental(s) 16, 122, 189
Elias 156
Elijah 156
Elphame 81
Enoch 130
   The Book of, 129
Enochian, 130
entheos, 219-220
Ephesians, 137
Ephesus, 237, 241
equinox, 115
Eve (Biblical), 130, 228-229
Exodus, Book of, 240

F
Fate, xii, 52, 86, 115-116, 135, 138, 144, 151-152, 154, 158, 169, 171, 184-185, 188, 199, 216, 218, 224, 253, 255
   -Dark Lady of, 184
   -Goddess of, 149, 151
Faust, 222-223
Feng Shui, 36
Fortune, Dion, 61-63, 109, 119, 136, 153, 164, 202, 204

-*Applied Magic,* 153, 202, 204, 208, 210
-*Aspects of Occultism,* 136, 164
-*Psychic Self-Defense,* 109
-*The Cosmic Doctrine,* 119
-*The Worship of Isis,* 136
Fowlmere, 35
fox (es), 105
Frazier, J.G., 139
   -*The Golden Bough,* 139
Freemasonry, 118, 229, 246

G
Gardner, Gerald, x-xii, 28, 60, 111, 135, 196-198, 203-204
Gardnerian Wicca, 55-58, 61, 63, 79, 82-83, 88, 135, 141, 173, 196-197, 203-204
geis, 218
Genesis, Book of, 129-130, 228, 254
German, 194, 222
Giantess's Apronful, 42
Giles, Norman, 33, 47, 56
Gilgamesh, 115
Gnostic, 122, 228
Gnosticism, 245
Goblin, The Universal, (Ted Holiday), 219
God(s), 245
   -Krishna, 115
   -Jehovah, 227-229
   -Lucifer, 140-141, 227-232, 240, 247, 249
   -Mammon, 145
   -Mercury, 180
   -Osiris, 162
   -Zeus, 130
Goddess, xii, 20, 26-27, 52, 58, 71, 79, 85-86, 97, 108, 133, 135-140, 142, 144, 152, 168
   -Aphrodite, 135
   -Aradia, 140, 200
   -Artemis, 135, 138
   -Asteria, 143
   -Bast, 135
   -Branwen, 68
   -Bridget, 184
   -Brigid, 135
   -Ceres, 163
   -Cerridwen, 108, 135
   -Charge of, 135

-Dark Mother, 149
-Diana, 135, 137-144, 157, 200
-Gracious, 135
-Great Mother, 145
Hecate, 139, 142-144, 147, 157, 184
-Hera, 180
-Hestia, 145
-Isis, 135-136, 163
-Kuan Yin, 135
-Melusine, 135
-Morrighan, 218
-Nemesis. 218
-of Death, 143-145
-of Fate, 149, 151
-of Fertility, 143, 145
-of Love, 135, 138, 145
-of Rebellion, 157
-of Sovereignty, 133, 218
-of the Crossroads, 142
-of the Hunt, 138
-of the Moon, 138, 140-142, 144, 146
-of the Underworld, 143
-of Wisdom, 147
-of the Witches, 143
-Our Lady, 58
-Black, 145, 147
-Great, 126, 136, 225
-White, 71, 86, 106, 122, 139, 144, 146-147, 216
-Three-fold, 190
-Vesta, 145, 147
-Virgin,
Golden Bough, The, J.G. Frazier 139
Golden Dawn, The Order of, 111, 173, 209
Golem, 12
Gospels, The (Biblical), 134, 170, 246
-Of John, 247
-Of Luke, 92
-Of Matthew, 247
Gospel of the Egyptians, 122
Gospel of the Witches, Charles Leland, 140
Grail (Graal), 128, 252, 254
Castle, 135
Grave, Robert, 71, 106, 122, 144
The White Goddess, 71
King Jesus, 128
Mammon and the Black Goddess, 145
Collected Poems, 146

Gray, William (Bill), 32, 45, 47
-*By Elder Tree and Standing Stone*, 32
-*Evoking the Primal Goddess*, 157
-*Magical Ritual Methods*, 32, 124, 200
-*Ladder of Lights*, 32, 255
-*Western Inner Workings*, 48, 81, 252, 254
Greco-Roman, 18, 137, 140, 180
Greek, 20, 22, 97, 129-130, 138-139, 145, 155, 169, 180, 188, 217-219, 241
Gros Fawr, 42, 197
guardian (s), 67-69, 108, 169, 178
-Ancestral, 204
-God, 108
-Goddess, 142,
-of humanity, 152
-of the gateway, 169
-of the inner planes, 183
-of the prtal, 45
-of the sacred hearth, 146
-of the threshold, 151
Guinness, 49, 51
Gwion Bach, 108

H

Hall, Manly P., 154, 162, 230
-*Magic: A Treatise on Esoteric Ethics*, 230
-*Reincarnation*, 154, 162
Hamlet's Mill, Giorgio de Santillana and Hertha von Dechend, 114
hare (s), 105-106, 108
Harlech, 68
hawk (s), 105, 108
Hawkins, Gerlad, 40
Stonehinge Decoded, 40
hazelnuts, 69
Hebrew, 122-123, 222
IHVH, 123
Jahve, 122
Hecate, 139, 142-144, 147, 157, 184
Heindel, Max, 154
The Rosicrusion Cosmo-conception or Mystic Christianity, 154
Hell (Christian), 17, 19, 150, 198, 223, 228, 230, 249-249
Henry VIII, 170, 248

INDEX

Hera, 180
Herme Post, 34, 100
Hermetic Tradition, 245
    -Corpus Hermeticum, 245
Hidden Company, The 32, 52, 67
Hindu, 140
    -Hinduism, 156, 251
History of Freemasonry, Albert Mackey, 118
Holiday, Ted
    -*The Goblin Univeral*, 219
Holy Blood, Holy Grail, Michael Baigent, Richard Leigh and Henry Lincoln, 127-129
Holyhead, 42
horn (s),
    -ram, 182
horned piper, The, 168, 174-175
hound (s), 106, 108, 138
    -greyhound(s), 106
Howard, Michael Jackson, 78-79, 85, 87
    -*Cauldron, The*, 79
    -*Pillars of Tubal Cain, The*, 85
    -*Roebuck in the Thicket*, 78

I

IAO, 122
Iceni, 179
IEOU, 122
incense, 15, 93, 144
Indian, 132
initiation, 183, 193, 196-196, 203, 208-210, 213
    -Gardnerian, 88, 196
Inquisition, The, 240
inquisition (s), 71, 105
Ireland, 68
Irish, 22, 133-134, 168
Isis, 135-136, 163
Islam, 251
    -Islamic, 130
Isle of Anglesey, 42
Israelites, 130
Italian, 45, 200, 243
Italy, 200

J

Jackson, Nigel, 80-81, 85, 87, 108, 221, 243

    -*The Call of the Horned Piper*, 80-81
    -*The Compleat Vampyre*, 108, 221, 243
    -*Masks of Misrule*, 81
    -*Pillars of Tubal Cain*, 85
Jehovah, 227-229
Jenny, Dr. Hans, 123
    C-ymatics, 123
Jeremiah, 156,
Jesus (Christ), 17, 20-21, 92, 109, 122, 127-128, 134, 156, 162, 247, 251
    -appearing to Mary Magdalene, 127
Jewish, 18, 123, 127-129, 169
John of Patmos, 246
John the Baptist, 155
Jones, Evan John, vii-viii, 49, 54, 64, 78-79, 173, 178, 184, 186, 197-198, 205-207, 253
    -*Sacred Mask, Sacred Dance*, 78-79
    -*Witchcraft: A Tradition Renewed*, 8, 64, 173
Joseph of Arimathea, 127-128
Joseph (husband of Mary), 134
Judea, 128
Judeo-Christian, 18, 28
Junrai, 177
Jupiter (planet), 152

K

karma, 151-153, 213, 224
Kathopanishad, 154
Key of Solomon, The Lesser, 16, 83, 131
King Jesus, Robert Graves, 128-129
King of the Woods, 139
King stone, 43
King, Sacred, 11, 50, 85, 108, 116, 127, 134, 139, 168, 174, 218, 247 – 254
kingship, 133-134
knife, 51, 53, 109, 173, 181-182, 190
knots, 29, 49, 53, 190, 206
Kondratiev, Alexei, 140
Krishna, 115
Kuan Yin, 135
Kullevro, 115
Kundaline, 117

L

Lake Nemi, 139
Lancaster, House of, 170
Lanyon Quoit, 41
Larkworthy, Peter, 63
Leadbetter, C.W., 161
    -*The Astral Plane*, 161
left-hand path, 118-119
Leland, Charles, 140-141, 200
    -*Aradia, Gospel of the Witches*, 140-141, 200
Lewis, C.S., 248
    -*Screwtape Proposes A Toast*, 248
Lucifer, 140-141, 227-232, 240, 247, 249
Lucifer Effect, The, 232
Luciferian, 83, 85, 87-89, 217, 231, 236, 241, 252
Lung Mei Lines, 36

M
Mabinogian, 68
Macbeth, 184
Mackey, Albert, 118, 229
    The History of Freemasonry, 118, 229
Magic: A Treastise...230
Man in Black, 49
Man-an-Tol, 42
Mars (planet), 152-153
Mary,
    -Magdelane, 127-128
    -of Bethany, 128
    -Virgin, 20-21, 128, 134-137, 139, 145, 162-163
    -The Three, 184
mask, 72, 76-82, 85-87, 97-98, 103-104, 109-111, 154, 197
    -leaf, 81
May Eve, 183
Mecca, 177
Medicine man, Sioux, 162
Megalithic Sites in Britain... 40
Melsuine, 135
Mephistopheles, 222-223, 242, 248
Mercury (God), 180
Mercury (planet), 152
Michell, John, 36-38
    The View Over Atlantis, 36-38
metempsychosis, 155
mill, 113, 115-119, 125, 175, 236

-of heaven, 116
-of magic, 113, 120
-treading the, ix, 29, 53, 57, 62, 66, 69, 97, 111, 115-120, 185-186, 188, 190, 192, 205
millstone, 114
Milton, John, 227, 230
    -*Paradise Lost*, 227, 230
Mac Neesa, Conchobhar, 133-134
Mac Roig, Fergus, 133
mistletoe, 51
moat, 113, 126
Moirai, 184
moon, x-xii, 40-42, 108, 136, 140-141, 144, 151, 153, 235
morals (morality), 17, 23, 25, 212, 229, 231-232, 240, 245
Moral and Dogma of the Ancient and...., 229
Morrighan, 218
mound, 32, 42, 88, 172, 190-192
    -Mound in the Dark Grove, 42
mouse (mice), 102, 107
Murray, Margaret, 198-200
    -*Witch Cult in Western Europe*, 198-200
Musgrave Ritual, 28

N
Naamah, 130
Nag Hammadi, 122, 128
Native America, xii, 27, 33
Nephilim, 130
Newgrange, 40
Newtimber, 50-51
Nirvana, 154, 252
Noah, 130
noose, 53, 190
Norfolk, 88, 178-179, 183-185, 187-188
Norman Conquest, 90
Norns, 184
Norse, 27, 129
North Berwick, 71, 199
north star, 115

O
oak, x, 51, 72, 139, 169, 172
Odyssius, 115
Old Straight Path, The Alfred Watkins, 36

INDEX

One: The Golden Toad, Andrew Chumbley 83-84, 256
Orpheus, 168
Osiris, 162
otherworld, vii, xii, 19, 25, 27, 29-30, 36, 45, 53, 86, 147, 159, 164-166, 168-169, 171, 175-176, 180, 189, 237
otter, 107-108
Oxfordshire, West, 31

P

Pagani, 224-245
Paradise Lost john Milton, 227, 230
Peddars Way, 88, 179
Pennick, Nigel, 34
Pennsylvania Dutch, 194
Penrhos-Feliw, 42
Phillips, Julia, 56
Pietro, Guido Fra. Angelicaplague, 242
Plato, 241
plow, 35
Pre-Christian, 22, 79, 198
Preselli Mountains, 42
Prometheus, 228
Protestant, 17, 22, 199, 228, 240-241, 243, 246
    -Calvinist, 241
    -Church, 228
    -Protestantism, 21, 251
    -Reformation, 21, 245
Psychic Self-Defense, Dion Fortune, 109
Ptolemey, 245

Q

Queen Nessa, 133
Queen of the Fairies, 170-171
Quetzalcouatl, 115

R

Rais, Giles de, 219-220
Rabbi, 128
ram, 182
raven (s), 68, 97, 105, 162
reincarnation, 154-156
Reincarnation, Manly P. Hall 154, 162
Republic, Plato, 241
Rex Nemorensis, 139
ritual,
    -Musgrave, 28
    -Rollright, 32-33, 43-44, 47, 205
Roebuck, vii, 54-55, 63-67, 71-73, 75, 78, 82, 205-206, 253-254
Rollright Ritual, The, 32-34, 43-44, 47, 205
Rollright Stones, The Rollrights, 30-33-43-44
Roman, 188, 244
Rome, 90, 139-141, 147, 177, 244
rose (s), 52, 88, 170-171, 174, 185-189
    -Compass, 187-189
    -Sub rosa, 170
Rose from the Grave, 88, 174
Rosicrusion, 164
Rosicrusion Cosmo-conception or Mystic Christianity, The, Max Heindel, 154

S

sacerdos, 139
Sacred King, 11, 50, 85, 108, 116, 127, 134, 139, 168, 174, 218, 247, 252, 254
Sacred Mask, Sacred Dance Evan John Jones and Chas Clifton 78-79, 81, 197
salmon, 97, 108
Samael Archangel, 130
Samson, 115
Sanders, Alex, x-xi
Sangreal, 128, 254, *see also Grail*
Sangreal Sodality Series William Gray, 48
Santillano, Georgio de, 114
Saturn, 152
Saxon, 36
Scottish, 40, 71-72, 105, 170
    -airts, 173
    -chieftan, 72
    -Rite, 229
    -throne, 72, 105, 199, 229
    -witch, 105
Screwtape Proposes a Toast, C.S. Lewis 248-249
serpent, 130, 147
    -Sacred, 254
Seth (Biblical), 130-131
Seventeen Thirtyfour (1734), 33, 52, 56-57, 167, 215
sex, 141, 162, 197, 200, 211, 222, 248
    -Gardnerian, 197
Shakespeare, 115, 184
shaman/shamanism, xii, 21, 25-27, 35,

39-40, 79-80, 86, 90, 92, 98-99, 104-105, 107-108, 165, 241, 246-246, 250-251, 255
  -bard, 108
  -Tlingit, 162
Shamanism and the Mystery Lines, Paul Devereaux, 38
shapeshifiting, 108-109
Sheela-na-gig, 35
sheep, 34, 68, 249
shew stone, 17, 19
Shinto, 177
Silbury Hill, 41, 190
Sioux, 26, 162
  -Medicine man, 162
skald, 167
skull, 29-30, 67-70, 88, 132, 190-192
  -Horse, 68, 182
  -Sheep, 68
Solinger, 51
Solomon, King, 18, 131, 146
  The Lesser Key of 16, 83, 131
  Temple of, 18, 58, 131
Spare, Austin, 82-83
spierings, 71
Spiral Castle, xii, 175
spirits, 17-21, 26-27, 30, 36-37, 83, 116, 154, 160, 163, 166, 171, 175, 204, 237
  -ancestral, 20, 27, 30, 163, 166, 237
St. Bruno's Church, 185
St. John Chrysostom, 137
St. Paul (Paul of Tarsus), 137, 246
stag, 97, 138, 142
  -antlers, 139, 183
stang, 9, 53-54, 65, 83, 174, 189-190
star (s), 41-42, 101, 110, 115-116, 121, 129, 188
  -north, 115
  -pole,
stigmata, 21, 109
Stonehenge, 34, 40, 42
Stonehenge Decoded, Gerald Hawkins, 40
Story of Civilization, Will and Ariel Durant, 274
Stuart, 67, 71
Stuart, Francis, 199
summoner, 55, 72, 76, 185
Sun, 40-41, 115, 118-120, 130, 140, 161
Swedenbourg, Emmanual, 175
sword (s), 15, 32, 60, 65, 73, 109, 182, 185, 192, 199, 214
  -Calling the, 60, 73

T

Tain bo Culaigne, 133, 218
Taliesin, 71, 108, 200
Tam Lim, 170
Temple of the Elder Gods, 56
Tetrabilbos, Ptolemy, 245
Thebes, 138
Thriplow, 35
Tlingit shaman, 162
totem, 39, 97-98, 163, 168, 170
treading the mill, ix, 29, 53, 57, 62, 66, 69, 97, 111, 115-120, 185-186, 188, 190, 192, 205
tree (s),
  -of Avalon, xiii
  -of Good and Evil, 229
  -of Knowleddge, 229
  -of Life, 152
  -world, 115, 190
Trefignath, 42
Trojans, 217-218
Tubal Cain, 64, 76, 88, 130-131, 202, 207
  -Clan of, 55, 57-58, 63-64, 66, 75-77, 85, 88, 111, 182, 197, 105, 207
  -Forge of, 33, 196
  -Pillars of, 85
Typhon, 83
Tyre, 83

V

Valiente, Doreen, vii, 48-50, 54, 56, 60, 64-65, 72, 82, 97, 135, 172, 197, 201-203, 216, 252
  -*Witchcraft: A Tradition Renewed*, 8, 64, 173
Vampyre, 108, 221-223, 225, 235, 239, 243-244, 255
Venus (planet), 22, 152
View Over Atlantis, the John Michell, 36, 38

W

Waite, A.E., 138
Wales, 22, 68, 83-84, 101, 171, 185
wand (s), 15-16, 206

Watchers, 89, 129-130
Watkins, Alfred, 35-36
    -*The Old Straight Track*, 36
Welsh, 22, 68, 72, 109
werewolf (werewolves), 235, 243-244, 249, 251
Western Inner Workings, William Gray, 48, 81, 252, 254
White Goddess, The Robert Graves, 71, 86, 106, 122, 139, 144, 146-147, 216
Whittlesford, 35
Wicca, 27-28, 56, 135, 141, 173, 196,
    -Gardnerian, 55-58, 61, 79, 83, 88, 135, 141, 173, 196-197
Wiccan Conference Canberra, 56
widdershins, ix, 69, 119, 121, 185, 189
    -dance, 82
Wilson, Joe, xii, 33-34, 48, 56, 71
Wilson, Monique and Scotty, 56
Witchcraft, A Tradition Renewed, Doreen Valiente and Evan John Jones64, 173, 253
wolf (wolves), 102, 105, 108-109, 233-234, 249
World Tree, 115, 190

Y
York, House of, 170

Z
Zeus, 130

BIBLIOGRAPHY

Hypostasis of the Archons (The Reality of the Rulers), from the Nag Hammadi Library

Aristotle, *Aristotle's Rhetoric, Treatise on the art of persuasion*, 4th century B.C.E

Baigent, Michael, *Holy Blood, Holy Grail, and, Richard Leigh and Henry Lincoln, Johnathan Cape Books, 1982.*

Barrett, Francis, *The Magus,* Printed for Lackington, Alley, and Co., Temple of the Muses, Finsbury Square, London,180.

Blavatsky, Helena, *The Secret Doctrine, First published by Theosophy Company. 1898.*

Chumbley, Andrew. *The Azoetia: A Grimoire of the Sabbatic Craft, Xoanon Publishing Ltd, 1992.*

Chumbley, Andrew, *One: The Grimoire of the Golden Toad, Xoanan Publishing, Ltd, 2000.*

Clifton, Chas, *Sacred Mask, Sacred Dance, and Evan John Jones, Llewellyn Publications, 1997.*

Cochrane, Robert, *The Roebuck in the Thicket, and, Evan John Jones, Michael Howard (editor), Capall* Bann Pub, 2002.

Cochrane, Robert, *The Witches' Esbat, New Dimensions, Vol. 2, No. 10,* November 1964.

Crowley, Aleister, *The Confessions of Aleister Crowley : an autohagiography, (Originally titled The spirit of solitude : an autohagiography) Mandrake Press, 1929.*

Davies, Owen, *Cunning-Folk, Hambledon and London, 2003.*

Dechend, Hertha von, *Hamlet's Mill: An Essay on Myth and the Frame of Time, and Giorgio de Santillana, Published by Gambit, Incorporated, 1969.*

Dee, John, *A True & Faithful Relation of What Passed for Many Years Between Dr. John Dee and Some Spirits, . (With a Preface Confirming the Reality as to the Point of Spirits) by Meric Casaubon)* published by D.Maxwell for T. Garthwait, London, 1669

Devereaux, Paul, *Shamanism and the Mystery Lines, W Foulsham & Co Ltd, 1992.*

Durant, Ariel and Will, *The Story of Civilization (11 volume set), Simon & Schuster,1935-1975.*

Evans-Went, W.Y., *The Fairy Faith in Celtic Countries*, London and New York; H. Froude, 1911.

Finnin, Ann, *The Forge of Tubal Cain*, Pendraig Publishing, Los Angeles, CA 2008.

Fortune, Dion, *Aspects of Occultism*, Aquarian Press, 1949.

Fortune, Dion, *The Cosmic Doctrine*, first published by The Society of The Inner Light, 1949.

Fortune, Dion, *Esoteric Philosophy of Love and Marriage*. First published: London, Rider, 1924.

Fortune, Dion, *Psychic Self Defense*, First published by Rider, London, UK, 1930.

Frazier, J.G., *The Golden Bough*, Published by Macmillan and Co., Limited, London, 1890.

Graves, Robert, *Collected Poems*, Garden City, N.Y., Doubleday, 1961.

Graves, Robert, *King Jesus*, Creative Age Press, 1946.

Graves, Robert, *Mammon and the Black Goddess*, Garden City, Doubleday, 1965.

Graves, Robert, *The White Goddess*, First published, Faber & Faber, Ltd, 1948.

Gray, William, *By Elder Tree and Standing Stone* by Llewellyn Publications, 1990.

Gray, William, *Evoking the Primal Goddess: Discovery of the Eternal Feminine Within*, Llewellyn Publications, 1989.

Gray, William, *Ladder of Lights*, originally published by Helios, 1975

Gray, William, *Magical Ritual Methods*, Helios Book Service, 1969.

Gray, William, *Western Inner Workings (The Sangreal Sodality Series Volume 1)*. First published, by Weiser Books, 1983.

Hall, Manly P., *Magic: a Treatise on Esoteric Ethics*, Los Angeles, CA.: Philosophical Research Society, 1978.

Hall, Manly P., *Reincarnation*, Philosophical Research Society, 1946.

Hawkins, Gerald, *Stonehenge Decoded*, Doubleday Books, 1965.

Heindel, Max, *Freemasonry and Catholicism*, The Rosicrucian Fellowship, 1921.

Heindel, Max, *The Rosicrusion Cosmo-Conception or Mystic Christianity*, L.N. Fowler, Imperial Arcade, Ludgate Circus, 1922.

Hesiod, *The Theogony, the Geneology or birth of the Gods, an ancient poem written by Hesiod, c. 700 B.C.E.*

Holiday, Ted, *The Goblin Universe*, Llewellyn Publications, 1986.

Homer, *The Iliad, Ancient Greek epic poem set during the time of the Trojan War, 762 B.C.E.*

Horowitz, Mitch, *Occult America*, Bantam 2009.

Howard, Jackson, *The Pillars of Tubal Cain, and, Michael Howard, and Nigel Jackson.* Capall Ban Pub, 2000.

Howard, Michael, *The Pillars of Tubal Cain, and, Jackson Howard, and Nigel Jackson.* Capall Ban Pub, 2000.

Howard, Michael (editor), *The Roebuck in the Thicket, and, Robert Cochrane, Evan John Jones,* Capall Bann Pub, 2002.

Jackson, Nigel, *The Call of the Horned Piper*, Capall Bann Pub, 1994.

Jackson, Nigel, *The Compleat Vampyre*, Capall Bann Pub, 1995.

Jackson, Nigel, *Masks of Misrule*, Capall Bann Pub, 1996.

Jackson, Nigel, *The Pillars of Tubal Cain, and, Michael Howard, and Jackson Howard.* Capall Ban Pub, 2000.

Jaynes, Julian, *The Origin of Consciousness in the Breakdown of the Bicameral Mind*, Mariner Books, 1976.

Jenny, Dr. Hans *Cynatics*, Basilius Presse Basel, Switzerland, 1967.

Jones, Evan John, *The Roebuck in the Thicket, and, Robert Cochrane, Michael Howard (editor),* Capall Bann Pub, 2002.

Jones, Evan John, *The Rose Beyond the Grave. Pomegranate: The International Journal of Pagan Studies.* 13. 48-52. 10.1558/pome.v13i5.48, 2012.

Jones, Evan John, *Sacred Mask, Sacred Dance, and Chas Clifton,* Llewellyn Publications, 1997.

Jones, Evan John, *Witchcraft: A Tradition Renewed, and Doreen Valiente. by* Phoenix Publishing, 1990.

Jung, Carl, *Man and His Symbols*, Doubleday & Company Inc., 1964.

Jung, Carl, *The Red Book*, W. Norton & Company, 2009.

Kondratiev, Alexei, *An Tríbhís Mhór: A Quarterly Journal of Celtic Spirituality (Imbas Journal),* 1997.

Leadbetter, C.W., *The Astral Plane*, Published by The Theosophical Publishing Society, 1895.

Leigh, Richard, *Holy Blood, Holy Grail*, and, Michael Baigent, and Henry Lincoln, Johnathan Cape Books, 1982.

Leland, Charles, *Aradia: Gospel of the Witches*, Charles Leland, Published by London: David Nutt, 1899.

Lethbridge, T.C., *Witches: Investigating an Ancient Religion*, Humanities Press, 1962.

Lewis, C.S., *Screwtape Proposes A Toast*, was first published in The Saturday Evening Post on December 19th, 1959.

Lincoln, Henry, *Holy Blood, Holy Grail*, and, Michael Baigent, Richard Leigh, Johnathan Cape Books, 1982.

Mackey, Albert, *History of Freemasonry* First published by Masonic History Company, USA, 1898.

Milton, John, *Paradise Lost*, Published by London: [Samuel Simmons for] Peter Parker, Robert Boulter & Mathias Walker, 1667.

Mitchell, John, *The View Over Atlantis*, First published, Sago Press, London, 1969.

Murray, Margaret, *Witch Cults in Western Europe: A Study in Anthropology*, Published by Clarendon Press, Oxford, 1921.

Pike, Albert, *Morals and Dogmas of the Ancient and Accepted Scottish Rite of Freemasonry*, published by the Supreme Council of the Scottish Rite, Southern Jurisdiction of the United States, 1871.

Plato, *The Republic is a Socratic dialogue about justice and order written by Plato c. 380 B.C.E*

Ptolemy, Claudius, *Tetrabiblos*, written in the 2nd century A.D. (C.E.) by Claudius Ptolemy is one of the oldest surviving texts on the philosophy and practice of Astrology.

Santillana, Giorgio de, *Hamlet's Mill: An Essay on Myth and the Frame of Time*, and Hertha von Dechend, Published by Gambit, Incorporated, 1969.

Steiner, Rudolph, *The Ahrimanic Deception*, Rudolf Steiner, presented 1919.

Steiner, Rudolph, *The Inner Nature of Music*, Lecture: S-5087, 1922.

Stoker, Bram, *Dracula*, Constable & Robinson Limited, England, 1897.

Thorn, Alexander, *Megalithic Sites in Britain*. Oxford: Clarendon Press, 1967.

Valiente, Doreen (editor), *Pentagram Magazine (Issue #2)*, BM/Elusis, London, W.C.I, 1964.

Valiente, Doreen, *Witchcraft: A Tradition Renewed*, and Evan John Jones. by Phoenix Publishing, 1990.

Watkins, Alfred, *The Old Straight Track*, Methuen & Co., London (1925)

Wilby, Basil, *New Dimensions Red Book: A Symposium of Practical Occultism.* Basil Wilby (editor) Toddington, UK: Helios Book Service Ltd., 1968.

Zimbardo, Philip, The Lucifer Effect, Philip Zimbardo, Random House, Rider, 2007.

*

www.ingramcontent.com/pod-product-compliance
Lightning Source LLC
Chambersburg PA
CBHW050321170426
43200CB00009BA/1403